GANDHI IN MODERN WORLD

About the Authors

Dr. Anil Dutta Mishra (1965) is a distinguished Gandhian scholar and writer. He started his career as Assistant Professor in the Department of Nonviolence and Peace Studies, Jain Vishva Bharati University, Ladnun, Rajasthan. He became Deputy Director of National Gandhi Museum and Honorary Professor, Centre for Gandhian Philosophy and Human Development, Gayatri Vidya Parishad Degree College [Autonomous], Visakhapatnam.
Dr. Mishra has held the post of General Secretary of Indian Society of Gandhian Studies, Alliance for Sarvodaya; Member Board of Studies, Nagpur and Punjab Universities; and is Member of Gandhian Studies Centre of different colleges and universities across India sponsored by UGC and Executive Member IIPA Regional Branch. He has authored/edited 30 books and published a number of research papers. His recent book **Reading Gandhi** is widely acclaimed.
Email: anilduttamishra@gmail.com

Nuti Namita (1970) did her Masters in Modern Indian History from University of Delhi and is working as Assistant Professor in the Department of History, Sri Venkateswara College, Delhi University. She has written several articles in reputed professional journals and newspapers including *Indian Journal of Public Administration*. She has presented Papers in National and International Seminars in India and abroad and is a member of many learning bodies. She has done a course on International Citizenship from the University of Birmingham,UK. She has visited Japan, Britain, France, Hungary, Austria, Spain, New Zealand and Korea.
Email: namita.nuti@gmail.com

GANDHI IN MODERN WORLD

Edited by
Anil Dutta Mishra
Nuti Namita

CONCEPT PUBLISHING COMPANY PVT. LTD.
NEW DELHI-110059

ISBN-13 : 978-93-5125-105-7

First Published 2015

Published and Printed by

Concept Since 1974

Concept Publishing Company Pvt. Ltd.
A/15-16, Commercial Block, Mohan Garden
New Delhi-110059 (India)
T: 25351460, 25351794, *F*: 091-11-25357109
E: publishing@conceptpub.com, W: www.conceptpub.com
Editorial Office: H-13, Bali Nagar, New Delhi-110 015, India.

Cataloging in Publication Data—*Courtesy:* D.K. Agencies (P) Ltd. <docinfo@dkagencies.com>

Gandhi in modern world / edited by Anil Dutta Mishra, Nuti Namita.
pages cm
Contributed articles.
Includes bibliographical references (pages) and index.
ISBN 9789351251057

1. Gandhi, Mahatma, 1869-1948—Political and social views. 2. Gandhi, Mahatma, 1869-1948—Philosophy. 3. India—History. I. Mishra, Anil Dutta, 1965-, editor. II. Namita, Nuti, 1970-, editor.

DDC 954.035 23

Preface

Gandhi was a unique and iconic personality. He changed the course of history and gave the world non-violent technique of protest, change, liberation and transformation. This technique was so powerful that it resulted in the end of the British Empire—An empire where Sun never set. Gandhi put ancient wisdom in modern form. His mind, methods and mission were old, nay ancient indeed, but they went against the main currents of his times. They made history, and set the agenda for generations to come.

Gandhi was a great man in every sense and many ways. His concerns were contemporary but timeless. Gandhi could interact with kings and prime ministers with the same ease as he could with peasants and artisans. He was not an academic in the ordinary sense of the word but he has become one of the major subjects of academic discourse in the contemporary time. He was a practical philosopher, an applied social scientist, a grassroots social worker, a political mobilizer, a revered national leader, a scientist and a saint, all at the same time. Gandhi changed the world he lived in and gave new direction to what is now known as development.

Gandhi is so much an inseparable part of our modern history that we cannot imagine an India without him. Gandhi worked all through his life to liberate India from British colonialism; but this mission of his was only a part of a larger and more encompassing mission of liberating humanity from the mythos that grip its soul, mind, and body. In real sense he was a *Karma Yogi* seeking knowledge and wisdom through action.

Gandhi tried to solve problems as they arose, following the law of Truth (morality), keeping in view the cultural background of the people, and good of the society at large. Presently, every discourse in Social Science starts and ends with Gandhi. Now Gandhi is at the centre stage in major global discussions. Testimony to Gandhi's global significance is provided by the books about him that constantly roll off the world's press.

The present book *Gandhi in Modern World* is an outcome of collaborative effort of like minded scholars. It took almost two years to take shape. This effort would not have been possible in the present form without the support and help from friends and well-wishers. We are indebted to all contributors for writing and sending their articles in time. We record our appreciation to them.

We cannot forget our family members for providing full support and cooperation when we were busy with the completion of this book.

Last but not the least, we would like to thank Shri Ashok Kumar Mittal of Concept Publishing Company Pvt. Ltd., for bringing out the book in the present form and that too within record time.

Anil Dutta Mishra
Nuti Namita

Contents

Our Contributors

Anil Dutta Mishra, Deputy Director of National Gandhi Museum and Honorary Professor, Centre for Gandhian Philosophy and Human Development, Gayatri Vidya Parishad Degree College [Autonomous], Visakhapatnam. He is the author of *Reading Gandhi*.

Anju Jham, Associate Professor in the Department of Political Science, S.P.M. College, University of Delhi, Delhi.

A.N. Panda, Associate Professor in the PG Department of Political Science Panchayat (Govt. Lead) College, Bargarh, Orissa.

Ashutosh Pandey, Assistant Professor, Department of Political Science, A.S. (PG) College, Lakhaoti, Bulandshahr, Uttar Pradesh.

Avanindra Kumar Jha, Associate Professor, Department of History, L.N.M.U., Darbhanga.

B.P. Mathur, former Deputy Comptroller and Auditor General and Director, National Institute of Financial Management. He has authored books on Economics, Finance and Governance-related issues.

B. Arun Kumar, Associate Professor in the Department of Political Science, Vardhaman Mahaveer Open University, Kota.

D. Venkateswara Rao, Professor and Head, PG Department of Public Administration, Sri Y.N. College, Narsapur, Andhra Pradesh.

Himanshu Bourai, Professor in the Department of Political Science, HNB Garhwal University, Srinagar, Uttarakhand.

Joseph Benjamin, Associate Professor and Head, Department of Political Science, St. Francis de Sales' College, Nagpur.

Nuti Namita, Assistant Professor, Department of History, Sri Venkateswara College, University of Delhi, Delhi.

Pravin Kumar, Associate Professor in the Department of History, Shyam Lal College, University of Delhi, Delhi.

Prem Anand Mishra, Assistant Professor in the Peace Research Centre, Gujarat Vidyapith, Ahmedabad.

Ram Binod Singh, former Professor of Economics, Lalit Narayan Mithila University, Darbhanga and President, Indian Society of Gandhian Studies.

Shakuntala, Reader, Department of English, HNB Garhwal University, Srinagar, Uttarakhand.

Y.P. Anand, former Chairman, Railway Board and Director, National Gandhi Museum, Rajghat, New Delhi.

Introduction

Mohandas Karamchand Gandhi, or Mahatma Gandhi, as he came to be revered later, immeasurably contributed to the emergence of India as an independent nation. Gandhi provided an alternative vision and strategy for attaining independence that became the prevalent discourse of the nationalist movement. His philosophy was as greatly inspired by the Western thinkers like Henry David Thoreau, John Ruskin, Leo Tolstoy as equally by the Indian philosophical tradition. Gandhi's novel political ideology, as Judith Brown has argued "appealed to few wholly, but to many partially", as everyone could find in it something to identify with. He honed and perfected his strategy in South Africa in the early years of his career as a lawyer and activist. Gandhi's twenty-one year stay in South Africa gave him world outlook and internal strength to develop and experiment the nonviolent technique of struggle. He went there as lawyer in search of livelihood and returned as Mahatma Gandhi. In India, he was reasonably well received when he began his Indian experiment in 1915.

Gandhi's invaluable contribution which he applied when he arrived in India was his sincere efforts to mobilize the masses in the nationalist movement against the colonial rule, which had, prior to 1915 primarily been limited to the small group of English educated professionals, who on the basis of belonging to certain castes, linguistic communities and specific regions, were able to take advantage of the opportunities provided by the British Raj. D.A. Low has described these classes as "the underlings of the British rulers". These leaders naturally did not represent the mass population of India; most of them were illiterate and poor. The Congress may ties with landlords ruled out the possibility of seeking peasant support by championing their interests. Theirs was mainly an elite politics whose social and economic goals were limited in their reach. Gandhiji worked to draw in the masses in the mainstream of freedom struggle. 'Inclusiveness' became "Gandhi's unique style of politics". This is not to discount the role played by the prevalent socio-economic and political circumstances in India after the First World War. The frustration of the educated youth, the economic backlash of price rise, disillusionment with the sparkle of the western civilization, all worked for the upsurge of the masses; they were ready, they just needed the firm hand of guidance, leadership and empathy, which was provided timely and judiciously by Gandhi. This mass nationalism with the attendant ideologies of *Satyagraha* and *Ahimsa* revolutionised the whole equation between the British rulers and the ruled. *Satyagraha* became Gandhi's tool for attaining his goal; non-violent resistance, a moral and philosophical mandate which he tried to rigorously impress upon the masses; *Swaraj*, his political aim and *Charkha*, his social symbol. One very notable achievement during this period was the involvement of the peasants in the mainstream national movement, who had earlier been aloof.

Usha Thakkar in her review of the book by Joseph Lelyveld *Great Soul: Mahatma Gandhi and his Struggle with India* gives credit to Lelyveld for identifying the four pillars on which Gandhi's structure of *Swaraj* stands. They were: the end of untouchability, Hindu-Muslim unity, the principle of non-violence for freedom, and transformation of villages by spinning and other self-sustaining measures. For Gandhi, constructive work was another side of the political struggle. Naturally, rebuilding villages, in accordance with the principles of self-sufficiency and decentralisation, was of crucial importance. His vision included productive employment for India's millions, schemes for rebuilding villages, promotion of *Khadi* and local handicrafts, village industries, and ensuring equality of opportunity for all. Gandhi was critical of the Western civilization based on large scale industrialization which he felt was at the root of conflict of interests; he advocated his own vision of society established on the premise of Indian civilization. In *Hind Swaraj* (1909), Gandhi offered a civilizational concept of Indian nation. This civilization, which was "sound at the foundation" and which always tended "to elevate the moral being" had "nothing to learn" from "godless" modern civilization that only "propagated immorality".

It is true that many of the ideologies that Gandhi enunciated could not be translated into government policy after independence; however, their significance and relevance cannot be disputed especially in today's world. Today in India there are issues like poverty, illiteracy, naxalism, scarcity of water and healthcare; and "Gandhian economics needs to be viewed in that sobering perspective before being written off as irrelevant in the era of globalisation".

His name and methods are often evoked during people's struggles and protests against authoritarian rule, Tunisia and Egypt being only few of the examples. Even in India, where all classes of the society felt hedged in and cheated by the corrupt and unresponsive government, Gandhiji became an inspiration to the likes of Anna Hazare who was able to organise mass based movement of the civil society. Gandhi's ideology of unpretentious, transparent, with many layered community governance system has many takers today. We can cite the latest example of the Aam Aadmi Party which tried to follow on Gandhi's ideas, achieving a miraculous victory in Delhi's State elections.

Satyagraha, civil resistance, removal of untouchability, Hindu-Muslim unity, spinning, uplift of village industries, sanitation, *brahmacharya*, and women's emancipation were not separate issues, but were closely interconnected with each other; all of them needed to be pursued with dedication. Most of the issues have relevance today. Many acknowledge their debt to him. He set high, almost impossible, goals during his life, ranging from freedom for India from the yoke of British rule to wiping every tear from every eye. India has not pursued many Gandhian prescripts, and we have a large number of poor and illiterates, and a wide chasm of inequality between the poor and the rich. However, equally there is the increasing partnership of women in Panchayati Raj institutions, legislations like the Right to Information Act, action for Human

Rights, mobility of various castes and attempts at self-reliance. The practice of untouchability is a legal offence and the *dalits* are making their presence felt. Lurking behind all these is Gandhi's vision. As he wrote in the *Harijan* of 25 March, 1933, Gandhi's ambition was to see "a complete regeneration of humanity".

The essays in this book present comprehensive and pertinent forays in different facets of a somewhat bewildering question: 'What made Gandhi?' The essays range over diverse themes, from abstract to mundane. Whether it be an essay on understanding Gandhi, or his socio-political ideas as discussed in *Hind Swaraj*, or deliberating about Gandhi's leadership calibre, or examining Gandhi's alternative to economic development, *Swadeshi* or his economic doctrines and his idea of economic independence, or something as simple as Gandhi's concept on beauty, women empowerment and corruption; all these issues are relevant today and need to be analysed and debated. This reader hopes to raise issues about Gandhian perspective, why it was more or less abandoned after independence and how it is now timely to implement some valid ideas of Gandhi into government policy.

In the first chapter by Anil Dutta Mishra, we get a pointer towards understanding Gandhi and his ideology which presents some challenges as Gandhi as a personality was complex. Notwithstanding this difficult task, the author delves deep into Gandhi's philosophy on varied aspects of life; his firm conviction on the value of Truth and *Satyagraha*; his unwavering support for non-violence; his pure love and respect for nature; and his deep scepticism of the western civilization based on industrialisation. Gandhi believed in the holistic development of humanity, he was a man of action rather than of words and his strategy for conflict resolution stemmed out of his ingrained understanding of the human psyche. Author concedes the complexity of understanding Gandhi but has managed to capture the essence of Gandhi and his ideology.

The second chapter by Anju Jhamb dwells on situating *Hind Swaraj* and reiterates that this book forms the foundation for understanding Gandhi. It was in *Hind Swaraj*, which Gandhi wrote on a ship journey in 1909, that he crystallised his philosophy. The author very eloquently dissects *Hind Swaraj* minutely by examining its context, text, interpretation and reaction. The theme of *Hind*

Swaraj is well brought out; *Swaraj* is understood as not only self-government but also as self-rule. Non-violent resistance or *Satyagraha* is seen as a means towards an end. *Satyagraha* has the element of proactiveness, not passiveness. Gandhi's critique of western/modern civilization takes shape in this book. He felt that modern civilization saps the moral energy of the humanity. He equated modern civilization with large scale industrialisation and believed that machinery is evil. Modern civilization breeds greed and thus gives birth to colonialism. He, however, was very appreciative of Indian civilization which he thought elevated the moral being of humanity. In *Hind Swaraj*, Gandhi also deliberates on the issue of national movement in India, the path it was taking and how it could be veered to take a middle path between the two extremes of 'mendicancy' of the moderates and the violent approach of the extremists. The author also goes into Gandhi-Nehru debate on the content of *Hind Swaraj*, how their different perspectives clashed with each other on some very vital issues, how it led to constructive criticism and fruitful discussions between the two. In the concluding remarks the author is of the view that *Hind Swaraj* is not only a book on *Swaraj* and 'Civilization', but it is also a spiritual book.

In the third chapter by Pravin Kumar we get a glimpse about Gandhi's views on the ideal human society based on the twin pillars of peace and stability. According to Gandhi, this was not an easy endeavour and could not be achieved through capitalist system or a socialist revolution. Gandhi felt that whereas the former bred social inequality and extreme class differentiation, on the other hand, socialism, though eradicated the misery of the working and other poor classes, it was based on dictatorship of the leader and in some cases bloodshed. Gandhi, therefore, evolved his own solution by relying on Indian tradition and religion. He advocated that the prevailing ills of the society could be cured by providing a moral leadership which depended as much on addressing the myriad socio-economic problems of India as on demonstrating the practical side of his philosophy through his own life and action. That is the true quintessence of a good leader and, therefore, people of India did not hesitate to follow him in his quest to oust the British rule.

The next essay by Prem Anand Mishra eloquently explores Gandhi's Concept of Beauty and infers that Gandhi did not equate beauty with the usual platitudes attributed to it. For him beauty is the extension of the metaphysics of truth and goodness. Further, Gandhi sees beauty in the things or activities which is closer to nature's law. He does not believe in artifice and thinks that for anything to be beautiful, it needed to be useful. In his view, art and beauty has no meaning if it does not help people in self-realisation. Thus, Gandhi's philosophy of beauty is essentially a moral beauty. Truth and simplicity form the hallmark for being beautiful.

In the essay by B.P. Mathur, the author discusses about Gandhi's alternative strategy of economic growth and goes on to demonstrate its relevance in today's world. He points out that Gandhi was opposed to mass industrialisation as it led to unemployment of many. His was an all inclusive economic philosophy in which welfare of each individual is taken care of and he is able to earn his bread in a dignified manner without relying on anyone's charity. Therefore, Gandhi favoured local and small production units to large scale industries; cottage industries to machine led industries. He reiterated time and again about the need to veer away from urban centric development model to rural-agriculture based civilization. He believed in the decentralised development model which leads to equitable distribution of profits and social harmony. Gandhi's belief in simple living, devoid of luxury, was instigated by his extreme abhorrence of consumerism, the main by-product of capitalism, and his realisation that greed not only destroys one's soul but it also has devastating impact on environment. Author also tries to situate Gandhi's economic ideology in the present day model of economic growth in India and seeks to establish its relevance even, nay, especially, in today's world.

Y.P. Anand attempts to invoke Gandhi's philosophy of non-violence, truth, brotherhood of all humanity and peace to address the pressing problem of terrorism and violence in the world today. The author is aware that the end of the Second World War which led to decolonisation, globalisation and interdependence should have also created a more peaceful world. However, contrary to that happened. The economic, social and political disparities between peoples of different nations, (sometimes of the same country), religion and race evokes a heightened sense of unfairness and injustice which create's situation for violence, terrorism and counter-terrorism. This state of affairs is facilitated by the easy availability of lethal weapons, religious fundamentalism, instant communication system and a chauvinistic sense of nationalism. The author realises the imperativeness of addressing this all-pervasive challenge and encourages to follow the path of *ahimsa* as shown by Mahatma Gandhi.

In the next chapter, Ram Binod Singh reflects on the relevance of Gandhian economic doctrines in a time when disenchantment with the science of economics has become acute, as reflected by the economic crisis witnessed all over the world. The author feels that since pure economics is based on an assumed human society, is not able to tackle the challenges of unequal distribution of wealth, mass poverty, unemployment and environmental degradation. It is in this context that Gandhi's views on economic behaviour becomes important. Although Gandhi was not an academic economist in the real sense of the word, his concepts, principally inspired by the *Gita* and *Unto this Last* by John Ruskin, still are applicable. His economic principles were based on the morality of the human beings; he equated economics with ethics. The salient points of Gandhi's economic doctrines were *Swadeshi*, *Sarvodaya*, trusteeship, decentralisation, and village based economic development. His was an holistic perspective in economics which boils down to this simple injunction: 'never advocate actions or policies that lead to material advancement at the cost of social, moral or spiritual impoverishment'. Gandhi was critical of technology which created unemployment for many. He was aspiring for a need based economy and not a greed based society; this dictum would take care of the major economic, social and environmental problems of the world.

A.N. Panda in his essay tries to assimilate the main ideas of Gandhi on economic independence. In Gandhi's view economic independence of an individual is crucial for him to perform his moral and social obligations to the best of his ability. He, however, believed that any economic activity of a person must have ethical foundation. Betterment of humanity should be the ultimate goal of any economic activity. The author goes on to enumerate the various principles on which Gandhi's economic activities were based. Gandhi knew the importance of village in the overall pattern of political-economic freedom. For him freedom should start at the bottom. For him, *Swaraj* was self-government of the poor. Further, he laid stress on the concept of *Swadeshi*, which would go a long way in elevating the poor masses from the shackles of poverty. He linked the country's loss of freedom with the ruin of the village economy. Thus, cottage industries, the propagation of *Khadi* became important symbols of economic independence of the country. He rejected the western concept of large scale industrialisation as he felt that it was detrimental to the country's economy, led to unemployment and snatched their economic independence. He was, therefore, in favour of trusteeship method of production. He advised that those who had property must regard it as a trust and must not use it for oppressing others. Economic activity should have a social and moral function which would ultimately lead to a just, equal and a peaceful society.

Gandhi's views on rights and duties are comprehensively described by D. Venkateswara Rao. The author is conscious of the contribution made by Gandhi towards the protection of human rights of individuals all over the world, thus, the honour of twentieth century *Man of Peace* has been bestowed on him. Gandhi's perspective on human rights was closely tied with social reforms; for him nationalist agenda of achieving independence from the British yoke would be incomplete unless the less privileged and the downtrodden of the society are treated as equals. Gandhi especially campaigned tirelessly for the social acceptance of the untouchables or as he renamed, *Harijans* (sons of God). Another vital aspect of Gandhi's perspective was that he laid as much stress on duties as on rights. He argued that if there were any rights at all, it could only be the result of well-performed duties. For the protection of the rights of the weaker sections of the society, Gandhi argued, it was important to impart education to the people at large. Gandhi considered education as the most powerful process to make people aware of their rights and duties.

Joseph Benjamin takes us on a journey exploring Gandhi's prescription to world peace. Author concedes the inadequacy of the institutions like United Nations to maintain world peace—A peace marked not only by absence of war and hatred but also by presence of cooperation, compassion and worldwide justice. For this purpose, author realises that *Gandhian* model of peace could be most effective. Gandhi believed that inner peace within an individual goes a long way in spreading peace in the world. Gandhi propagated non-violence (*Ahimsa*) and *Satyagraha* as the two most important tools for attaining peace. For him, non-violence was the supreme virtue and he felt that with the practice of non-violence the worst enemy could be conquered. Mahatma Gandhi, the martyr of peace, chose the way of love, non-violence and forgiveness on the road towards harmony in the world.

In the next chapter, B. Arun Kumar attempts a comparison between the strategies of protest against colonial rule of Gandhi on one hand and those of Gopal Krishna Gokhale and Bal Gangadhar Tilak on the other hand. The author recognizes that Gandhi, who arrived later in the freedom struggle than these two stalwarts of nationalist movement, was inspired in his political strategy by them.

However, it was not blind adoption and Gandhi did bring in his own version of fighting against the British. Gokhale, who belonged to the moderate stream of nationalist movement, recognized the need for an active protest against the unjust and oppressive rule. However, he denounced violent and revolutionary tactics for this purpose and advocated moderation and constitutional protest. Tilak on the other hand was an extremist and was more militant in his views. He believed that an unjust rule which fostered inequality and suppression of freedom should be resisted actively by an individual; it was his moral duty to maintain his dignity. Therefore, he recognized *Swaraj* as the birth right of every individual and emphasized upon achieving it at all cost. Gandhi borrowed heavily from them. However, he moulded the tactics of protest as the situation demanded. When recourse to constitutional means failed to secure desired results, he advocated the use of agitation or *Satyagraha*. However, Gandhi was clear in one thing, that the agitation howsoever intense and wide ranging, should conform to the principles of non-violence and truth. As his protest movement became more defined, Gandhi believed more and more in the idealised vision of his spiritual enterprise.

Himanshu Bourai and Shakuntala discuss about Gandhi's view on women empowerment. They realize that for Gandhi, individual was the basic unit of a society and in that respect women should have freedom and rights as that of a man. However, non-violence and truth should form the basis of any of their agitation. Gandhi believes that women have attributes of self-sacrifice and patience, therefore, they should utilize their strengths in fighting for freedom. In his view, women would make better *satyagrahis*. On other issues affecting women, that is, widow remarriage, child marriage, *sati*, education for women, Gandhi applauded the work of the social reformers who were fighting for these causes. Gandhi was vehemently opposed to child marriage, he considered it immoral and inhuman. He favoured widow remarriage if so desired by the widow. Enforced widowhood was a sin. Gandhi also believed in the emancipating role of education for women and said that there should be universal education for all in their pre-adolescent years. He advocated equal inheritance rights for women. Gandhi considered women as individuals in their own right and, therefore, should have freedom to take their own decisions with purity of heart and inner conscience.

Ashutosh Pandey, in his essay on *Gandhian Perspective of Democracy and Satyagraha*, deliberates on these two concepts as understood by Gandhi. Gandhi believed that *Satyagraha* and *Swaraj* were essential tools for achieving the holistic development of humankind. He considered *Satyagraha* to be the best weapon for the evolutionary process of social change. Gandhi tried to relate *Satyagraha* with Democracy. He thought that *Satyagraha* was compatible with democratic political process. On the concept of democracy, Gandhi was of the view that Parliamentary Democracy as practised in the western nations leads to centralisation and a politics from top which is not conducive for the betterment of all the people in the society. In his view democracy must be accompanied by decentralisation as manifested in the Panchayati Raj Institutions, growth of village and cottage industries, removal of untouchability, communal harmony and non-violent organisation of labour. For Gandhi, Democracy should be consistent with the goal of achieving human happiness combined with full mental and moral/spiritual growth.

Further, Anil Dutta Mishra strongly denounces the prevalence of rampant corruption in our daily life; the nexus between politicians, bureaucrats and industrialists, which breeds corruption of the highest order and he reiterates that Gandhi detested corrupt practices and spoke vehemently against it. He equated corruption with misgovernment. For Gandhi, corruption was an evil which he believed could be eradicated if the public became aware and vigilant. Gandhi advocated simple and ethical living, laid stress on personal integrity and lastly and most importantly had absolute faith in *Satyagraha* to fight corruption and for establishing good governance.

Avanindra Kumar Jha gives an interesting comment on the concept of 'Politics of Power' by comparing the views of Gandhi, M.N. Roy and Jay Prakash Narayan. He believes that there is an underlying similarity among them on their views of reconstruction of politics by minimising the gap between power and the community. Whereas Gandhi felt that a decentralised pattern of political structure implemented with the precept of 'self- rule' and 'self-control' would usher in an ideal state. Panchayati Raj was an important institution which would facilitate a flexible response and action to local requirements. M.N. Roy considered the organised local democracy as the foundation of the pyramidal structure of the state. Jay Prakash Narayan was also concerned about rural upliftment and thought that healthy development of democracy depends upon the minimum dependency upon state. He was of the view that essential reforms were needed for establishing local participating democracy. To achieve this goal he stressed upon the role of education in this venture. Both M.N. Roy and J.P. were inspired by Gandhi and aspired to coalesce politics of power with politics of humanity.

In the last chapter on *Swadeshi* in contemporary times, Nuti Namita attempts to determine the relevance of Gandhian concept of *Swadeshi* in the present scenario. While explaining and elucidating about the true meaning of *Swadeshi*, she makes copious use of Gandhi's own ideas as quoted in several of his texts. According to Gandhi, *Swadeshi* is based on the twin pillars of self-reliance and freedom. He was absolutely certain that the economic enslavement of the Indian nation was an essential precondition of India becoming a colony. Gandhi's insistence on using India made products and resources was not an unequivocal denial of everything foreign. He realised the importance of using those goods and technology not available in India. However, he said that cottage industries not only saves livelihood of millions of people in India but it also creates demand for food products within the country, thus ensuring the survival of both the village handicraft industry and agriculture. For Gandhi, *Khadi* and *Charkha* became the underpinnings of the *Swadeshi* movement. The author effectively brings out the debilitating effect of globalisation and liberalisation and how they perpetuate poverty and income disparities in developing countries. It becomes, therefore, essential to revisit Gandhi's thoughts on *Swadeshi* and try to adopt them in present times.

CHAPTER 1

Understanding Gandhi

ANIL DUTTA MISHRA

Gandhi was a unique and iconic person. Gandhi was a simple person and whatever he has written can be understood by the illiterates and literates alike. Yet his was a complex personality. Behind the veneer of simplicity, there was a complex Gandhi—A Gandhi who can be understood only if we tune our life to that of Gandhi. His mind, methods and mission were old, nay ancient indeed, but they went against the main currents of his times. They made history, and set the agenda for generations to come. He could interact with kings and prime ministers with the same ease as he could with peasants and artisans. He was not an academic in the ordinary sense of the word but he has become one of the major subjects of academic discourse. He was a practical philosopher, an applied social scientist, a grassroots social worker, a political mobilizer, a revered national leader, a scientist and a saint, all at the same time. His was a simple but complex personality. No matter how deep we penetrate his writings and life, we fail to understand him for we can neither relive his times nor can we disentangle ourselves from the myths, experiences, and prejudices of the past. To understand him, we have to read and re-read Gandhi, meditate over what he said and did and why; and above all to understand his experiment with truth and non-violence to resolve the problems we face with similar, if not the same, resolve, dedication, and mission. Gandhi changed the world he lived in and gave new direction to what is now known as development.

To understand Gandhi we have to be objective and analytical but at the same time strive to be synergic, interdisciplinary and holistic.[1] Unfortunately, we are trained to be specialists; we see the parts but not the whole. But, if everything is related to everything else, and nothing stands apart, knowing the part alone would lead to knowing the whole. Universe is a system of which the solar system is a subsystem; in the solar system, the earth is sub-system; in the earth as a system, lithosphere, hydrosphere, ionosphere, atmosphere and biosphere are sub-systems; in the biosphere, human species form a sub-system; in the human species each family and individual forms a sub-system. This being the case, to understand even an individual in full, we have to treat him as a part of the whole universe. True, he is more closely related to the systems nearer to him but he is influenced by thoughts and deeds not only of his fellow human beings, but also all that surrounds him, nature included. All that we do has its implication far wider than we realize. This is how the problem of global warming and climate change has emerged. Real Gandhi is a systems man and unless we see him that way, we cannot understand him.[2]

Further, Gandhi is so much an inseparable part of our modern history that we tend to be emotional about him and refuse to hear anything critical of him although those who see nothing great in him are not few. On the one hand, he is treated as the father of Indian Nationhood, on the other there are many who think that he wanted to take India to primitive days; who consider him an impractical man, and a man who mixed up religion, politics, and economics. We can understand Gandhi only if we distance ourselves, both physically and intellectually from dogmatism, fanaticism, and barren logic; if we see life in its all manifestation, and as a part and parcel of other life forms in general and human beings in particular.[3]

Gandhi worked all through his life to liberate India from British colonialism; but this mission of his was only a part of a larger and more encompassing mission of liberating humanity from the mythos that grip its soul, mind, and body. He lived so simply not only because he wanted to identify himself with the poorest of the poor, but also because he followed the dictum of simple living and high thinking. Gandhi saw unity in diversity; unity of souls and diversity of bodies with oscillating minds in between. Gandhi had no enemies; he had no hatred for anyone. He accepted differences of opinions, perceptions, thoughts, and approaches as natural, for each individual saw the truth differently. These and other differences can be transcended and ironed out when the contenders are overflowing with love for each other and talk to each other as brothers and sisters.[4]

He was at once saint and revolutionary, politician and social reformer, economist and man of religion, educationist and *Satyagrahi*; devotee alike of faith and reason, Hindu and inter-religious, nationalist and internationalist, man of action and dreamer of dreams.[5] He was a great reconciler of opposites and he was that without strain or artificiality. Rabindranath Tagore called him Mahatma, Subhash Chandra Bose 'Father of the Nation'; Lord Mountbatten, 'One Man Boundary Force'; Hindu fundamentalists 'Pro-Muslim', M.A. Jinnah 'Pro-Hindu', and Winston Churchill called him 'naked fakir'.[6] Whenever, he went wrong, he stopped, looked around, retraced his steps and then moved again. Each of us has the potential to become something like him, by experimenting with Truth, as we move forward on the road to higher levels of consciousness.

Gandhi was not a theorist or model builder. He was a *Karma Yogi* seeking knowledge and wisdom through action. When people asked him to put his experiments in writing, he replied: "I am not built for academic writings. Action is my domain."[7] Yet he wrote copiously. As we scan through the 100 volumes of his Collected Works, we are struck by the depth and breadth of his reach. We wonder how this man of action wrote so much in so short a time. Even a four line letter he wrote contains pearls of wisdom. Yet, he was so humble as to say "There is no such thing as 'Gandhism' and I do not want to leave any sect after me, I do not claim to have originated any new principle or doctrine. I have simply tried in my own way to apply the eternal truths to our daily life and problems...Well, all my philosophy, if it may be called by that pretentious name, is contained in what I have said. You will not call it 'Gandhism': there is no 'ism' about it".[8] He climbed step-by-step to transcend all isms and proclaimed Truth is God.

Gandhi tried to solve problems as they arose, following the law of Truth (morality), keeping in view the cultural background of the people, and good of the society at large. He was often accused of being inconsistent, which he indeed was because "At the time of writing I never think of what I have said before. My aim is not to be consistent with my previous statements on a given question, but to be consistent with truth as it may present itself to me at a given moment. The result has been that I have grown from truth to truth; I have saved my memory an undue strain; and what is more, whenever I have been obliged to compare my writing even of fifty years ago with the latest, I have discovered no inconsistency between the two. But friends who observe inconsistency will do well to take the meaning that my latest writing may yield unless, of course, they prefer the old. But before making the choice they should try to see if there is not an underlying and abiding consistency between the two seeming inconsistencies".[9]

Not many have been able fathom his depth. Gandhi believed in the unity of human life, which is a synthetic whole. It cannot be divided into separate, watertight compartments—religious, moral, political, economic, social, individual and collective. Gandhi said "Drops in separation could only fade away, drops in cooperation made the ocean which carried on its broad bosom ocean greyhounds".[10] "A drop torn from the ocean perished without doing any good. If it remained a part of the ocean, it shared the glory of carrying on its bosom a fleet of mighty steps."[11]

Gandhi changed his approaches to conflict resolution depending on the nature of problem, people involved, and the circumstances that surround it; certain timeless laws he followed and adhered to ever that remained his guiding stars. *One*, he firmly believed that the process of evolution that Darwin unravelled did not stop with the chimpanzees turning into Homo sapiens. Once the physical evolution was over, the evolution of the inner self began and it would continue until the humans evolve into super-conscious beings. Anything that took man backward to his animal past was regressive, and that which took him to the next milestone of consciousness was progressive. *Two*, Truth and non-violence were the driving forces of this evolutionary journey to higher consciousness. *Three*, everything was related to everything else, and hence nothing stands independent and isolated. All that we feel, think, and act upon, has wider implications. Those nearer us are affected more than those at distant places. *Four*, since the journey of life adds new experiences, truth is not absolute; it is relative. As such all of us can be victims of truth or untruth depending on our perception of the reality. One should, therefore, change one's views as new truths come to light. One should not be dogmatic. *Five*, all life is a united whole; humans have to love not only their fellow human beings but also the nature—the plants, insects, and animals, and all that is created by the cosmic force otherwise known as God. And *Six*, "there is enough on this earth to satisfy everyone's need but not everyone's greed"[12] and hence follow the dictum of simple living and high thinking.

Gandhi lived in a world of wars, colonialism, survival of the fittest, and eye for eye, Gandhi's truth and non-violence appeared to many, as weapons of the weak. They gathered around him as co-workers and followers only when it appeared to work as a potent force against violence appearing in different garbs: injustice, exploitation, colonialism, and wars, to mention a few. Gandhi's weapons proved more powerful but least destructive *vis-à-vis* the conventional weapons of war. His *Satyagraha* evoked worldwide attention and crossed the borders of India to reach many other countries, the USA, Russia, China, EU, and South Africa included. It proved beyond doubt that his means of fighting injustice ennobled both sides and left them in win-win situation. Globalization of Gandhian praxis did not go far enough to usher in a civilization of peace and harmony. It remained a movement which petered off when war mongering returned with a big bang in the form of modernization and globalization. Modernization means westernization and globalization means deprivation of the rights of the people to fully participate in production and consumption of the goods and services they need and use. It converts people from being producer to consumers.[13]

Rejection of Gandhian ways began soon after India became independent. It proved too difficult for the leaders of the time, even though they followed Gandhi during the freedom struggle, to carry forward his legacy of truth and non-violence. Gandhi was soon enshrined in museums spread over different parts of the country, and Gandhi Bhawans of select universities. He became a research topic and a name to be prefixed with institutions, organizations and individuals to acquire prestige. Many development schemes sponsored by the Central and State governments are being named after Gandhi. But in all these cases it is name, not the spirit of Gandhi that pervades.[14]

Gandhi advocated development from below. He wanted each village of India to function as an autonomous republic. The situation today is just the same as it was during the British days. It is development from above. Development is delivered by the Central and State governments to the people; it is not created by the local government—the Village Panchayats and city municipalities. It is clear from the fact that two-fifths (42%) of the public expenditure on salaries is claimed by the Central Government employees; a little more than that (45%) by the state government employees; and only one-sixth (12-13%) goes to local governments which are closest to the people; in China it is 43 per cent. It is not to suggest that more money will make local governments better. But it points how far we have followed Gandhi.[15]

Education and health are the most basic functions of the local government. But what is the situation on both of these fronts? We have failed to make people literate and those who claim to be literate (around 65%) are literates only in name. Functional literacy rate would be less than 50 per cent. How tragic it is that the village panchayats have no say in schooling of the children, the future of our country. There is a plethora of officials who are supposed to inspect the schools, but rampant corruption has crippled them. Pay a monthly amount to the Basic Shiksha Adhikari (BSA), and you do not have to go to school or you can appoint a proxy to do the work you are supposed to do. Gandhi advocated Hindi and mother tongue as the medium of instruction. But in the land of Gandhi, English occupies the top choice of parents and children alike. Even those leaders who advocated Hindi as the medium of instruction, sent their children to UK and USA but asked the people to learn and love Hindi. Israel introduced Hebrew, a defunct language and made it national language. But we have failed to revive our living languages, Hindi included.[16]

The same is the case with Primary Health Centres (PHCs). Most doctors go to the centres only once in a week or month. Pay the district Chief Medical Officer (CMO) a fixed amount each month and run your private clinic in the city or nearby town fearlessly. British are gone but the British system of administration continues. The only major change is incursion of corruption in a big way. Worst is the situation with regard to law and order. Police stations do not register First Information Report (FIR) as they want their areas to be crime free. The bureaucracy all the way from Central Secretariat to Panchayat Samitis has gone corrupt. It is not that we do not have honest and able civil servants, but the rot is spreading very fast. What has gone wrong is the nexus between corrupt politicians and corrupt bureaucrats. Had they been honest, India would have gone far ahead of China; there would have been no illiterates in the country; and abject poverty would have been a thing of the past. This is just a sample of how Gandhi has been sidelined, and the common people who constitute more than 75 per cent of the population of the country have been robbed of their livelihood. Unless we return to Gandhi, at least, in broad perspectives we would make India a land of perpetual violence.[17]

Summing Up

A number of approaches to the study of Gandhi's thought are in practice today – the Nationalist, the Marxist, the Oriental, the Post-colonial and the Subaltern, etc. To understand Gandhiji amidst his conflicting statements, one has perhaps to go into the meaning of meaning. To know their deeper significance, going by the literal meaning of the words would be futile and burdensome.[18] Even Vinoba Bhave, the spiritual heir of Gandhi failed to comprehend his *guru*. "Gandhiji…laid bare his mind in its fullness before the world. For his part, he had permitted no secrecy. Even so, I must confess, the last chapter of his life, which I have called the 'Swargarohan Parva', or the chapter of the 'Ascent to Heaven', remains a mystery to me. Indeed, in my eyes, it stands equal to the last phase of Lord Krishna's *Leela*. To unravel its mystery, it may become necessary for Gandhiji himself to be born again."[19]

NOTES

1. Mishra, Anil Dutta, *Understanding Gandhi: Speeches and Writings That Reveal His Mind and Mission*, New Delhi, Concept, 2012, p. 14.
2. *Ibid*., p.14.
3. *Ibid*.
4. *Ibid*., pp. 14-15.
5. *Ibid*., 15.
6. Mishra, Anil Dutta, *Reading Gandhi*, Delhi, Pearson, 2012, p. 1.
7. *Harijan*, 3-3-1946, p. 28.
8. *Ibid*., 28-3-1936, p. 49.
9. *Harijan*, 30-9-1939, p. 228.
10. *CWMG*: 89: 97.
11. *Ibid*., 87: 23.
12. Mishra, Anil Dutta and Ravi Gupta, *Inspiring Thoughts of Mahatma Gandhi*, New Delhi, Concept, 2008, p. 63.
13. Mishra, Anil Dutta, *Understanding Gandhi: Speeches and Writings That Reveal His Mind and Mission*, New Delhi, Concept, 2012, pp. 17-18.
14. *Ibid*., p. 18.
15. *Ibid*.
16. *Ibid*., pp. 18-19.
17. *Ibid*., p. 19.
18. *CWMG*: 93: 153.
19. *Ibid*., 86: IX-X.

CHAPTER 2

Hind Swaraj: Text and Contexts

ANJU JHAMB

Introduction

Hind Swaraj is a foundational text for understanding Gandhi's Socio-political ideas. It is perhaps the most systematic exposition of Gandhi's ideas of State, Society and Nation. Although *Hind Swaraj* is an original tract, while writing it Gandhi was heavily influenced by some of the leading western thinkers and his experiences in India and South Africa. In this manner, *Hind Swaraj* is an 'outcome of a cross fertilization of ideas, both Indian and Western'. It is in *Hind Swaraj* that we find Gandhi first announcing his own life mission "This life mission was nothing other than showing the way for the moral regeneration of Indians and the political emancipation of India."[1]

Hind Swaraj laid the most crucial theoretical foundation of his entire strategy for winning *Swaraj* for India. On the other hand it is a severe condemnation of modern civilization. It declares this civilization a systemic disease, which could be eradicated only by systemic change in human life. This civilization promotes material development and does not even consider moral development as one of its focal concerns. *Hind Swaraj* presents a way for the freedom of mind and the evolution of human beings from material beings to moral beings. T.K. Mahadevan in his preface to book "*DVIJA: A*

Prophet Unheard" said, "Read *Hind Swaraj* if you love the human family and this earth which is our home. Read it if you wish to do your little bit to halt man's mad race towards self extinction".[2]

Hind Swaraj was originally written in Gujarati, in ten days, between 13 and 22 November, 1909, on board the ship 'Kildonan Castle', on Gandhi's return voyage from London to South Africa. It was serialized in two instalments in December 1909 in the Gujarati edition. In January 1910, it was issued as a booklet in Gujarati and on 24 March, 1910, the Government of India proscribed it as it "contains matter declared to be seditious."[3]

Gandhi responded by issuing a translation, for he felt he owed it to his "English friends" that they should know its contents. *Hind Swaraj* was also sent to Tolstoy, who recorded in his diary on April 20, 1910: "Read Gandhi about civilization, wonderful." The whole manuscript was written on the ship's stationery and the writing went on at such a furious pace that when the right hand got tired, Gandhi continued with the left: 40 of the 275 manuscript pages were written by the left hand. And he wrote as if under inspiration.

Hind Swaraj was written in Dialogue Method. This method was influenced by Plato's, *The Republic* as well as the dialogue between Krishna and Arjuna in *Bhagwad Gita*. In *Hind Swaraj* the dialogue is between the 'Editor' of a newspaper and the 'Reader'. The text of *Hind Swaraj* consists of the "entire argument as it took place" during Gandhi's conversation with avowed anarchists (Pran Jiwan Mehta, Shyamji Krishan Verma and V.D. Savarkar). Gandhi felt that dialogue method 'suits Gujarati Language' and it is the best method of treating difficult subjects.

It was not just the moral inadequacy and extravagant pretensions of modern civilization, but its treacherously deceptive, hypnotic and self-destructive tendency that was the 'theme' of *Hind Swaraj*. *Hind Swaraj* raises some very important questions for the reader. What is the general conception of *Swaraj*? How does Gandhi define this *Swaraj*? Do we get real *Swaraj* just by thrashing out Britishers from India? Does *Swaraj* mean only political Independence and Economic prosperity? Where are we reaching with this modern civilization? Why is India a subject nation? What are the central problems of Indian Economy? Where are the solutions: in agricultural and community oriented programmes or in

Industrialization? *Hind Swaraj* is a remarkable constructive and inward looking programme based on ethical and moral values. John Middleton Murry described it as a "spiritual classic" and even more extravagantly, as "the greatest book written in modern times."[4]

Hind Swaraj—Why?

Anthony J. Parel grouped the intentions of Gandhi for writing *Hind Swaraj*. It is addressed to a mixed audience: the expatriate Indians greatly attracted to terrorism and political violence, the extremists and moderates of Indian National Congress, the ordinary Indians as well as the new emerging middle class.

As to why he wrote the book, his intentions were clear. First of all, there was the question of "inner illumination" and the "consequent urge to communicate." On 14 October, 1909, Gandhi wrote to his friend Henry Polak "The thing was brewing in my mind, therefore, I feel that I should no longer withhold these ideas. These ideas are not new but they have now assumed such a concrete form and taken a violent possession of me."[5] Even the foreword of *Hind Swaraj* reflected the same urgency. "I have written because I could not restrain myself. Just as one cannot help speaking out when one's heart is full, so also I had been unable to restrain myself from writing the book since my heart was full."[6]

- The second reason was to clarify the meaning of "*Swaraj.*" *Swaraj* was the basic concept of Gandhi's political philosophy, more basic than is even non-violence, a concept with which his name is universally associated. The fact remains that non-violence is only a 'means' to *Swaraj* whereas *Swaraj* is the 'end' and "a state of being."[7] In *Hind Swaraj*, Gandhi used the concept of *Swaraj* in two different ways—*Swaraj* as self-government and *Swaraj* as self-rule. *Swaraj* as 'self-government' means a quest for home rule and *Swaraj* as 'self-rule' means quest for self-improvement. Gandhi wrote in *Hind Swaraj* "It is, *swaraj* when we learn to rule ourselves. It is, therefore, in the palm of our hands. Don't consider this *Swaraj* like a dream".[8]
- Thirdly, Gandhi believed that through *Hind Swaraj* he would

be able to give a practical philosophy to Indians. He tried to redefine the concept of '*Dharma*'. Gandhi said "This is not a mere political book. Though I have used the language of politics but I have tried to offer a glimpse of *dharma*". If someone asks me about the meaning of *Hind Swaraj*, I will answer it as the 'rule of *Dharma*' or '*Ram Rajya*'. We may read '*The Gita*', or '*The Ramayana*' or '*Hind Swaraj*', but we have to learn, the desire for the welfare of others.

- Fourthly, Gandhi was anxious to teach the Indians that modern civilization posed a greater threat to them than did colonialism. Ordinary Indians takes it for granted that modern civilization was a blessing and colonialism an evil forgetting that colonialism itself was a product of modern civilization. "It is not the British that are responsible for the misfortunes of India but we who have succumbed to modern civilization." The key to an understanding of *Hind Swaraj* lies in the idea that worldly pursuits should give way to ethical living. Gandhi again said "the western civilization which passes for civilization is disgusting to me. I have given a rough picture of it in *Hind Swaraj*. Time has brought no change in it"[9].
- And fifthly, Gandhi found that some Indian anarchists are adopting the method of violence for the achievement of *Swaraj*. Gandhi felt that "they are following a suicidal policy". Political violence is not the remedy for India's ills. Her civilization required the use of a different and higher weapon for self-protection.

These are few exalted aims of writing the book *Hind Swaraj*. Gandhi wanted to show the picture of modern India in which politics and ethics can be combined together.

Structure/Text of *Hind Swaraj*

The text of *Hind Swaraj* is divided into 20 small chapters. At the first glance we do not find any coherence in the chapterization. It looks as if the theme of each chapter is unrelated to the other. But after the deep study one can understand that the first three chapters make the background/Introduction of the *Hind Swaraj*. In other sixteen chapters Gandhi presented his views on different subjects and the last chapter presents a way for future India. According to Anthony J. Parel, eleven chapters out of these twenty are related to historical views and nine chapters present the philosophical views of Gandhi. Most of these twenty short chapters of *Hind Swaraj* continue in an uncompromisingly critical vein about the political and social institutions of modern civilization, the glaring gap between its lofty claims and its unedifying conduct, and the destructive impact of an imperialistic, commercial system upon a traditional rural culture.

The title of the first chapter is "The Congress and its Officials." An attempt has been made to understand the popular concept of 'national independence' and of the 'home rule wave sweeping over India'. It is described what Congress had done to make India one nation. On the other hand, the issue of widespread disillusionment of the youth with regard to the methods adopted by the moderate leadership of the Congress party presents the views of 'Reader'. Gandhi argues that it is ungrateful on the part of youth to forget the contributions made by the early leaders in rousing the consciousness of Indians. "The Congress brought together Indians from different parts of India and enthused us with the idea of nationality"[10]. "The grand old man of India (Dada Bhai Naoroji) prepared the soil...Gokhale occupies the place of a parent. What does it matter if he cannot run with us .... Justice Tayabji was one of those who, through the Congress, sowed the seed of home rule."[11] We shall become useless, if we lack respect for our elders.

Second and third chapters are related to each other entitled 'The Partition of Bengal' and 'Discontent and Unrest'. Gandhi agrees with the 'reader' that the division of Bengal led to real awakening of India. *Swadeshi* movement was already there. "People do not fear now", they were ready to go to jails. Gandhi said "After the partition, people saw that petition must be backed by force, and that they must be capable of suffering."[12] After this partition, gradually the discontent and unrest spread. This discontent and unrest was against British rule and their policies. Gandhi said, "This discontent is a very useful thing. As long as man is contented with his present lot, so long it is difficult to persuade him to come out of it".[13]

The actual agenda or manifesto of *Hind Swaraj* starts from Chapter Four, entitled 'What is *Swaraj*'. Gandhi states that *Swaraj* for him did not stand for replacing British rule with the rule by Indians and adopting the form of government or institutions of the British. What you call *Swaraj* is not *Swaraj* because "we want English rule without English men. You want tiger's nature but not the tiger, that is to say, you would make India English.... This is not *Swaraj* that I want".[14] Gandhi differentiates between *Swaraj* as self government and *Swaraj* as self-rule. *Swaraj* in political sense means self-government and this was the popular form also, but for Gandhi *Swaraj* means self-government that is in tune with Indian culture and traditions. Governance by indigenous people using foreign means and methods is not *Swaraj*. Secondly, *Swaraj* also means self-control. It means a person should have control over his senses and animal passions. For Gandhi this is self-rule and this is the kind of *Swaraj* Gandhi wants.

In the fifth chapter of *Hind Swaraj*, Gandhi criticised the Parliamentary system of Britain. The title of this chapter is "The Condition of England". Though it has been said that English Parliament is the mother of all parliaments but it is like a "sterile woman and a prostitute".[15] First because despite being a sovereign institution, it cannot enact a Law according to its own judgement but is constantly swayed by outside pressures, and the second because it continually shifts its allegiance from one set of ministers to another depending on which is more powerful. Gandhi objects to the entire structure of politics and government in which each individual is having his own individual interest. Gandhi agreed with Carlyle's remark that it is "the talking shop of the world". Next in the line of attack is the much flaunted free British press. The press keeps on changing its stand frequently thereby misleading people who tend to follow it blindly.

'Civilization' is the title of the sixth chapter of *Hind Swaraj*. Gandhi's anger against this modern civilization is quite evident. Several others also gave the similar views—Tolstoy, Ruskin, Henry Maine, Blount and many more. Gandhi was highly influenced and impressed by their works. Edward Carpenter in his book "*Civilization: Its Cause and Cure*" called modern civilization a 'disease'. Gandhi also accepted the view but felt that "the cure of this disease is possible. This civilization makes man a prisoner of his craving for luxury and self-indulgence, releases the forces of unbridled competition, and thereby bring upon society the evils of poverty, disease, war and suffering. It is precisely because modern civilization looks at man as a limitless consumer and thus sets out to open the floodgates of industrial production that it also becomes the source of inequality, oppression and violence on a scale hitherto unknown in human history".[16] It is only a complete change in moral values that will change our perception in our social needs and thus enable us to set deliberate limits to social consumption. Gandhi considered Indian civilization a true civilization because it aims at moral upliftment of man. A true civilization would carry man towards peace and harmony and towards love and compassion.

The seventh chapter of *Hind Swaraj* is "Why was India Lost?" The question now arises that if civilization is a disease then how Englishmen have been able to take India and how they are able to retain it? Here Gandhi clarifies "The English have not taken India, we have given it to them. They are not in India because of their strength, but because we keep them… . They came to our country for purposes of trade…. They had not the slightest intention at the time of establishing a kingdom. Who assisted the Company's officers? Who was tempted at the sight of their silver? Who bought their goods? History testifies that we did all this. When our princes fought among themselves, they sought the assistance of Company Bahadur. The object of Britishers was to increase its commerce and to make money. We created the circumstances that gave the Company its control over India. Hence, it is truer to say that we gave India to the English than that India was Lost. Gandhi accepted that we lost not because of the weaknesses of our traditional civilization. Nor English civilization and their social system is better than us. We lost because of our greed. English rule is the product of irreligious, unethical civilization. The day we will stop supporting and assisting them, they will be bound to leave our country.

Chapters eight to twelve of *Hind Swaraj* clarifies 'The conditions of India' during British rule. Which factors are responsible for the impoverishment of India? Gandhi said "under modern civilization India is becoming irreligious".[17] Gandhi was in favour of that "Religion which underlies all religions".[18] Different religions preach to limit our worldly desires and emphasise that only our religious ambitions should be unlimited. In modern civilization we are engaged in more and more worldly pursuits.

In the next chapters, Gandhi attacked the very institutions which we have hitherto considered to be good—Railways, Lawyers, Doctors, Hospitals, Allopathic medicines all have impoverished the country. The railways have been responsible for the continuance of British rule in India and their effective control. Earlier, diseases like plague would be confined to our region only. Railways have assisted their rapid spread. Railways have encouraged people to sell their grains at far off places for higher prices thereby leading to famines in villages. Earlier people used to take pilgrimages out of the holy motives, now because of the comfortable journeys, pilgrimage has taken the form of tourism. The 'Reader' of *Hind Swaraj* raised the issue of spreading nationalism in India because of railways but Gandhi said that 'we were one nation before they came to India" they only divided us.

In the series of 'the condition of India' chapter ten points out the issue of Hindus and Muslims. It has been propagated that India is not a nation. Hindu and Muslims can never live with each other peacefully. There are so many differences in their religious beliefs. Gandhi makes it clear, "In no part of the world are one nationality and one religion synonymous terms, nor has it ever been so in India".[19] India cannot cease to be one nation because people belonging to different religions live in it. If the Hindus believe that India should be peopled only by Hindus, they are living in a dreamland. Even two brothers living together often fight. Different religions are different roads converging to the same point. Gandhi firmly believes that the existing mutual distrust between the two communities could be dissolved by creating mutual confidence and trust.

Gandhi was highly critical of the modern judicial-legal system. In chapter eleven, he criticized Lawyers by saying "my firm opinion is that Lawyers have enslaved India, have accentuated Hindu-Mohammadan dissensions and have confirmed English authority".[20] The very process of Law which thrives on conflict creates a vested interest among legal practitioners to perpetuate social divisions and indeed to create new ones. They advance quarrels instead of repressing them. Without Lawyers the courts could not have been established or conducted and without the latter the English could not rule.

In chapter twelve, Gandhi discusses how doctors and the modern medical system have ruined India. "Doctors and Hospitals are institutions for propagating sin". The spirit of scientific inquiry and technological innovation too is aimed more towards physical self-indulgence and Luxury than towards the discovery of Truth. The science of medicine on whose behalf the tallest claims are made by the propagators of modernity, concerns itself more with enabling people to consume more than with the removal of disease. "I overeat, I have indigestion, I go to the doctor, he gives me medicine. I am cured. I overeat again, I take his pills again."[21] And this only perpetuates the disease, it does not cure it. Allopathic medicines also violate our religious instinct because all sorts of animal parts and alcohol are used in the preparation of these medicines. No religion sanctions this. There is no real service of humanity in this profession. In this direction Gandhi supported Naturopathy, Homoeopathy, Dietary reforms as other alternatives to allopathic medicines. Even with the help of *Yoga*, change in living habits, eating habits, one can lead a healthy life.

Two more issues can be related with the evils of modern civilization. Both these issues are very controversial for a country like India. Even though in the coming years we find certain changes in the view point of Gandhi on these issues. But while writing *Hind Swaraj* Gandhi's views were negative on these two issues—education and machinery. In chapters eighteen and nineteen these two issues are discussed.

On education system, Gandhi criticized the British system of primary education. He even considered higher education imparted in India to be worthless because it does not deal with or teach the student values of life. Real education is about character building and performing one's duty towards family and society. "True education is that when we train our body to serve on our will, true education is that when one's mind is stored with knowledge of the fundamental truths of nature, true education is that when our senses are in our control. When man is in harmony with nature, he will make the best of it."[22] Gandhi pleaded for ethical education as the first and necessary component of education. To give millions knowledge of English is to enslave them. It is very sad that we speak of Home Rule in a foreign tongue. It is true that we cannot reject English outrightly. "Those English books which are valuable, we should translate them into various Indian languages." We should learn the education of religion, of ethics and morality.

The issue of 'machinery' is raised in chapter nineteen of *Hind Swaraj*. "Machinery is the chief symbol of modern civilization; it represents the great sin.... It is machinery that has impoverished India. Machinery is like a snake hole which may contain from one to a hundred snakes."[23] Again Gandhi said, "A snake bite is a lesser poisonous than machines and factories. The former merely destroys the body but the latter destroy body, mind and soul".[24]

In 1921, Gandhi remarked that he was not trying to destroy all machines and mills. He was only trying to contain its use so that the sufferings of the people is minimized. Machinery, that displaced people from work, that could be used to destroy human dignity and freedom and that generated mechanical mentality and made humans less human was rejected by Gandhi. Machinery, the chief symbol of modern civilization, is working against the welfare and wishes of comman people. Now the question arises that if this modern civilization and its various institutions are bad then which is the true civilization.

After pointing out at the evils of modern civilization, Gandhi proceeds to describe his views on "what is true civilization"—chapter thirteen of *Hind Swaraj*. "Civilization is that mode of conduct which points out to man the path of duty. Performance of duty and observance of morality are convertible terms. To observe morality is to attain mastery over our mind and our passions. In this way, we know ourselves and this is civilization."[25]

As the tendencies of Indian civilization aims at the moral upliftment of people, it is true civilization. The 'Reader' of *Hind Swaraj* raised the question about the weaknesses prevalent in Indian Society—child marriage, *Sati Pratha*, untouchability, caste system, animal killing, *Devadasi* system, etc. To answer this question Gandhi clarified "in no part of the world and under no civilization have all men attained perfection. The tendency of the Indian civilization is to elevate the moral being, that of the western civilization is to propagate immorality. The latter is Godless, the former is based on the belief in God. So every lover of India should cling to the old Indian civilization as the child clings to the mothers breast".[26]

Some other questions came to our mind. First as India is in the hands of Britishers then how can India become free? What methods we should adopt for the attainment of *Swaraj*? Can we adopt bad means for a good end? The answers to these questions, we can find in the chapters 14, 15, 16 and 17 of *Hind Swaraj*. The answer of question one "How can India become free"? In this chapter, Gandhi makes us understand that so far as the freedom of India is concerned we should not forget that we brought the English here and we keep them. We are adopting their civilization, so they are present in India. The day Indians left the attraction of modern civilization, we shall be free. Our hatred should not be for Britishers but for their civilization. "Indians were seduced by the glitter of modern civilization that they became a subject people. What keeps them in subjection is the acceptance by leading sections of Indians of the supposed benefits of civilization. As long as Indians continue to harbour illusions about the 'Progressive' qualities of modern civilization, they will remain a subject nation. Even if they succeed physically in driving out the English, they would still have English rule without the Englishman, because it is not the physical presence of the English which makes India a subject nation, it is civilization which subjects."[27] In this lesson Gandhi also clarifies the meaning of *Swaraj*. "It is *Swaraj* when we learn to rule ourselves. It is in the palm of our hands." This *Swaraj* is not a dream.

The important question now is that what methods we should adopt to win freedom. The example of Italian freedom movement is given in chapter fifteen where Garibaldi, a great warrior, gave arms in the hands of every Italian for struggle of independence with Austria. On the other hand Mazzini was a great saint. Gandhi's struggle was not like Garibaldi, he wanted *Swaraj* with the help of *Satyagraha*, *Ahimsa* and Truth.

Importance of 'ends and means' is discussed in chapter sixteen, though the title of this chapter is 'Brute Force'. The question of Ends and Means is the essence of Gandhian philosophy. "The means may be likened to a seed, the end to a tree; and there is just the same inviolable connection between the means and end as there is between the seed and the tree."[28] Violence breeds violence and so long as man uses violence as a means to settle his disputes, he would continue to suffer violence. Means and ends are not discrete, they constitute a continuum and they are interdependent. Both means and ends must be pure. One cannot achieve pure ends by impure ends. For an 'end' like '*Swaraj*' the 'means' should be truth and non-violence not the brute force. "The force of arms is powerless when matched against the force of Love or the Soul."[29]

The issue of "Passive Resistance" has been analysed in chapter seventeen. It means opposing whatever is evil without use of physical force, i.e., by soul force; self suffering. "It is a method of securing rights by personal suffering; it is the reverse of resistance by arms." Everybody admits that sacrifice of self is infinitely superior to sacrifice of others. Only the person using it suffers. He does not make others suffer. It implies that one should break the Laws, which are unjust, and be prepared to undergo the punishment for breaking the Law.

Gandhi later used the term *Satyagraha* in place of 'Passive resistance' as it has an element of force applied to the Soul of the opponent; whereas brute force is applied to the body of the opponent. *Satyagraha* has the element of proactiveness, not passiveness. It is not the weapon of the weak. It needs far more training, will power and self-control, than the use of physical force. It is an all-sided sword. Without drawing a drop of blood it produces far reaching results. Everyone knew that India achieved its independence with the power of *Satyagraha* and non-violence.

In the last chapter, Gandhi presented a way for future India. "*Swaraj* is not possible only by driving Britishers out, we have to achieve it for ourselves. We should have to overcome our weaknesses and shortcomings. We should be away from greed. Our senses should be in our control. We should use English language only in compulsion. We have to leave English institutions and system. We should not temper with nature. We should change our life style, eating habits. We should understand the importance of manual labour. In the direction of achieving *Swaraj*, we should be prepared to go to jails without any fear." In the end, Gandhi states that "Real home rule is self-rule or self-control; which could be achieved only through passive resistance; which requires the use of *Swadeshi*; and this could be achieved not by hating the English but by convincing them that their system and civilization was harmful".[30]

Context of *Hind Swaraj*

Intellectual/Philosophical Context of Hind Swaraj

Although *Hind Swaraj* is an original tract, while writing it Gandhi was heavily influenced by some of the leading western thinkers. As he himself admitted "whilst the views expressed in *Hind Swaraj* are held by me, I have but endeavoured humbly to follow Tolstoy, Ruskin, Thoreau, Emerson and other writers besides the masters of Indian philosophy".[31] The views expressed in *Hind Swaraj* are the result of deep study by Gandhi. Appendix-I of *Hind Swaraj* lists twenty books which remain the ideal starting point for discussion on Gandhian thought.

Indian Sources

Gandhi accepted in his 'Autobiography' that "The knowledge of my own religion is meagre; though I am a Hindu by birth, yet I don't have much knowledge of my own religion".[32] He had not even read the *Gita* until persuaded to do so in England by two theosophists. "They were reading Sir Edwin Arnold's translation—'The Song Celestial' and they invited me to read it. I felt ashamed as I had read the divine poem neither in Sanskrit nor in Gujarati. I was constrained to tell them that I had not read the *Gita*."[33] For the rest of his life, *Gita* became an infallible guide of conduct. It was a ready solution for all his troubles and travails. Gandhi's ideas on *aparigraha* (Non-possession) and *Nishkam Karma* (detached activity) were influenced by *Gita*. A play, seen in his childhood "Harishchandra" also captured his heart. He asked himself day and night that "why should not all be truthful like Harishchandra."[34] "Shravana Pitribhakti Nataka" also influenced him and left an impression on his mind. 'Here is an example for you to copy and do your duty'.[35] *Ramayana* also left a deep impression on Gandhi. During the days of his father's illness—a visitor 'Ladha Maharaj' regularly read *Ramayana*. Even the Family nurse Rambha taught him that "*Ram nam* is the remedy for all fears".[36] All this laid the foundation of Gandhi's deep devotion to the *Ramayana*. He regarded "The *Ramayana* of Tulsidas as the greatest book in all devotional literature".[37] He described the India of his dreams as *Ramrajya*. Even at the time of his death, the last words were 'Hey Ram'.

Gandhi was greatly influenced by Rajchandra on Indian philosophy. He was a Gujrati Jain, Bombay jeweller but his knowledge about *Dharma* and *Vairagya* impressed Gandhi. Gandhi accepted, "In my moments of spiritual crisis he was my refuge".[38] In a state of confusion, Gandhi once asked Rajchandra 27 Questions[39]. On God, soul, liberation, the *Vedas*, the *Gita*, the *Bible*, incarnation, Brahma, Vishnoo, Mahesh, devotion, etc. Rajchandra tried to answer these questions in detail.[40] On the meaning of *dharma* (religion) Rajchandra said, "*Dharma* does not mean any particular creed or dogma. Nor does it mean reading or learning by rote books known as *Shastras* (Sacred text) or even believing all that they say. *Dharma* is the quality of the soul present in every human being. *Dharma* is the mean by which we can know ourselves. We may accept this means from wherever we get it whether from India or Europe or Arabia".[41] Although Gandhi never accepted Rajchandra his spiritual *Guru* but his idea of a "religion which underlies all religions"[42] has its source in Rajchandra.

Western Sources

Gandhi's introduction to Western thought began in 1888 with his legal studies in London. He studied some fundamental texts these days – Broom's 'Common Law', Shell's 'Equity', White and Tudor's 'Leading Cases', William and Edwards's 'Real Property'. One thing he learnt forever, "moral law is superior to any constitutional Law." His practical skill in preparing petitions to government, drafting resolutions for various political bodies was because of his training in western jurisprudence. Gandhi used this skill very efficiently not only in India but also in South Africa.

Vegetarianism was also an important issue for Gandhi. Before leaving for London Gandhi took three vows; not to touch wine, woman and meat, on the insistence of his mother. He read variety of books on this subject: Anna Kingsford's *The Perfect Way in Diet* and Howard William's *The Ethics of Diet*. William's countered the myth that vegetarianism was the cause of defeat of Hindus at the hands of beef eating foreigners. Only prejudice, ignorance or sophistry will argue this way.

Tolstoy—The influence of Tolstoy on Gandhi is widely recognized. Gandhi directs the readers of *Hind Swaraj* to read six of Tolstoy's works, Listed in Appendix. These books cover four broad topics—critique of the new industrial civilization, colonial question in India, Christianity as an ethical religion and aesthetics.

In 1894, Gandhi read a book "*The Kingdom of God is within you*." He was deeply influenced by this. Tolstoy presented the case for Christianity as an ethical religion. At the heart of its teaching is the ethic of 'The sermon on the mount' which teaches the doctrine of non-violence. 'New Testament' raises many questions regarding temptations, agony, death, resurrection, violence and truth. We find answer to at least one question, i.e., violence in the world; how to settle the conflict between people. In this context, the solution taught by Christ is the only viable solution which is based on 'non-violence'. 'The Kingdom of God is within you' was mandatory reading for members of Phoenix settlement. Later Gandhi translated it into Gujarati.

Three other works of Tolstoy *How Shall We Escape?*, *The Slavery of Our Times* and *The First Step* mainly criticisms of the various aspects of the new industrial civilization. They deal with the evils of exploitation of workers, the degradation of the peasants, the rampant consumerism as the feature of modern life and the absence of virtue. Gandhi fully endorsed these views. In *Letter to a Hindoo* Tolstoy explained colonialism in India. Indians are as much responsible for this situation as are the Britishers. "It is not the English who have enslaved the Indians, but the Indians who have enslaved themselves. If the English have enslaved Indians it is because the latter recognized force as the fundamental principle of social order. For the Indians to complain about the English is like the alcoholic complaining about the wine merchants." In 'What is Art', Tolstoy accepted that there is a connection between aesthetics, ethics, symbols and political action. "Spinning wheel" the symbol of Gandhi communicated the value of solidarity between the rich and poor, of manual labour and appropriate technology.

Another writer who had deep influence on Gandhi was John

Ruskin. Gandhi derives the basic principles of his economic philosophy from Ruskin. Ruskin's book *A Joy Forever and its Price in the Market* was a critique of new industrial civilization as it provides luxury goods only for the few. It is not able to satisfy the basic needs of the many as food, shelter, clothing, education, health facilities. Ruskin said that "Blankets must come before silk laces" – "as long as there is cold and nakedness, there can be no question of splendour in dress".[43] Gandhi adopted Ruskin's dictum to India in the form of his doctrine of Appropriate Technology.

Ruskin's other book *Unto this Last* had more profound impact on Gandhi. In the chapter "The Magic Spell of a Book"[44] of his *Autobiography*, Gandhi wrote, "my friend Mr. Polak gave me this book to read during the journey (Johannesburg to Durban, 24 hours journey) and the book was impossible to lay aside once I had begun it, it gripped me".[45] Gandhi determined to change his life in accordance with the ideals of the book. Later on Gandhi translated it into Gujarati entitled *Sarvodaya* – the welfare of all. The teachings of *Unto this Last* were:

1. That the good of the individual is contained in the good of all.
2. That a lawyer's work has the same value as the barber's, inasmuch as all have the same right of earning their livelihood from their work.
3. That a life of labour, i.e., the life of the tiller of the soil and the handicraftsman, is the life worth living.[46]

The immediate result of reading this book was the establishment of 'phoenix settlement'. Later on Tolstoy Farm, (1910), Sabarmati Ashram (1915) and Sevagram, Vardha (1930) were established. Ruskin saw the value of handicrafts even in an industrial society. Gandhi saw the value of the spinning wheel, *khadi* and handicrafts for India.

The last chapter of *Sarvodaya* is like a prelude to *Hind Swaraj*. Gandhi felt that Indian middle class was clamouring for *Swaraj*, which is identified with political power to be gained by driving out the British by force and with economic prosperity brought about by rapid industrialization. This notion of *Swaraj* was not acceptable to Gandhi. Gandhi said, "Real *Swaraj* required not only political power and economic prosperity but also moral development among the people.... The new Indian middle class had not yet reached that level of moral development... If every Indian makes it, a point to follow truth always, India will achieve *Swaraj* as a matter of course".[47]

Gandhi's concern for modern civilization and *Swaraj* expressed itself in his deep interest in the revitalization of India's villages. He included Henry Maine's *Village Communities in the East and the West* in the Appendix. Gandhi said "*Swaraj* would mean little for India if the lives of the poor in the villages saw no significant improvement".[48] In a letter to his friend Henry Polak (October 14, 1909) Gandhi said, "Bombay, Calcutta and other chief cities of India are the real plague spots".[49] An over populated country like India which is heavily dependent on agriculture, the villages held the key to economic and political development. Maine felt that traditionally villages were representative institutions and they enjoyed certain judicial and legislative powers. But now these powers are shifted to lawyers and courts. In chapter Eleven of *Hind Swaraj*, Gandhi condemned the new breed of Lawyers.

Edward Carpenter's *Civilization: Its Cause and Cure* is mentioned in Chapter six of *Hind Swaraj*. Carpenter said "Civilization is a stage through which every society passes".[50] He used the metaphor of 'disease' for civilization. Gandhi retains the metaphor but modifies its use—'Modern Civilization is a curable Disease', and Gandhi presumably its doctor, as far as India is concerned.

Thomas Taylor's *The Fallacy of Speed* also influenced Gandhi. It is divided into three short chapters—"Speed and Population", "Speed and Profit" and "Speed and Pleasure". This book challenges the prevailing assumption that "faster is better." Here Gandhi related speed with railways and machines. Because of this speed people are shifting from rural areas to urban areas for opportunities, without thinking the results. Taylor concluded that "On the whole healthy conditions are less readily available under the reign of speed than they were under the reign of a slower pace".

Robert Harborough Shefard in his work *White Slaves of England* prescribed a harrowing account of the life of the average industrial worker in England. They share a common horrible slavery, poor wages and poor health care. The condition of women in the new factories is unimaginably appalling. Gandhi also presented the similar picture in *Hind Swaraj*. "Women who should be the queens of households, wander in the streets or they slave away in factories. Half a million women in England alone are labouring under the miserable circumstances in factories."[51] Gandhi was hopeful that a moral revolution in the hearts and minds of the rich and powerful is possible and this change is real *Swaraj*.

Godfrey Blount's pamphlet "A New Crusade" also appealed to Gandhi. Its motto was "simplicity, art and aspiration". This pamphlet was based on the principles like "machinery is the Devil's instrument, life without work is guilt, handicrafts and agriculture are conducive to human well-being, the betterment of the society begins with the betterment of the individual", etc. Gandhi also started his crusade for the *Khadi* (compulsory for members of different Gandhi Ashrams to wear *Khadi* and to use hand made goods).

Max Nordau's name is also included in the appendix. He wrote two books—*Conventional Lies of Civilization* and *Paradoxes*. Gandhi read both the books and felt that "pessimism was the keynote of the nineteenth century European civilization. Pessimism is there in art, literature, religion, economics and politics. The reason for this is the lack of truth in our lives. Today, the cities grow at the expense of the farming population. The attitude towards manual labour is reprehensible. The modern liberal professions, lawyers and doctors are parasitic since they draw on both rich and the poor.

Henry David Thoreau remained a source of life long inspiration for Gandhi. His 'Principles of Civil Disobedience' was paraphrased and published in *Indian Opinion*. Gandhi was heartened to read that conscience should have the ultimate say in judging what is politically right and wrong. Thoreau said that while it is not one's duty to eradicate evil, it is certainly one's first duty not to give support to it. Though the genesis of *Satyagraha* had occurred independently of him, Gandhi did find confirmation for his new philosophy. Thoreau's second book *Life Without Principles* is also listed in the Appendix. Gandhi agreed with it that "Politics without virtue is a kind of vegetation. What modern politics needs most is a high and earnest purpose".

After reviewing the impact of western intellectual sources on Gandhi, one can say that he was not completely opposed to Western civilization. Earnest Barker said, "his attack was limited to certain unhealthy tendencies in modern western civilization and this attack was not motivated by any narrow nationalism or anti-colonialism". In *Hind Swaraj* he shared the views of many western thinkers in defence of true civilizational values.

Historical Context

The Question of Modern Civilization

Gandhi's critique of modern civilization is one of the main contribution to modern political thought. It is important to note that though his attitude towards modern civilization is highly critical but it is not completely negative. He welcomes a number of its contributions like civil liberty, equality, rights, liberation of women from tradition and religious toleration. But this welcome is conditional as rights are to harmonise with duties, liberty with *Swaraj*, religious toleration with religious belief and economic development with spiritual progress.

Gandhi has his own definition of civilization. In *Hind Swaraj* Gandhi wrote "Civilization is that mode of conduct which points out to man the path of duty".[52] By modern civilization he meant that mode of conduct which emerged from the industrial revolution. This revolution brought into being a new mode of life. It changed people's outlook towards nature, religion, ethics, science, knowledge, technology, politics and economics. Nature now is mastered and possessed at will for the satisfaction of human needs and desires. The desire for economic prosperity became the main object of politics. The industrial revolution altered the concept of Labour, accepted mainly to produce profit, power and capital. Manual labour was looked upon as fit for the backwards only. Now, machines became the masters and man became a slave.

With modern civilization two types of political theories emerged—Liberalism for the industrialized societies and imperialism-colonialism for the non-industrialized societies. World is divided into rich and poor, industrialized and non-industrialized or civilized and 'non-civilized'. Gandhi felt that in this modern civilization there is no place for religion and ethics. This civilization is based on bodily comforts and responsible for all kinds of exploitation.

Gandhi felt that modern civilization and industrialization work together. Machinery is the chief symbol of this civilization and it represents a great sin. It has changed the concept of labour and man has become lazy. In this civilization, the conditions of labour class are worst. Gandhi said "A snake bite is lesser poisonous as it merely destroys the body but machines destroys body, mind and soul".[53] There is a difference between 'true civilization' and the 'civilization based on machines'. True civilization is based on religion, ethics and morality while factory civilization is based on greed and exploitation. "The tendency of the Indian civilization is to elevate the moral being that of the Western civilization is to propagate immorality. The latter is Godless and the former is based on a belief in God."[54] Our greed and desires gave birth to colonialism and imperialism which ultimately is responsible for exploitation. Colonialism and industrialization are complementary to each other and harmful for human society.

Gandhi felt that for an ordinary Indian, railways and other means of transport represents speed. Hospitals, doctors and allopathic medicines represent modern health system. So, people are forgetting nature cure and dietary reforms. Courts and Lawyers are representing modern judicial system. So, traditional Panchayati Raj system is vanishing. English education became the symbol of modern education system and machines became the symbol of development and production. Besides all these, Indians are accepting parliamentary system as an alternative. The emerging middle class is accepting all the things which are western. Gandhi was not happy with this trend and he supported our traditional civilization based on truth, morality, compassion, religion and justice.

The Politics of South Africa

Gandhi's critique of modern civilization took a concrete shape not in India but in South Africa. He first acquired his vision of Indian nationalism in South Africa. Even his unique political philosophy and political techniques developed in Transvaal and Natal and not in Khera, Bardoli or Champaran. In this context, his leadership role in *Natal Indian Congress* and *Transvaal British Indian Association* is important. Initially, Gandhi went to South Africa just for two years for a Muslim firm but after seeing the conditions of Indians, he remained there for 20 years. The campaign against the discriminatory Legislation against Indian labourers, traders and settlers, the starting of *Satyagraha* and its different techniques, his career as a lawyer and a journalist, running the weekly journal *Indian Opinion* and the establishment of Phoenix settlement and Tolstoy Farm, all these things happened in South Africa only.

Some more issues associated with South Africa need highlighting. First, it was in South Africa Gandhi became aware of the fact that modern civilization was the root of the colonial problem. If Lenin connected colonialism to capitalism. Gandhi went one step further and connected colonialism with modern civilization. Gandhi accepted in his *Autobiography* "Western Civilization is predominantly based on force."[55] In a question to Gandhi, it has been asked "Supposing the whites carry out their threats, how will you stand by your principle of non-violence? Gandhi replied, I hope god will give me the courage and the sense to forgive them".[56]

Modern civilization rested on two fallacious maxims—'might is right' and the 'Survival of the fittest'. But these maxims are centrifugal and lacked a 'goal'. On the other hand Indian civilization had set goals (Truth, Love, Justice, Religion, Ethics, Compassion, Non-violence). It was 'adaptive' and 'contemplative'. "A Civilization or a condition in which all the forces fly away from the centre must necessarily be without a goal, whereas those who converge to a point have always a goal."[57] In *Satyagrah in South Africa* Gandhi wrote it was neither vulgar racism nor trade jealousy that motivated him, the motivating force was his concern for modern civilization. The whites considered themselves the representatives of modern civilization. They want to protect and promote this civilization at any cost. Indians are disliked not for their vices but for their virtues—simplicity, patience, perseverance. On the other hand Westerners are impatient, enterprising and engrossed in multiplying their material wants. They were afraid that allowing Indians to settle in South Africa would be like "Cultural Suicide".[58]

The second issue associated with South Africa was the relative "Social freedom". Because of this freedom, Gandhi conducted his social and political experiments for India easily. He found himself "free from certain restrictions from which our people suffer in India".[59] The establishment of Phoenix settlement and its experiments were not possible without this social freedom. Here Indian women were free from a number of social taboos. Gandhi wrote "Phoenix is a nursery for producing right men, women and Indians. It is a more suitable place for making experiments and gaining proper training. There are no undesirable restraints in Phoenix. Indian women would never have come out so boldly as they are doing at Phoenix".[60]

Thirdly, Gandhi acquired the diplomatic skills, necessary for dealing with the British political establishment in London. During these visits Gandhi came into contact with many expatriate Indians living abroad. These were the new converts to modern civilization. Their uncritical acceptance of modern civilization bothered Gandhi. The harmful effects of this western/modern civilization when imported to India and propagated by Indians themselves were incalculable.

The Indian National Movement

As the historical context of *Hind Swaraj*, various aspects of Indian national movement are important. For Gandhi, India is a nation and it has its own identity. Indian nationalism should never legitimize violence as a means of National Liberation. *Hind Swaraj* opens with an analysis of the Indian National Congress. In 1885, Congress was established and its leadership was in the hands of moderates. These moderates were demanding certain political reforms with the help of constitutional methods. But after the Partition of Bengal, 1905, an important change in Indian national movement came. Leaders like Lala Lajpat Rai, Bal Gangadhar Tilak, Vipin Chander Pal, Arvind Ghosh were in total contrast with moderates. They demanded '*Swaraj*'. Tilak said, "*Swaraj* is my birth right". The *swadeshi* movement was also gaining momentum. Dissatisfaction against the policies of Britishers was there.

As a lawyer and as political activist Gandhi was well informed of what was going on in India. He felt that a large number of politically conscious Indian middle class were being strongly attracted to modern civilization and political violence. The moderates stood for *Swaraj,* defined as self-government within the Empire, achieved through constitutional means granted by the imperial parliament gradually. Gandhi knew from his South African experiences that mere constitutionalism did not get you anything. The extremists stood for *Swaraj* defined as complete sovereignty achieved through constitutional means if possible but through other means if necessary. (While the names of some moderates—Dada Bhai Naoroji, Gopal Krishna Gokhale, Badr-ud-Din Tayabji are mentioned with respect in *Hind Swaraj*, no extremist is mentioned by name) Gandhi was aware of what Tilak and Arvind Ghosh were writing in their newspapers—The '*Kesari*' the '*Maratha*' and '*Vande Mataram*'. Tilak's revival of Ganpati festival and the memory of Shivaji, Arvind Ghosh's concept of *Shakti* in its violent form, mythologised by Durga, Kali and Bhawani, did not help the cause of a composite Indian nationalism that Gandhi was trying to promote.

While no work by the extremists is included in the appendix, two works by the moderates appear in it. ('*Poverty and Unbritish rule in India*' by Naoroji and '*The Economic History of India*' by R.C. Dutt) These works set the tone of the argument against the evils of colonial rule. (The colonial economic policies served primarily the interests of alien investors and only secondarily those of the average Indian). In short, the moderates began well with good intentions but with time they rethought their goals, methods and priorities. *Hind Swaraj* is an alternative to both uncreative constitutionalism and violent extremism.

In the whole episode of Indian national movement, there was also the question of Indian Muslims. Gandhi worked in close harmony with Muslims in all his South African campaigns. On his London trips he was accompanied by Muslim leaders of the Indian community. He had no reason to think that Indian Muslims would turn away from the general direction that Indian nationalism was taking. That is why Gandhi supported Morley-Minto recommendations for special electoral status for Indian Muslims. His conception of nationalism and *Swaraj* were neutral as far as religion as sect was concerned. He saw first all Indians as members of a single nation and then members of a sect or a caste or a region.

The Immediate Context

The Politics of Expatriates

Hind Swaraj was definitely a critique on modern civilization but the violent activities of young Indians were also there in the mind of Gandhi. Gandhi wrote in *Hind Swaraj* "The bravery of these Indian anarchists impressed me. But their zeal was misguided by adopting violent methods, they are following a suicidal policy."[61] In the starting of 20th century, some Indian youth settled in England, US, Canada or Japan to prepare themselves for careers in science, technology, law, medicine, etc. They were nationalists but their disenchantment with the Indian National Congress can be seen. They were attracted to various European revolutionary movements – Marxism, Irish home rule movement, terrorism, etc. Some of them were active supporters of Indian Secret Societies like 'Abhinav Bharati' of Bombay and 'Anushilan Samiti" of Bengal. While abroad, they continued their support by sending to India, manuals for making bombs and other weapons of destruction. To Gandhi they appeared to be misguided Indians committed to 'modern civilization' who wished to fashion India on the model of Great Britain, Itlay or Japan.

The most important name in these expatriates was Shyamji Krishna Verma. He came to England to work for Indian nationalist cause. He was influenced by the views of Herbert Spencer. Verma started various scholarships for Indians. The object behind this was to bring bright Indian youth to Europe and America for training in theory and practice of violent revolution. He was also the founder of "India House" 1905 (To offer residential facilities to young Indians. Gandhi also stayed there for few days in 1906 and had conversations with Verma) He also started a monthly *The Indian sociologist* dedicated to the ideas of Herbert Spencer. "Resistance to aggression is not simply justifiable but imperative. Non-resistance hurts both altruism and egoism".

V.D. Savarkar was another name behind this group of expatriates. He came to London in 1906 on Tilak's recommendation. He was arrested for revolutionary activities. In London he produced two works—one, a translation of Mazzini's life from English into Marathi and the other *The Indian War of Independence of 1857*. It was a militaristic interpretation of events of 1857.

The most prominent among the revolutionaries to be influenced by Savarkar was Madanlal Dhingra. His assassination of Sir William Curzon Wyllie (The ADC to the Secretary of State for India) on 1st July, 1909, a few days before Gandhi's arrival in London, shook London and Gandhi also. For Gandhi it was an act of terrorism legitimized by nationalism. Actually, Savarkar was the man who incited Dhingra to commit the murder. Madam Bhikaji Rustom Kama, U. Chattopadhyaya, Tarak Nath Das, were others in this series. The main question for Gandhi as well as for these expatriates was how to attain *Swaraj*? While Gandhi said that non-violence is the only legitimate means to achieve this end. The expatriates opposed it. The arguments of *Hind Swaraj* are certainly in response to these expatriates. By 1909, Gandhi had integrated all the essential ingredients of his ideas, experiences and experiments into a coherent whole in the form of a booklet *Hind Swaraj*.

Discussions on *Hind Swaraj*

Hind Swaraj did not get a favourable response in India initially. It was proscribed by the then Government of Bombay Presidency stating "It had the potential of spreading disaffection among the people of India against the British Government".[62] Gopal Krishna Gokhale, whom Gandhi considered his political *Guru* said that "this book is so crude and hastily conceived".[63] He prophesied that Gandhi himself would destroy the book after spending a year in India. In 1921 Gandhi said, "With deference to the memory of the great teacher, I may say that his prediction has failed to come true".[64]

The first evaluation of *Hind Swaraj* or "Indian Home Rule" took place in 1938 *via* volume IX, September 1938 issue in '*Aryan Path*' by nine western writers and intellectuals (Frederick Soddy, G.D.H. Cole, C. Delisle Burns, John Middleton Murry, J.D. Beresford, Hugh Fausset, Claude Houghten, Gerald Heard and Irene Rathbone). Professor Fredrick Soddy, a well known economist said, "In this little booklet Gandhi expounds the principles of Non-violence and non-cooperation".[65] He suggested that people should read *Hind Swaraj* and make their own opinion about it. "If you want to know anything about anyone outstanding probably the worst thing to do is to read other people's impressions about him and his work."[66] But Soddy refers to Gandhi's criticism of modern civilization as destructive, the railways, lawyers and doctors, "the very institutions we have hitherto considered to be good".[67] Gandhi wanted "No Lawyers, no Courts, no English". Soddy said that having just returned from a visit to India, I saw little outwardly to suggest that the doctrine inculcated in the book had attained any considerable measure of success. But one thing is sure "anyone who wishes to change the world, would do well after studying this book".[68]

G.D.H. Cole said that this book has "a deep power to disturb our minds".[69] Gandhi saw weaknesses in Western civilization (Western ideals, western action, standards of value). He was repudiating these things not only for India but also for humanity. Western law, western medicine, western machinery, all these things had weaknesses. But Indian civilization is also full of weaknesses (Child marriage, *Sati*, Prostitution, Sacrifice of animals in the name of religion). Cole was unable to understand that how this Western civilization is working against 'Human Soul'. He did not accept that world will be in safer and better position without scientific inventions or without hospitals and doctors. But Cole accepted that this small booklet has "a deep power to disturb our minds".

C.Delisle Burns expressed his views in two ways. First welcoming the book Burn said that the governing principles of Gandhi's thought are valid and undeniable. "Moral distinctions between good and bad, right and wrong, justice and injustice, are of fundamental importance, as compared with more superficial distinctions between men in race, sex, religion on political opinion. No civilization at all is possible unless this is admitted".[70] Gandhi's concept of Ends and Means (right end must be achieved through rightful means) is also acceptable. But Burns notes some serious problems with regard to Gandhi's choice of doctors, lawyers, machines, etc., of as manifestations of Western civilization. In the West, there is a great tradition of music, arts, drama, and poetry. There are examples of religious and moral insight and enthusiasm which are not less great than those of any other types of civilization.

Another mistake in Gandhi's teaching is his 'condemnation of machinery as evil'. "This is a fundamental philosophical error. It implies that we are to regard as morally evil any instrument which may be misused ..... But it is ridiculous to treat as morally good or evil the mechanism which can be used equally by saints and villains."[71] Any mechanism may be misused. But if it is the moral evil, it is in the man who misuses it, not the mechanism.

Johan Middleton Murry called *Hind Swaraj* the "Spiritual classic." "*Hind Swaraj* is the greatest book that has been written in modern times."[72] But he finds certain contradictions also. First, his criticism of Parliamentary democracy was scathing but his corporate life was devoted to the attainment of Parliamentary *Swaraj*. Second, his condemnation of the technical civilization of Europe as evil was not acceptable to Murry. "Machine is only a tool; it is not evil; much depends on who uses it and for what purpose." But even after all these disagreements and contradictions, *Hind Swaraj* is a great book and Gandhi the greatest teacher.

J.D. Beresford not only appreciates but accepts for personal practice the doctrine of "Soul force".[73] *Hind Swaraj* was written in 1909 and after almost thirty years nothing has been changed or altered. Because there was nothing to alter. The lessons it taught were not about political issues (ever changing) but they were moral issues (Non-violence, Love, Compassion, Truth, Religion). Nobody can find faults with these issues. Even when he said, "machinery is one of the false gods worshipped by modern man, a god that will ultimately help to destroy him. The craze for greater speed, increasing restlessness, the demand for distraction, can only lead to destruction".[74] The condemnation of machinery is becoming a familiar outcry now-a-days. The truth is that "We can still practice in our own lives, the law of love to mankind".

Hugh A. Fausset considers *Hind Swaraj* as a bold attempt to save India from "Modern civilization which is eating into the vitals of the west."[75] There is a need to save India not from Englishmen but from the modern civilization. Mr. Gandhi claims that "Civilization requires the use of a different and higher weapon for self-protection than that of brute force". Fausset said, "This is a profoundly revolutionary little book that is addressed not only to Indians but for Englishmen also".

With time, Gandhi was ready to tolerate parliamentary home rule, railways, hospitals, law courts, machinery and mills as at best necessary evils, which will die a natural death. When enough people come into the possession of their true selves. Fausset also agreed with Gandhi that "machinery represents a great sin". For him, "*Hind Swaraj* is one of the best modern hand books of the real revolution, which must happen in us all, if we are to fulfil the creative purpose of life".[76]

For Gandhi, the real home rule is self-rule and the way to achieve it is 'Passive resistance" that is soul force and love force. He not only preached passive resistance but practiced it in thought and act. To a world, rapidly becoming quite irreligious he taught here the practice of the "religion which underlies all religions".[77]

Claude Houghton clarifies that *Hind Swaraj* deals with a number of subjects—Home Rule for India, lawyers, doctors, machinery, railways, education, etc., but essentially it revolves around two themes. One Western civilization, with all its skyscraper glories, is a plague and India would be infected by it. Two, the main theme is that Love alone has power. It is madness to fight evil with its own weapons. One must resist it passively. "Passive Resistance is a method of securing rights by personal suffering..... If I do not obey the Law and accept the penalty for its breach, I use soul force, it involves sacrifice of self."

To fight evil with its own weapons is to deny the righteousness of God. With this booklet Gandhi teaches us the path of duty. He said "civilization is that mode of conduct which points out to man the path of duty".[78] Duty! Not right, not ambition, not self glorification. Gandhiji's main contention is that if we have inner freedom, no one has power over us. If we are slaves to any one or anything, we have created this slavery. "If we become free, India is free. If we serve evil, we become the slaves of evils."[79] Gandhi wrote in *Hind Swaraj* "Our enemies are not outside the gates, but within them". Pride, envy, lust, sloth, inertia, greed – these are our enemies, because we have served them. They are the cause of the misery of man. Self rule is the only freedom.

Gerald Heard compared *Hind Swaraj* with Rousseau's *Social Contract* and Karl Marx's *Das Capital* and considered it superior to both. "*Hind Swaraj* is more significant because it does not mark an end of an age but the beginning of a new order."[80] Gandhi opened a new path. He put into practice new means, "the right means which alone can lead to right end". Wrong and evil methods can only lead to wrong and evil results. Gandhi has attempted to solve the economic issue also, by making every peasant his own manufacturer. If our self will is strong, we can attain this work order.

Irene Rathbone describes *Hind Swaraj* as an 'enormously powerful' booklet. It has forced her "by its tremendous honesty to search my own honesty", therefore, I would implore people to read it. Gandhi said that "this book replaces violence with self-sacrifice, it pits soul force against brute force". Gandhi's doctrine of "Passive Resistance does not mean that its practice is easy. It requires a more stringent training and a greater fearlessness, than the warriors. Its appeal is potent".[81]

But Rathbone fears that the system in which we live and the forms which evil is taking now in the world are so subtle and atrocious that it is no longer a matter of suffering one's own death, but the death of one's children. The modern tyrant says if you won't obey me or refuse to accept my rules, your family shall pay the penalty. Which human being would see his/her children being torn to pieces, if by bowing to the tyrant and denying one's own conscience, the children could be saved. That question Gandhi did not answer. But Gandhi beautifully said, "Strength lies in absence of fear, not in the quantity of flesh and muscle we may have on our bodies". No doubt there is tremendous honesty in the book to search one's own honesty.

Thus on the whole the book appealed to all those European authors who even expressed their doubts on many of Gandhi's formulations as Gandhi's prescriptions presented in *Hind Swaraj* were not political, they were spiritual and ethical.

Gandhi-Nehru Debate/Discussion on Hind Swaraj

Both Gandhi and Nehru were pre-eminent founders of modern India. They agreed as well as disagreed on many issues. At the heart of their disagreement lay the basic thesis of *Hind Swaraj*, which they debated frequently. In a letter to Nehru, Gandhi wrote on 5th October, 1945 that "I still stand by the system of government envisaged in *Hind Swaraj*..... I am convinced that if India is to attain true freedom, then sooner or later the fact must be recognised that people will have to live in villages, not in towns, in huts, not in palaces. Crores of people will never be able to live at peace with each other in towns and palaces. They will have to resort to violence and untruth. I hold that without truth and non-violence there can be nothing but destruction for humanity. We can realize truth and non-violence only in the simplicity of village life.... The essence of what I have said is that man should rest content with what are his real needs and become self-sufficient. If he does not have this control he cannot save himself. The village of my dreams is still in my mind. My ideal village will contain intelligent human beings. They will not live in dirt and darkness as animals. Men and women will be free and able to hold their own against anyone in the world. There will be neither plague nor cholera, nor small pox; no one will be idle, no one will wallow in luxury. Everyone will have to contribute his quota of manual labour".[82]

In his reply to Gandhi, Nehru wrote on 9th October, 1945 that "the question before us is not one of truth *versus* untruth, or non-violence *versus* violence. The whole question is how to achieve this Society and what its content should be. I do not understand why a village should necessarily embody truth and non-violence. Normally speaking, a village is backward intellectually and culturally and no progress can be made from a backward environment. Narrow minded people are much more likely to be untruthful and violent. It seems to me inevitable that modern means of transport as well as many other modern developments must continue and be developed. I do not think, it is possible for India to be really independent unless she is a technically advanced country. There is no question of Palaces for millions of people. But there seems to be no reason why millions should not have comfortable homes.

It is many years ago since I read *Hind Swaraj* and I have only a vague picture in my mind. But even when I read it 20 or more years ago it seemed to me 'completely unreal'. "It is 38 years since *Hind Swaraj* was written. The world has completely changed since then. Of course, there are problems and evils in modern civilization, but how to get rid of this evil and yet to keep the good in the present as in the past is our problem. Obviously, there is good too in the present".[83]

On 13 November, 1945, Gandhi again wrote to Nehru and said that "there is not much difference in our outlook".

- The real question, for Nehru is how to bring about man's highest intellectual, economic, political and moral development. Gandhi agreed on it entirely.
- Both agreed that there should be an equal right and opportunity for all.
- There should be equality between the town-dwellers and the villagers in the standard of food and drink, clothing and other living conditions. In order to achieve this equality today people should be able to produce for themselves the necessities of life.
- Man is not born to live in isolation but is essentially a social animal independent and interdependent.

In another attempt, to bring out some Indian opinions on *Hind Swaraj* a symposium was organized by Gandhi Peace Foundation in 1973. A special issue in *Gandhi Marg* was published, with the title 'Towards a Counter Civilization'. The main purpose of this symposium was to assess its relevance to the then situation in India and to draw lessons from it for India's future development. Among the participants were Sugata Das Gupta, Devdutt, R.R. Diwakar, R.C. Majumdar, D.R. Mankekar, R.K. Patil, Mohit Sen, Badr-ud-Din Tayabji and others. The discussion centred about the question of suitability of Gandhian model of development. The central theme in *Hind Swaraj* is that "Modern technology is destructive of human autonomy and freedom and that the affluence and power it brings is not worth the candle".[84] Through *Hind Swaraj* Gandhi called upon India to reject modern civilization and to return to her ancient ways. He wanted a total cultural revolution. The question now is —Can India yet return to the vision of Gandhi?

Sugata Das Gupta felt that "Gandhi has beckoned us not to the past but to a future society—a solid rational system based on reasoning and resource".[85] His recipe was global though he was mainly concerned with Indian liberation. Explaining Gandhian model, Sugata Das Gupta said, "The goal of all tne developed and developing countries of the world today is 'development'. Development here means high standard of living, accompanied by 'consumption baskets' constructed by big advertising consortiums, provide the dynamic definition of this new phenomenon". Gandhi said, development was not desirable because it was feasible only in a non-egalitarian, exploitative framework and not where principles of equality were practised. The logic here is based on arithmetic. If development has been possible in the USA, it is because of the fact that six per cent of the world population have been using seventy per cent of its resources. So, it is not possible for the 70 per cent of the third work to develop with the ten per cent of resources, now at their disposal. Assuming theoretically, that the world's resources are equitably distributed and every person could use one per cent of resources, how could they attain 'development' as we understand it today? So, aiming at a 'no poverty' and 'no development' Society, Gandhi's design provides the only rational and realizable goal. Gandhi's logic of development should be the talisman for the nations of the third world. But so simple an arithmetic is often so difficult to grasp. So, development is a pernicious doctrine aimed at the systematic exploitation of the masses.

Devdutt points out that although *Hind Swaraj* was written in 1909, it reflects the essential conditions of India today. In this sense, Gandhi's prescriptions have considerable contemporary relevance.

So far as the conditions of India are concerned it can be said:

- The culture of our people is being poisoned by imitative westernism and unreflecting industrialism.
- Moral decadence permeates the centres of power and this erosion of values is unprecedented.
- The new means of communication are growingly becoming disseminators of evil.
- Tyranny, hypocrisy, double talk, double think, open cut throat competition and unethical politics are rampant.
- Communal conflicts and caste antagonisms are also there.
- The English speaking and English knowing people have completely enslaved India, middle classes are enlarging and there is danger of embourgeoisiement.

And for these problems Gandhi provides us with an approach, i.e., "India has nothing to learn from anybody else". There is a need to recover our faith in our own civilization. Some prescriptions are given by Gandhi, for the attainment of a new Society.

- Discourage, the process which enlarges the base of the middle classes and promotes middle class values. Reject the present system of education, abandon the present laws and legal process, deflate the importance of parasitical professionalization and commercialization.
- The craze for industrialism must be overcome. Gandhi wants to neutralize the dehumanizing, enslaving and exploitative tendencies of machines. "Today machinery helps a few to ride on the backs of millions."[86]
- In *Hind Swaraj*, Gandhi makes a plea for the gospel of love and aims at replacing violence with self-sacrifice. This is essential today.

Hind Swaraj is a comprehensive enunciation of the conditions of India, of what should be our approach to deal with our sickness and what action should be followed to build a new society. Now-a-days, there is a growing awareness of the hazards of rapid and large scale industrialization. Ecological consciousness is increasing (Environmental degradation, pollution, global warming, naturopathy, Ayurveda, Organic food, *Yoga*, meditation, vegetarianism). *Hind Swaraj* provides definitely an answer to all these problems.

R.R. Diwakar clearly stated that India has not accepted Gandhi and his philosophy as a whole. All religious and spiritually oriented leaders and cults from the beginning of history have dreamt like Gandhi and they have failed. Gandhi was totally against partition, but partition happened and new problems arise as Gandhi warned. Now, the question comes of Gandhi's opposition to modern civilization, as stated in *Hind Swaraj*, based on science and technology and the multiplication of wants. It is very true that "man is a tool maker, but every tool makes him a slave, as he has to depend on it".[87] There is an old saying that "every dependence is a source of sorrow and every self-reliance is a source of joy".[88] But today's advanced science and technology have not come from outside. A total rejection is neither possible nor advisable. What is necessary is for man to remain the master and not to succumb to their overwhelming influence. Rejecting them would mean rejection of man's own potentialities without trial. "Making the instruments, trying them, using them without becoming their slaves is a way of the creator. Rejecting them out of fear and apprehension is a weakness."[89] Even Gandhi was never for total rejection. He said, we should invent, accept and use science and technology without exploitation and without losing mastery over them. His views about the uses of science and technology were quite clear—use them if they were consistent with human values and the spiritual betterment of man, not of a few but of the whole of humanity. Non-exploitation of man by man and decentralization of power are the keystones of his human philosophy and they flow from the dictum: attainment of truth through non-violence alone.

Durga Das described the title of the symposium as "Towards a Human Civilization" instead of "Towards a counter civilization". Gandhi's *Hind Swaraj* is based on eternal values. It has been ignored by his disciples and successors, for they were enamoured by the products of western civilization. The world has so far lived on the opiate provided by religion. Technology and science have destroyed man's blind faith in religion, but they cannot provide a substitute. It is for us to find another 'opiate'. It should be based on a proper balance between man's physical needs as ordained by modern conditions and his spiritual impulses. And this is possible if we pool the world's resources for economic regeneration, social well-being and human fulfilment.

Prabhakar Machwe felt that we Gandhians are responsible for making Gandhian principles and programmes as rituals. There is a need to change our social behaviour. "How many of us interdine, inter-marry, encourage inter-caste friendship and harmony?" We live in a nation where northerner hates the southerner and *vice versa*. Gandhi emphasized that physical labour ought to be respected and treated at par with the so called intellectual labour. But even after independence, the subtle caste system still plagues us. Technocrats and bureaucrats still rule over the dumb masses of workers. There is a disparity in the incomes which is unbridgeable. Corruption has gone deep into our system. This situation has to change. Charity begins at home. We should live more naturally, tidying up our surroundings, make one illiterate, literate and so on. Change will definitely come.

D.R. Mankekar said that our country is passing through an intense moral crisis—a crisis of character and credibility. So, it is right that our nation should turn for solace and refuge to the ideals of Gandhi. But there are certain questions to be asked:

1. Is it possible to turn our backs on the modern scientific age. Without large scale industrialization, can we really solve our unemployment problems?
2. Can we do agrarian reforms and maximize food production without modernizing agriculture?
3. When the security of our country is at threat from close and distant neighbours can we work on "Sermon on the Mount" principles?

It is very true that we refused to rely on non-violence to defend our hard won independence. We are not prepared to accept Gandhian theory of trusteeship in industrial relations. For our problems going back to the Gandhian ethics and values in public and private life seems imperative. But such a transformation of Indian society is impossible without a whole scale change in the "Leadership."

"A good leadership could have easily moulded the Indian people into a great nation by eliminating their civic weaknesses, quickening their sense of public duty and social conscience and fostering social discipline in them".[90] These qualities have been eroding among the Indian people. So, there is need to start with a radical change in the leadership of the country. "Clean administration, honest leaders and return to the rule of Law, is the need of the time. Such a leadership alone can generate an entirely new atmosphere of right conduct and Gandhian values."[91]

R.K. Patil, on the one hand, accepted that India is facing problems like high prices, unemployment, corruption, unplanned urbanization, tendency of violence, etc. But even after all these problems, India has adopted the path of modern industrialization for its all-round development and not that of *Hind Swaraj*. Even

Gandhi wanted India's development through parliamentary system, i.e., decentralized democracy. So, in the due course, problems must arise. It is easy to suggest a change and ask for a return to "the vision of Gandhi. But to adopt it in the concrete would require another Gandhi, another leadership and perhaps another people".[92] India has decided to sink or swim with the rest of the world and accepted development and progress through industrialization.

On the other hand, Patil also said that it will be a mistake to assume that Gandhi has no relevance today. His Constructive Programme can be re-examined with the changing circumstances. The fight against untouchability and caste, communal unity, Leprosy work, national Language programme, all are relevant even today. Even khadi and village industries, basic education can be reinterpreted in the modern context. As a nation, we have to introspect and question ourselves about the causes of the present malaise and evolve remedies dictated by our reason and perception.

Mohit Sen accepted the sickening moral crisis pervading in the Indian society. We are seeing that "millions starve but monopolists hoard foodgrains". The remedy is not the preaching of morals but drastic social surgery – the removal of these breeding grounds of a thoroughly immoral situation. Though we have achieved economically in the last few years but we failed also on many points; the remedy lies not in preaching of morals but the proclamation of a programme of struggle against the morally decayed order.

Badr-ud-Din Tayabji also accepted that the present state of affairs in our country has reached one of its lowest points. "Gandhi's whole philosophy lies in its advocacy of the ideal of self-sufficiency." He did not want a complete turning of the face to the progress of technology and man's mastery over matter. He wanted man to use technology and material progress for its true purpose, i.e., to enable man to live in this world in a manner that would help him to feel at peace with himself and with other living beings and the environment. For this purpose there has to be a harmony between means and ends.

For Indian masses, Gandhi suggested a system of production of which they are masters not the slaves. That is why, he was against the importation of foreign techniques of industrialization and manufacture which turn the worker into nothing more than a slave. The classic example of this was his attitude towards the *charkha*. He wanted village production to rise leading to the establishment of small scale village industries. Even today, if the state would devote itself of providing us with the foods which, without either enslaving each other or corrupting ourselves, make us the master of our own destiny, India will become a happier and more prosperous nation.

P. Kodando Rao was not convinced with the ideas proposed in *Hind Swaraj*. He said, Gandhi is a prophet to be worshipped but most of his concrete policies do not seem to have universal relevance. The main purpose of *Hind Swaraj* was the demand of home rule for India. Gandhi said "British rule had introduced the Western and modern civilization into India and he claimed that our own ancient civilization was superior. He advocated the rejection of modern civilization and the restoration of the ancient Indian civilization. But it is not very clear that what is the precise definition of modern civilization and what constitutes the ancient Indian civilization.

Gandhi advocated truth and non-violence but these principles are as old as humanity itself. Gandhi did not invent the ethical imperative. Non-violence is a universal phenomenon and everybody is not at everybody's throat everyday. Gandhi was not the creator of non-violence. All religions and prophets have preached it, Gandhi also preached it and practiced it. Gandhi believed in God but his definition of God was not consistent (Sometimes he said God is truth then truth is God then God is love).

The proposals contained in *Hind Swaraj* were pronounced to be impracticable. He himself said that "India was not ripe for the kind of *Swaraj* which he projected". He postulated that English was the language of foreign British rulers. He said that it was imposed by Englishmen for their own convenience. But the fact is that no less a statesman and patriot than Raja Ram Mohun Roy invited the introduction of English into India to give Indians access to modern experimental science. So, Gandhi can be worshipped like Buddha but his principles are not acceptable.

R.C. Majumdar is not very comfortable with Gandhi's ideas presented in *Hind Swaraj*. For him *Hind Swaraj* is an old fashioned or quaint book and has produced very little effect upon the people for whom it was meant. For him, the object of this symposium is to discuss that "as there is deterioration in every sphere of life, has the time come to give a trial to the remedy suggested by Gandhi and to respond to his call to reject modern civilization in total and return to the ways of life followed in India before the arrival of British".[93]

Majumdar said that after reading *Hind Swaraj* I found that "Gandhi was a victim of the mental disease of intoxication in respect of the ancient civilization of India". He denounced almost everything modern and held out a rosy picture of almost everything that preceded it. "This illogical, unreasonable and unhistorical attitude has vitiated almost all his conclusions and recommendations."[94]

His quaint ideas which I am sure most of the Indians would reject straightaway, is furnished by his strong denunciation of lawyers, doctors and railways, Gandhi said, "These have impoverished the country". It is my "firm opinion that the Lawyers have enslaved India". As regard to doctors, Gandhi does not refer to the progress in surgery, remedies for intractable diseases, which has been discovered in modern days only. For Gandhi, "Hospitals are the institutions for propagating sin". For him "It is beyond dispute that railway propagate evil" and "English education has enslaved us". He ignored the fact that the railways and English education are the most important factors in bringing together the most diverse peoples of this vast subcontinent and creating the spirit of nationalism unknown before. The above views and statements are so quaint and palpably absurd that any conclusion based on them cannot be taken seriously. Apart from this, one vital objection of Majumdar is that "the remedy for this is to reject modern civilization and go back to the old way" which is theoretically wrong and impracticable.

The fact is that the evils/problems today are inefficiency, indiscipline, immorality and degradation. India under the modern civilization would definitely find its way to economic prosperity and moral and intellectual progress. The necessary changes and adjustments between our ancient ideals and modern practices would automatically follow.

Nageshwar Parsad's 'Hind Swaraj – A Fresh Look'

In 1985, Nageshwar Parsad, a Gandhian and a scholar, edited a book, *Hind Swaraj–A Fresh Look* for 'Gandhi Peace Foundation' in New

Delhi. This book contains papers presented in a seminar on *Hind Swaraj* at the Gandhian Institute of Studies, Varanasi in April 1982. It was designed to offer guidelines for the government to manage its business on Gandhian lines. The discussions hovered around *Hind Swaraj*. It has been said that "*Hind Swaraj* cannot be taken to be the final blue print along which Gandhi wanted to refashion Indian society as well as the world order".[95] Although Gandhi maintained all through his life that he had nothing to change in the text because what he had written had stood the test of time, he did make some changes from time to time. It did not thus present a final blue print even if the principles it enunciated were eternal. It presented the ideal conditions for an ideal state but his was an evolving model. In Gandhi's own words: "I am not at all concerned with appearing to be consistent. In my search after truth, I have discarded many ideas and learnt many new things. What I am concerned with is my readiness to obey the call of truth, my God, from moment to moment, and therefore, when anybody finds any inconsistency between any two writings of mine—he would do well to choose the latter of the two on the same subject".[96] Even Mahadev Desai said "the views expressed in the first edition of *Hind Swaraj* have remained in substance unchanged, they have gone through a necessary evolution".[97]

The substance of Gandhi's attack in *Hind Swaraj* is 'Machinery' that is, technology. "It is the chief symbol of modern civilization; it represents a great sin."[98] What we are witnessing today is a civilizational crisis. The entire system of machine technology is in crisis. Gandhi was the first in the present century who realized the deeper and long range implications of this technological progress. His whole response to it is one of "caution, restraint and limitation".[99] In Gandhi, man emerges at the centre of all social, economic and political development. There must be certain conditions for such a man to develop. Since Gandhi challenged the technological basis of modern civilization, he presented alternative technique also, "which should meet the basic human needs, which should not be based on unlimited depredation of earth's resources, which should not lead to environmental pollution, which should not displace human labour, and in which man becomes its master".[100] Gandhi was not in favour of unlimited multiplication of wants or needs.

Hind Swaraj is a warning against indiscriminate large scale mechanization of life. The rudimentary model presented therein is not static, it is dynamic. Gandhi's thinking becomes global in character through time, *Hind Swaraj* must be placed within the framework of Gandhi's thought as it developed through his active life.

Concluding Remarks

Gandhi considers modern civilization as a phase in human history. This phase is overpowering because it is global in coverage. It is the task of whole humanity to overcome it and put the spiritual progress of man on the rails again. In this sense *Hind Swaraj* is not only a book on '*Swaraj*' and 'Civilization' but also it is a 'Spiritual' book. It teaches us that there is a link between inner life and outer achievement. It offers the means to reach the goal of self-realization. It makes us understand that "The means and ends of modern civilization are not the ultimate means and ends of humanity".[101]

The cornerstones of the Gandhian philosophy in *Hind Swaraj* are—truth, morality, non-violence, love, compassion and welfare of all. "The force of love and pity is greater than the force of arms." Non-violence has its source in soul force and violence in body force. *Hind Swaraj* shows us a way that moral values sustain human life and differentiates humans from animals. Gandhi said, "To me God is truth and love; God is ethics and morality; God is fearlessness.... God is conscience". He envisioned true civilization which supports Individuals in their search for moral virtues. *Hind Swaraj* is a valiant attempt to weave these virtues in the fabric of the freedom struggle. "*Hind Swaraj* is primarily a call to religious reawakening and only secondarily a political document.[102]

Modern civilization discouraged self-realization and was far from being a vehicle for spiritual growth and freedom. True civilization for Gandhi meant the presence and creation of structures and institutions where not only a human being's basic needs were met, but also the place where 'a sense of spiritual and social obligation is fused with a spontaneous sense of natural reciprocity'. Since institutions are an embodiment of their values, it was impossible to change them without changing their inherent moral values. Gandhi concluded that modern civilization as represented by the West should be rejected; otherwise, Indians were only freeing themselves from one yoke while firmly subjecting themselves to another. For Gandhi morality implied sharing of resources, concern for the neighbour and society and compassion in dealing with human weaknesses.

Hind Swaraj is a fervent moral plea by Gandhi to all Indians to reflect deeply both on their morality and that of the economic, political and social institutions they wish to set up, as a consequence of gaining *Swaraj* and in keeping with their moral selves. *Hind Swaraj* was written not so much by prophet of righteousness as by a righteous revolutionary. Gandhi's profound discontent led him to a daringly sanguine view of how politics may be purified, how absolute standards may be upheld in all human relationships and how individual conscience may be combined with heroism in society.

NOTES

1. Pare l, Anthony J., *Hind Swaraj and Other Writings*, Cambridge, Cambridge University Press, 1997, p. XIV.
2. Mahadevan, T.K., DVIJA: A prophet Unheard.
3. *CWMG*, Vol. 10, p. 245.
4. *The Aryan Path*, Vol. IX, September 1938, No. 9, p. 437.
5. *CWMG*, Vol. 9, p. 478.
6. *CWMG*, Vol. 32, p. 489.
7. Parel, Anthony J., *Gandhi, Freedom and Self Rule*, 1993, p. 1.
8. Gandhi, M.K., *Hind Swaraj or Indian Home Rule*, Ahmedabad, Nav Jivan Publishing House, September 2004, p. 56.
9. *CWMG*, Vol. 40, p. 300.
10. Gandhi, M.K., *op cit*., p. 21.
11. *Ibid*., pp. 18-19.
12. *Ibid*., p. 23.
13. *Ibid*., p. 24.
14. *Ibid*., p. 26
15. *Ibid*., p. 27.
16. Chatterjee, Partha, "The moment of manoeuvre – Gandhi and the critique of civil society" in '*Nationalist thought and the colonial world*', Oxford University Press, 1986, p. 87.

17. Gandhi, M.K., *op cit.*, p. 34.
18. *Ibid.*, p. 36.
19. *Ibid.*, p. 43.
20. *Ibid.*, p. 47.
21. *Ibid.*, p. 51.
22. *Ibid.*, p. 76.
23. *Ibid.*, p. 83.
24. *Ibid.*, p. 82.
25. *Ibid.*, p. 53.
26. *Ibid.*, p. 55.
27. Chaterjee, Partha, *op cit.*, p. 6.
28. Gandhi, M.K., *op cit.*, p. 62.
29. *Ibid.*, p. 66.
30. *Ibid.*, p. 90.
31. Parel, Anthony J., *op cit.*, p. 6.
32. Gandhi, M.K., "*An Autobiography* – The Story of My Experiments with Truth", Navjivan Publishing House, Ahmedabad, November 2000, p. 58.
33. *Ibid.*, p. 57.
34. *Ibid.*, p. 6.
35. *Ibid.*, p. 6.
36. *Ibid.*, p. 27.
37. *Ibid.*, p. 28.
38. *Ibid.*, p. 75.
39. *CWMG*, Vol. 7, pp. 90-91.
40. *CWMG*, Vol. 32, pp. 593-602.
41. *CWMG*, Vol. 32, p. 11.
42. Gandhi, M.K., *Hind Swaraj*, *op cit.*, p. 36.
43. Parel Anthony J., *op cit.*, p. XI.
44. Gandhi, M.K., *Autobiography*, *op cit.*, p. 248.
45. *Ibid.*, p. 249.
46. *Ibid.*, p. 250.
47. *CWMG*, Vol. 8, pp. 373-375.
48. Parel, Anthony J., *op cit.*, p. XIII.
49. *CWMG*, Vol. 9, p. 479.
50. Parel, p. XIII.
51. Gandhi, M.K., *Hind Swaraj*, *op cit.*, p. 33.
52. *Ibid.*, p. 53.
53. *Ibid.*, p. 82.
54. *Ibid.*, p. 55.
55. Gandhi, M.K., *Autobiography*, *op cit.*, p. 159.
56. *Ibid.*, p. 159.

57. *CWMG*, Vol. 8, p. 244.
58. *CWMG*, Vol. 29, p. 77.
59. *CWMG*, Vol. 5, p. 290.
60. *CWMG*, Vol. 9, p. 382.
61. Gandhi, M.K., *Hind Swaraj*, p. 15.
62. *Ibid.*, p. 13.
63. *Ibid.*, p. 13.
64. *Ibid.*, p. 13.
65. Aryan Path, *op cit.*, p. 425.
66. *Ibid.*, p. 424.
67. *Ibid.*, p. 425.
68. *Ibid.*, p. 428.
69. *Ibid.*, p. 429.
70. *Ibid.*, p. 433.
71. *Ibid.*, p. 436.
72. *Ibid.*, p. 441.
73. *Ibid.*, p. 442.
74. *Ibid.*, p. 443.
75. *Ibid.*, p. 445.
76. *Ibid.*, p. 446.
77. *Ibid.*, p. 447.
78. Gandhi, M.K., *Hind Swaraj*, *op cit.*, p. 53.
79. *The Aryan Path*, p. 449.
80. *Ibid.*, p. 450.
81. *Ibid.*, p. 453.
82. Shirer, William L., *Gandhi: A Memoir*, New York, 1979.
83. Nehru, Jawaharlal, 1958, *Old Letters*, pp. 507-510.
84. *Gandhi Marg*, October 1973, Gandhi Peace Foundation, New Delhi, p. 261.
85. *Ibid.*, p. 262.
86. Gandhi, M.K., *Hind Swaraj*, p. 8.
87. *Gandhi Marg*, p. 270.
88. *Ibid.*, p. 271.
89. *Ibid.*, p. 271.
90. *Ibid.*, p. 279.
91. *Ibid.*, p. 280.
92. *Ibid.*, p. 281.
93. *Ibid.*, p. 274.
94. *Ibid.*, p. 275.
95. Prasad, Nageshwar (ed.), *Hind Swaraj: A Fresh Look*; Gandhi Peace Foundation, New Delhi, 1985, p. 12.

96. *CWMG*, Vol. 55, p. 61.
97. Gandhi, M.K., *Hind Swaraj*, p. 5.
98. *Ibid.*, p. 94.
99. Prasad, Nageshwar, *op cit.*, p. 24.
100. *Ibid.*, p. 25.
101. Mishra, R.P., *Hind Swaraj*, Concept Publishing Company, New Delhi, p. 269.
102. Pinto, Vivek, *Gandhi's Vision and Values – The Moral Quest for Change in Indian Agriculture*, Sage Publications, New Delhi, 1998, p. 30.

CHAPTER 3

Gandhi: A Leader Beyond Modernism or Socialism

PRAVIN KUMAR

Searching meaning and relevance of life in Gandhian framework has been a difficult task but unavoidable one, for all of us. This subject was really a difficult subject to understand and ponder over, even for a man of the stature of Gandhi, himself. Very few political leaders of colonial India had time and patience to dwell upon this theme. But one in million, an extraordinary one, such as Gandhi, took this risk and decided to explore the world of unknown while experimenting with truth of life and thus by default and also by a conscious choice opted for metaphysical reasoning in order to achieve a concrete answer to the problem. It was an inward journey where Gandhi probed into internal cosmos of the body and by doing so it became possible to find out an internal kind of solar system with sun, moon, and other planets at their respective place. What was required was to synchronize the external world with that of internal. For that, one was advised to move upward from *mooladhar* to *sahastrar* in Indian *yogic* tradition and by doing so it was possible to help the process of melting *karmic* crust over soul and thereby cleansing the wrong doings by one in the present life and the long previous past. It was simply setting the internal sense of religion in motion.

But, how to achieve this aim, however, is a problem in challenging social life of modern era. Socialist and Capitalist ways of living and the challenges they had been throwing to the human kind had made it difficult to move in the above mentioned direction, despite one's commitment and internal craving. There was no denying of the fact that the very champions of the capitalist mode of production were successful in digging its own grave, deep and wide. But it was also a fact that the revolutionaries, emerging from that very contradiction, helped in creation of an alternative order based on party discipline and dictatorship of the leader was equally distrusted by the people. One, therefore, ended in sharp social inequality in one scheme of living and in deep bloodshed in another. Peace and stability could be lost in both the cases. This was unacceptable to Gandhi and, therefore, he underlined: "I am a man of peace, I believe in peace".[1]

One thing was, however, clear that one needed to enter into altogether a very different mindset to tackle such a sensitive issue. If one opted to go into pages of history it was not very difficult to understand the root cause of instability and uncertainty of human mind. It all started with the beginning of class differentiation and social stratification which began with a relatively more developed mode of production and needed to mobilize surplus production forcefully with the aid of state apparatus and the muscle power at its command. The trend started sharpening with the appearance of more developed modes of production. Iron, coal, steel, electricity, rail, chemical, and computers had complicated the situation. Knowledge growth and technology upgradation succeeded in sharpening the contradiction to the extreme level. This is what Gandhi understood and appreciated and, therefore, argued: "The railways, telegraph, hospitals, lawyers, doctors, and such like have all to go, and the so called upper classes have to learn to live consciously and religiously and deliberately the simple life of a peasant knowing it to be a life giving true happiness".[2] This understanding of Modernity forced Gandhi to pen down the critic of modernization in the form of his famous pamphlet, the *Hind Swaraj*. Here Gandhi put forward a systemic criticism of modernization, a theory for which theorists and philosophers worked overtime since Passive Renaissance to convince future generation about its validity, longevity and rationality. Gandhi did it as the process of modernization resulted in extreme individualization at the cost of societal collectivism. Capital created inflated ego in neo emerging class of super rich individuals at the cost of labourers, farmers and colonial underprivileged masses. Gandhi, with his human approach and gradual learning about various contours and underlying agenda of modernity, enabled himself with a thorough diagnosis of prevailing ills of the society and also the most suitable prescription to cure the prevailing disease of the modern society. Thus, emerged what is known today is Gandhism which is nothing but an art and attempt of convincing us about absurdness of continuous feeding of our self ego and making a move to make society prosper as a unit. In a prosperous and healthy society, everyone is bound to become peaceful, contented and realized. If one is really interested in going deep into the process of making of his persona peaceful, one needs to dwell deep into the above mentioned diagnosis of societal ills. It is only in this context, we can appreciate the influence of *Gita* and *Ramcharitmanas* on Gandhi.

Gandhi, being an original thinker and open to all the possible ideas, studied law in English University, created points of contact with thinkers and philosophers of his time, exchanged notes with them, grasped the essence of the guiding words of Western Civilization such as Rule of Law, Liberalism, Freedom, Equality, Right, Constitutionalism, Egalitarianism, Enlightenment, etc., with its grammar and syntax. Not only on the level of ideas and understanding, but for fashion and dressing, young Gandhi opted for Western attire and appearance for himself, a true English Gentleman! However, the honeymoon with westernization proved to be a deviation, at the best, not the norm of the life. The question, therefore, arises as to why did Gandhi allow such a summersault in his mental makeup and total appearance when he prepared himself, and also, the people of India, for the struggle in the last years of the second decade of twentieth century. We require finding an answer for that.

South African experience taught Gandhi few lessons about real nature and essence of Colonialism and Racialism. He was able to understand and recognize the dual face of the structure, the Englishmen were trying to create in whole of the British Empire. Theoretically, they were justifying their presence in India, or any other country in Asia and Africa, in terms of their civilizing mission and self-imposed white-men's burden.[3] Practically they were grabbing huge land mass outside their sovereign boundary to provide solidity to their neo-emerging capitalism by making the colonial economies subservient to their specific need of capital, cheap labour, raw material, and huge market with the help of the most brutal and the most barbaric tool of repression.[4] While in India and at the probation for his long future political career, he came into contact with nationalist voices of Ranade, Surendra Nath Banerji, Firoj Shah Mehta, etc., on the one hand, Bankim Chandra Chatterji, Aurobindo Ghosh, Lala Lajpat Rai, etc., on the other. Gandhi was reaffirmed about the brutal realities of modernizing influences so carefully and caringly imported to the worlds of Asian and African people. In the mean time, he also decided to cover length and breadth of colonial India to collect the first hand information about the country and the people. It is not very difficult to note that the 'economy of enclaves' which colonial regime was trying to craft was not in the interest of majority Indians except few compradors and clients of the *Raj*. He was able to observe the fact that the rails, banking and insurance companies, shipping and plantation, mining and indentured labour, etc., were to serve the interests of the British Capitalist Class, at the cost of indigenous people. The arteries of Industrialization and subsequent Capitalist development functioned in the Colonies as channels of drain that sucked the life blood of Indian Economy.

An alternative to Modernization and Capitalism was Communism, formulated and developed by Marx and Engel, modified and employed by Lenin and later by Mao-tse-Tung. When Gandhi was on probation for his political career in India, world witnessed a Bolshevik Revolution, first political experiment to install a Communist order in Russia after a bloody armed revolution which, after a huge human cost, established a government ruled by a party in the most dictatorial manner with no civil rights whatsoever to the people. Though farmers and labourers gained something in economic terms, other section of the people were simply suppressed and butchered. Nationality and Religion were the casualties of the change. Gandhi did not like the alternative.

The question that needs to be answered then as to what kind of the strategy of growth and development India required at that time to undo the miseries that was thrusted upon by the colonial masters. The answer for that lay at least, not in both of the models, Communist and Capitalist, of growth. Gandhi, therefore, looked backward. It was for everyone to note that without these two generators of growth, India still succeeded in becoming the most prosperous economy in the world and that too under the so called Muslim rulers that came here from outside India like the Company rulers and the British Crown. Gandhi surely understood the fact that India grew exceptionally well in the past with its indigenous resources at her hand. The only problem with this growth story was that it was unequal and caste linked. The goal of eradicating inequality without bloodshed required a little help from God and religion. Gandhi, therefore, turned to Hinduism and underlined the fact that five *vikaras,* namely *kama, krodha, lobha, moha,* and *ahamkara*, which created a sense of Individuality in the individual were needed to be overcome if one wanted to attain Salvation, a cherished goal for every Hindu. While overcoming these *vikaras,* one could move from individual plane to the collective one. Here philosophy of *niskam karma* of *Gita* was of great help. Unlike capitalist ways and thinking, here we were needed to involve ourselves in productive process wholeheartedly without any expectation of return or profit. With this little support from religion and scripture, it was easier for Gandhi to move towards the principle of trusteeship to successfully tackle the question of inequality prevailing in Indian society. And now he was in a position to declare: "My ideal is equal distribution, but so far as I can see it cannot be realized. I, therefore, work for equitable distribution". Gandhi's imperative here was to create a sense of partnership between men of property and power and men without property and power so as to achieve the utopian goal of *Ramrajya* where people were supposed to live collectively without any fear of divine, physical, or body related curse.

Along with mutual partnership stated above, Gandhi also tried to strengthen the position of the people living on margin through various other initiatives which included village reconstruction programme, eradication of untouchability and reframing of the name of the related class as *Harijans*, economic empowerment of the poor through *khadi* and *charkha,* etc. Gandhi was always ready to mediate between landlords and the peasants, capitalists and the workers with a more sympathetic attitude towards the latter. If he was committed for revival of the handicraft industry for which India was once famous, it was for the empowerment of the poor and also for creating a more equitable society. Even though he was committed to the interests of the poor, Gandhi still hesitated following class politics despite being a patron and leader of leftist youth like Jawaharlal Nehru and Subhash Chandra Bose for the reason already hinted above. Instead Gandhi opted for moral politics. Unlike Communists for whom religion was just an opium and unlike Rationalist Enlightened Individuals for whom religion and politics must operate in two distinct domains and a marriage between the two was bound to drag the humanity back into barbaric medieval age. Gandhi understood the potential of moral politics in building and rebuilding of a tottering state. Slowly and gradually he succeeded in projecting himself as the champion of all the Indian religions including Islam and Sikhism. One can easily interpret the inclusion of Khilaphat and Akali issue with that of Non-Cooperation in this reference. A *naked fakir* gradually became messiah with miraculous power as the belief of his followers goes in the pages of History. A bridge that Gandhi built between the two was proved so formidable that it finally overthrew the mighty Raj from her Indian territory.

In another sense too, it helped him to operate his political activity from altogether a different plane from where Gandhi positioned himself as spiritual *guru* of all the masses of India. In Sikhism and Islam, and also in Hinduism, *Guru* had been equated with God. Once Gandhi succeeded in establishing himself to that position, he became undisputed leader of Indian masses. Even after committing Himalayan blunders, no one ever dared to question his decisions. In the history of the Indian National Movement, he remained the supreme leader with dictatorial powers at his hand. As *Guru* is empowered to choose and nominate other worthy ones as group leaders and so on, Gandhi in Congress helped in the emergence of a hierarchy of leadership with complete control in his hand. A well cultured and lubricated model of *Ashram* leadership that History offered, Gandhi grabbed with folded hands and modelled the struggle for National Emancipation of it.

If one decides to revisit the last seventy years or so, one could find the emergence of many different kinds of protest movements obviously against ever exploiting British Raj. Brahmo Samaj, Arya Samaj, Prarthana Sabha, etc., Movements by Hindu middle class and Aligarh Movement or Deoband Movement by the Muslim community developed gradually at cultural level; constitutional agitation was similarly initiated by the Moderates of the Congress Party and from this very movement and Party gradually emerged in two different factions of Extremists and Revolutionaries at political level. Parallel to the Congress Party, the Raj encouraged the making of the Muslim League so as to counter balance the emerging nationalist Hindu threat as per their newly formulated strategy of Divide and Rule. Beneath the upper and middle layer of politics were also developing the popular movements of insurgency against their immediate oppressors by peasants, labourers and *Dalits*. Need of the hour was, therefore, to develop an umbrella kind of leadership which could accommodate different types of struggle into one unified movement and that too against the Raj, leaving aside all the class and community contradictions that existed in the Indian society. A difficult task indeed but Gandhi succeeded in doing that authoritatively and skilfully.

It was interesting as all the stakeholders of Indian politics were busy in developing their respective models of leadership to enable their respective brand of politics in controlling the levers of power politics in India. Decision-makers in the power corridors of the Raj tried their level best to convince the poor Indian masses and elites of the society that they alone were capable of providing progressive leadership to the decaying and declining society which was at the verge of becoming moribund. It was underlined that it was because of their effort and sacrifices that the disintegrating India had been successfully restored to the world map as a nation with full physical entity. It was they who were trying hard to inject a dose of modernism through their concept of Rule of Law, liberal economic philosophy, constitutionalism, English education, etc., to help ignorant Indian masses in becoming part of the mainstream modernity. And it was impossible, without political and economic integration of this vast geography, to turn it into a vibrant nation. That was precisely the reason, the information industry of the Raj tried her best to convince us, as to why Company and Crown Raj came into existence in India. After all, as the leader of World Civilization, it was their responsibility to drag Indian aboriginals into the realm of Civility,.... A Whiteman's burden indeed! Administrators of the Raj legitimized their Indian Colony in these precise words only. A pseudo kind of cultural leadership was thus crafted over to undercover their actual motive of bleeding Indian resources in the interest of British Capital and people.

The Nationalist alternative that evolved over time as a result of and in reaction to the specific policies of the Raj gradually succeeded in creating an anti-thesis of the colonial ideology to get rid of colonialism itself. Though a child, a problem child, of the colonial structure as it created the great Indian Middle Class to become its flag bearer in India as native administrators, policemen, clerks, professionals in British Establishments with fluency in English language and their availability at the cheapest price possible with expectation that it would fit itself into the role of junior partner in their scheme of bleeding India white in the interest of British Capitalism, the Great Indian Middle Class finally succeeded in decoding the actual motive of the colonialist administrators and formulating a counter strategy to turn the table against their mentor and the master. Two different brands of politics emerged as a result of this growing sensibility among the leaders of newly emerged middle class as differences of opinion on the form of counter strategy did exist in this body. A faction, Moderates, which was more British in their attitude, opted for a leadership of constitutionalist kind with emphasis on prayer, petition, persuasion, and if needed, a well organized constitutional protest. Another faction known as Extremists did not believe in Moderates and went for a strategy of mass-mobilization against colonialist power in India and created a mass-leadership for the people to dislodge them from power with slogan that *Swaraj* is our birth right and needed to be earned as early as possible. Unfortunately, however, none of them succeeded in dislodging the British Power from her Indian territorial possession and dethroning them from their crowning glory. Thus it became clear that a very different kind of strategy and altogether a different kind of leadership were the need of the time if India was serious about her emancipation from English bondage. Gandhi provided both, a strategy of popular mobilization and mystic leadership from the pages of *Gita* and *Ramayana*.

Through the experiments of Non-Cooperation, Civil Disobedience and Quit India Movement, Gandhi succeeded in demonstrating the World that mighty regime of the British Crown in India could be overpowered with his not so modern tactics like those used during French or English Revolution nor with strategy used by Comrades during Russian Revolution. What Gandhiji offered was searched meticulously from the ancient treasure of Indian metaphysics and applied to the tottering and crumbling Indian society of early twentieth century under English weight. Taking clues from *Gita*, Gandhi dissolved his personal ego and personal self in the interest of humanity. Competition, individualism, marketism, capitalist sense of profit making, communist sense of bloody class-revolution, etc., had no place in Gandhian reasoning. Child like simplicity, treasure of love in the heart for everybody around, removal of all the *tapas, daihik, daivik and bhautik,* were some of the ideals, Gandhi stood for. Aim of life for him was to engage himself in continuous experiment with the truth in order to reach the level of the ultimate truth which according to the ancient Indian spirituality was to reach a stage of Unison of soul with *Brahman* and that to with the clear understanding that all the souls are *amsa* of *Brahman,* and eternal in the same way. *Ahimsa* in this model could only be the medium of communication and action and *Satyagraha* could be only form of demand (read demand as movement) in the interest of both Indian people and the English overlord. And, therefore, Britishers were not to be hated but to be elevated to the level of their ultimate salvation in Gandhian scheme of things.

What was unique about Gandhi was not that he was able to place a philosophy of societal behaviour before the people of India and world in twentieth century but also succeeded to demonstrate the practical side of this philosophy through his own life and action. That is how Gandhi succeeded in becoming a saint and *mahatma* for common Indian people. Now his words became commands from the God Himself. And it was in the domain of the knowledge of every Indian public that the God never falters and if looked faltering then only because of our ignorance and limitation. That is why

Gandhi gave the call, people of India followed him with utmost sincerity. The day Gandhi came out with the call of Quit India for the English overlords, the independence of India was earned in the same day in the popular mind.

It is in this background, a new understanding of Gandhi needs to be developed, surely beyond the realm of socialist and capitalist contours of thought. Again we also need to disagree with the view that the marriage between politics and religion, and for that matter between morality and rationality, is always dangerous to the health of the society. The life history of Gandhi could provide a brilliant case study for this subject.

NOTES

1. *The Gandhian Way of World Peace*, p. 8.
2. Bose, N.K, *Selections from Gandhi*, Ahmedabad, Navjivan Puplishing House, 1948.
3. A thorough analysis of the Imperialist sensibilities, best expressed in the works of Rudyard Kipling, has been made by Prof. Suhash Chakravarty in his book, *The Raj Syndrome*, published by the Penguin, India.
4. Prof Bipan Chandra has brilliantly painted the real picture of Colonial Contribution to Indian economy through his books such as *Rise and Growth of Economic Nationalism in India*, etc.

CHAPTER 4

Exploring Gandhi's Philosophy of Beauty

PREM ANAND MISHRA

Mrs. Millie Graham Polak, Gandhi's fellow worker in South Africa, records a conversation with Gandhi in her book:

> "....Another subject we almost contended about was what I called Mr. Gandhi's love of the *uncomfortable*.
> "I do not know why you always want to choose the most uncomfortable way of doing a thing", I once said to him [Gandhi].
> "But it is not uncomfortable to me", he replied. "What are you complaining about?"
> "It must be uncomfortable to do so many of the things you do, not because you have to do them, but out of, what seems to me, a strange idea of principle. If you have to go from one place to another, you always look to see if there is a *stony* path to walk over, rather than the *soft grass*."
> "Ease and comfort are often the paths from God. We must not let the body have its own way when it asks for sensuous ease."
> "But God does not mean you to whip your body all the time."
> "And He does not mean you to lose sight of Him because of it."
> "No, I admit that, but I cannot help believing that God

> makes the flower-decked path for our enjoyment. I cannot believe He meant us to ignore these *flowers* and hunt for *jagged stones* to cut our feet on."
>
> "Our danger is of putting the comfort of our body and serving it before the service of God."
>
> "But", again I urged, "We are not denying God because we appreciate the beauty of His world. Are the stones more His than the grass"?
>
> "The *temptation* to seek ease and slothfulness is always with us and we have to guard against it."
>
> "But it was no use arguing with Mr. Gandhi when he was in these moods. His bent was naturally *towards the ascetic* and *not towards the aesthetic*. And it must be admitted that this tendency and his constant practice of the hard and simple life stood him in good stead when he had to endure the discomfort and privation of prison-life. He could adjure his followers so to live in times of peace that they might be able to endure hardship in times of struggle."[1]

This piece of conversation might be reduced in a set of binary oppositions as comfortable/uncomfortable, soft grass/stone, flowers/jagged stones, enjoyment/service of God, temptation/restraint. This set of binary oppositions obviously represents two different views to look life and the world—ascetic and aesthetic.

Being very specific, Mrs. Polak also attempts to judge Gandhi's life from two matrixes—ascetic and aesthetic—in which she finds Gandhi making 'constant practice of the hard and simple life' accepting discomfort 'to endure hardship in time of struggle'. Thus she concludes, Gandhi purposefully accepted ascetic life, thus, there was no place of aesthetic sensibility in his life.

Mrs. Polak is not alone in such an interpretation who wrote about the lack of aesthetic bent in Gandhi's life. As Suhrud puts, "Even during Gandhi's life time itself it was a widely shared belief that art, literature, or music had no place in his ascetic life".[2]

Because of Gandhi's bent towards asceticism, sometimes it is also argued that Gandhi never welcomed a 'wholesome outlook on beauty and art'.[3] Furthermore, as his ascetic life gave substantial importance to *Brahmacharya,* thus, it prevented him to express his views on *Sringar* that is dominant emotion in art and beauty. One might well wonder; did Gandhi really have no aesthetic sensibility as Mrs. Polak and other critics described? Or if he had any view on aestheticism, what was it and how did he locate his philosophy of beauty in his entire system of thought? Furthermore, what was Gandhi's own position on this issue of asceticism or aestheticism posed by critics?

I wish to explore these questions in the light of the following quotation of Gandhi:

> Asceticism is the highest art. For what is art but beauty in simplicity and what is asceticism if not the loftiest manifestation of simply beauty in daily life, shorn of artificialities and make-believe? That is why I always say that the true ascetic, not only practices art but lives it.[4]

By this statement, Gandhi opens a new debate on the issue of aestheticism or asceticism as he does not see binàry opposition between them but *relates* them in his own fashion. However, this further opens a new set of questions. First of all, on what basis does Gandhi relate his asceticism with aesthetics? What is the nature of the relationship between aesthetics and asceticism and how does he define objects whether they are beautiful or not? Furthermore, was it Gandhi's original position or he borrowed it from some cultural traditions?

To unpack these questions, it is essential to explore Gandhi's philosophy of beauty. Assuming that a person's philosophy is the result of his/her cultural locations, we need to look at different cultural spheres inhabited by Gandhi in different parts of life. This brings us to briefly examine two different aesthetic traditions— Indian and Western— and to place Gandhi in them if we can.

Locating Gandhi's Aesthetics

Although beauty is impossible to define,[5] yet, both Western and Indian philosophical traditions have sought to develop notions about beauty. In Western tradition, the pre-Socratic Greeks tried to define beauty in spatial and quantitative terms.[6] Plato (424/423 BC) in his discussion on beauty merged the beautiful in a sublime identity with the good. Aristotle (384 BC-322 BC) tried to define beauty in terms of symmetry, proportion, and in organic order of parts in united whole.[7] Later on Kant (1724-1804) and Schopenhauer (1788-1860) argued: beauty becomes that whereby an object pleases us regardless of its use, stirring in us a will-less contemplation, a disinterested happiness.[8] For Hegel (1770-1831), beauty is again unity in variety, the conquest of matter by form, the sensuous manifestation of some metaphysical ideal.[9]

In Indian philosophical tradition, in this context one might refer to the notion of trinity of absolutes called *Satyam* (Truth), *Shivam* (goodness) and *Sundaram* (beauty) which are interrelated with each other. According to this, the absolute idea conceived by the human intellect is the highest *truth*; realized in practice is the greatest *good*; and manifested in man and nature is the supreme *beauty*.[10] Although, some modern western aesthete like Keats relates truth with beauty, however, Indian aesthetics underline the importance of goodness also in the aesthetic experience. Especially in *Vedantic* tradition, there is an idea of *Satchitanand* (*Sat*, infinite existence; *chit*, knowledge; *anand*, supreme joy) that opens up new and expended notion of beauty. According to *Vedantins*, beauty is not outside; true beauty consists of that inner harmony underlying all diversities of experiences.[11] This true beauty is the ultimate reality which appears in the form of *Ananda*. In Indian philosophical tradition, *Ananda* is not only recognized as "essence of beauty, but enable us to differentiate between spurious and authentic beauty".[12] Further, in Indian thought there are three categories of *Ananda*. The first variety is called *Priya* which is obtained by the unsophisticated and simple experience of the beautiful, second type is called *Moda* which is received through conscious enjoyment. It is a kind of experience which is obtained by free play of imagination. The third kind of *Ananda* is called *Pramoda,* the loftiest joy. This comes to an individual through his active participation in the creative expression of beauty.

At the very outset, it needs to be clarified that Gandhi did not write systematically anything on beauty. However, he studied life as an integrated whole and was concerned with every aspect of life, so it was quite natural for him to express his views about the place of beauty and art in life. Thus, one may extract his idea of beauty and art from his voluminous writings. As far as the nature of his writings on beauty is concerned, it seems to be influenced by the idea of Tolstoy (1828-1910), Ruskin (1819-1900) and Emerson (1803-1882),[13] that have been termed as 'other West' in Gandhian scholarship. Besides these influences, even the cursory look at his scattered writings on beauty also suggests that his view of beauty echoes Indian ascetic tradition which is spiritual in outlook.

To understand the relation between Gandhi's asceticism and aestheticism, it is proper to first deal with his distinct view on asceticism. Gandhi's asceticism is based on his interpretations and understanding of *Gita*. He used two terms from *Gita* to describe his way of looking at oneself and the world—*sthitpragnya* and *nishkama*. Gandhi's lifelong quest was to attain this state of *sthitpragnya*. According to *Gita*, a *sthitpragnya* is one who puts away all the cravings that arise in mind and find comforts for himself only from the *Atman* and one whose senses are reined in on all sides of object. This was so important for Gandhi that eighteen verses from the second discourse of the *Gita*, which describes the characteristics of a *sthitpragnya*, became an essential part of his daily prayers in Ashram. Especially the verses 62 and 63 of the second discourse made a deep impression on him. These verses are:

> Dhyāyto viṣayān puṁsaḥ, saṅgasteṣūpajāyate
> saṅgātsañjāyate kāmaḥ kāmātkrodhobhijāyate
> Krodhādbhavati sammohaḥ sammohātsmṛti-vibhramaḥ
> smṛti-bhraṁśād buddhi-nāśo buddhi-nāśātpraṇaśyati
> (*Gita*: II: 62, 63)

> "In a man brooding on objects of the senses, attachment to them springs up; attachment begets craving and craving begets wrath. Wrath breeds stupefaction, stupefaction leads to loss of memory, loss of memory ruins the reason, and the ruin of reason spells utter destruction."

If these verses are so influential for Gandhi to shape his outlook, then it is logical to assume that his aesthetics must have evolved from these verses. In fact, one might see the crux of Gandhi's notion of relation between asceticism and aestheticism here. Gandhi, following the Indian spiritual tradition, was able to understand how 'ponders on objects of the sense' may lead to ruin. Further, this verse must have led Gandhi to think that 'attraction', attributes of an object, is not beauty as many aesthetes (especially Western aesthetes) consider but actually it 'saps' mind.

Then, how does Gandhi see the objects of the world?

He again quotes *Gita* on this question,

> Viṣayā vinivartante nirāhārasya dehinaḥ
> rasa-varjaṁ raso'pyasya paraṁ dṛṣtvā nivartate
> (*Gita*: II: 59)

> "Sense-cravings subside in a man who refrains from gratifying them, but pleasure in their objects remains; it vanishes only when he has had a vision of the supreme."

Getting inspiration from this verse Gandhi argues, "If beauty consisted in shape or colour, we would have gratified our sight by looking at statues. *Beauty lies in virtue* and this is not a thing which can be perceived by the senses".[14]

Yet one might ask: if beauty lies in virtue how can things without a moral quality be beautiful? For instance, is there truth in a sunset or a crescent moon that shines amid the stars at night?

Responding to such questions, Gandhi answers, "...Indeed these beauties are truthful, inasmuch as they make me think of the Creator at the back of them". (CWMG: 25:79)

Two things emerge from this discussion. First, Gandhi saw the things of the world from this *sthitpragnya* state of mind (free from longing after desire) and second he establishes a relation between beauty and creator, what he called God or Truth.

It needs to be pointed out here that Gandhi rejects the idea of beauty purely based on matter and senses. It means he also rejects *'priya'* and *'moda'* described in category of *Anand* described above. Further, Gandhi rejects western aesthetic value system that sees beauty in proportion, intuition, symmetry and harmony as important ingredients of beauty. On the other hand, in Gandhi's view, the *atmashuddhi* or purification of oneself is an important ingredient in the realization of true beauty.

Although Gandhi tries to establish a relation between asceticism and aestheticism on the ground of mental state of *sthitpragnya*, yet, one vital question merits explanation at this point as to what is the source of Gandhi's notion of beauty?

As discussed above, Gandhi sees a relation between beauty and creator (Truth or God). Then, what kind of relation does exist between beauty and truth? Following Indian spiritual tradition, Gandhi argues that truth is first thing which is followed by beauty. He wrote:

> Truth is the first thing to be sought for, and Beauty and Goodness will then be added unto you. Jesus was, to my mind, a supreme artist because he saw and expressed Truth; and so was Muhammad, the *Koran* being, the most perfect composition in all Arabic literature—at any rate, that is what scholars say. It is because both of them strove first for Truth that the grace of expression naturally came in and yet neither Jesus nor Muhammad wrote on Art. That is the Truth and Beauty I crave for, live for, and would die for.[15]

Thus, truth is supreme in Gandhian scheme and everything is just manifestation of that. Unlike Keats (1795-1821) who said 'beauty is truth, and truth beauty', Gandhi perceives beauty *in* truth and *through* Truth. He wrote:

> I see and find Beauty *in* Truth or *through* Truth. All Truths, not merely true ideas, but truthful faces, truthful pictures or songs are highly beautiful. People generally fail to see Beauty in Truth; the ordinary man runs away from it and becomes blind to the beauty in it.[16]

At this point one might recollect Ruskin's idea of beauty who wrote beauty:

> ... is either the record of conscience, written in things external, or it is the symbolizing of Divine attributes in matter, or it is the felicity of living things, or the perfect fulfilment of their duties and functions. In all cases it is

> something divine; either the approving voice of God, the glorious symbol of Him, the evidence of His kind presence, or the obedience to His will by Him induced and supported.[17]

All beauty, then, relates to the nature of God, and, Typical Beauty, according to Ruskin,—"the symbolizing of divine attributes in matter"— most directly partakes of the Holy.

Like Ruskin, Gandhi also divides a thing's aspects in two categories 'outward' and 'inward'. He argues, "There are two aspects of things—the outward and the inward. The outward has no meaning except in so far as it helps the inward. All true Art [beauty] is thus an expression of the soul. The outward forms have value only in so far as they are the expression of the inner spirit of man.[18] However, internal or inward is so important in Gandhi's notion of beauty that Gandhi warns that even when outward looks ugly, yet it may be beautiful. In Gandhi's view:

> To a true artist only that face is beautiful which, quite apart from its exterior, shines with the Truth within the soul. There is... no Beauty apart from Truth. On the other hand, Truth may manifest itself in forms, which may not be outwardly beautiful at all. Socrates, we are told, was the most truthful man of his time, and yet his features are said to have been the ugliest in Greece. To my mind he was beautiful, because all his life was a striving after Truth, and you may remember that his outward form did not prevent Phidias from appreciating the beauty of Truth in him, though as an artist he was accustomed to see Beauty in outward forms also.[19]

Further, unlike Keats who saw a trinity of Truth, beauty and power in correlation, Gandhi seems following the Vedantic tradition in which Truth (*sat*), knowledge (*chit*) and bliss (*anand*) are interrelated. He wrote:

> And where there is Truth, there also is knowledge which is true. Where there is no Truth, there can be no true

> knowledge. That is why word *Chit* or knowledge is associated with the name of God. And where there is true knowledge, there is always bliss (*Ananda*). Their sorrow has no place. And even as Truth is eternal, so is the bliss derived from it. Hence, we know God as *sat-chit-ananda*, one who combines in Himself Truth, Knowledge and Bliss.[20]

In fact, like Truth, the idea of God is also central in Gandhi's notion of beauty. For him, 'God manifests Himself in innumerable forms, in this universe, and every such manifestation commands my spontaneous reverence'.[21] Thus the nature is expression or manifestation of God or all pervasive reality or Truth. This nature and other nature's object or heavenly bodies are beautiful, according to Gandhi, because they are truthful. He said:

> These beauties [a sunset or a crescent moon that shines amid the stars at night] are truthful, inasmuch as they make me think of the Creator at the back of them. How else could these be beautiful, but for the Truth that is in the centre of creation? When I admire the wonder of a sunset or the beauty of the moon, my soul expands in worship of the Creator. I try to see Him and His mercies in all these creations. But even the sunsets and sunrises would be mere hindrances if they did not help me to think of the soul is a delusion and a snare; even like the body, which often does hinder you in the path of salvation.[22]

The spiritual beauty of these heavenly bodies that Gandhi emphasizes seems influenced by his reading of Emerson's essay *Nature* in which Emerson echoes, "Nature's beauty enhances the grandeur of noble deeds and increases spirituality".[23]

Gandhi seems to suggest that anything which is closer to nature is closer to God/Truth and thus beautiful. This idea is further reflected in his discussion of art and beauty. Thus, in contrast to these heavenly bodies which are 'the eternal symbols of beauty in nature' man's art works are nowhere. In very glowing term Gandhi claims,

> What conscious Art of man can give me the panoramic scenes that open out before me, when I look up to the sky above with all its shining stars?... I personally feel how inadequate these [production of man's art] are compared with the eternal symbols of beauty in Nature. These productions of man's Art have their value only in so far as they help the soul onward towards self-realization.[24]

The last sentence of above quote naturally leads to a corollary in which art is seen as method of self-realization or self-purification. In fact, Gandhi like Tolstoy rejected any definition of art based on a conception of beauty.[25] Thus, in Gandhi's view like Tolstoy, the only clear definition of art depends upon its function, and can be judged on how well it transmits feelings and the value of the feelings transmitted (truth or goodness). Consequently, Gandhi rejects the notion of 'art for art sake', and places its importance only to the extent it is helpful in realization of the ultimate. Further, Gandhi does not see art only for some people but he wants "art and literature that can speak to the millions".[26] Here again Gandhi seems influenced by Tolstoy who claimed that a great work of art is only great if it can be understood by everyone.[27]

In fact, Gandhi wanted art to fulfil a distinctive role. The artist should fashion his artistic expression in such a way that it should uplift the moral and spiritual level of society. This idea of Gandhi can be traced in his reading of Tolstoy's *What is Art* in which Tolstoy wrote:

> The destiny of art in our time is to transmit from the realm of reason to the realm of feeling the truth that well-being for men consists in their being united together, and to set up, in place of the existing realm of force, that kingdom of God—that is of love.[28]

However, this discussion leads one to draw attention towards the relation between beauty and utility that Gandhi seems addressing in the following passage:

> Why can't you see the beauty of colour in vegetables? And

> then, there is beauty in the speckless sky. But no, you want the colours of the rainbow, which is a mere optical illusion. We have been taught to believe that what is beautiful need not be useful and what is useful cannot be beautiful. I want to show that what is useful can also be beautiful.[29]

Gandhi's this idea is unlike Kant who says as soon as any idea of usefulness is attributed to the aesthetic sense, it starts disintegrating. Gandhi's idea is to establish the fact that utility might be explained in terms of beauty. Although Marxist aesthetic has also this assumption like Gandhi as they say that beautiful and useful are not incompatible, but for them beauty belongs to cultural superstructure and it is determined by socio-economic condition, especially economic condition. However, for Gandhi beauty is not product of socio-economic condition but the God or Truth is the original source of beauty.

The correlation between beauty and utility is central in Gandhi's discourse of beauty. As seen above, he tries to show that what is useful can be beautiful. In this regard, he introduces the concept of honest labour in definition of beauty as far as human artistic products are concerned. This might be seen as radical departure from the traditional concept in which beauty was delinked from the idea of utility. Madan Gandhi points out:

> Among human artistic products Gandhiji sees beauty in those that involve honest labour, reflect no greed and exploitation and intended to fulfil the purpose of good of all. ....for him there is no beauty apart from goodness and no aesthetics which does not have ethical foundation.[30]

Thus, for Gandhi, beauty is not only an abstract idea but a concrete thing that could be seen and utilized or practiced for the welfare of all. Gandhi's this notion is a challenge to those who limits beauty to intellect or some artifacts. Because of his idea of insertion of utility in beauty, it was quite natural for him to see spinning wheel—a human instrument that characterizes honest labour—as the symbol of beauty. It might be recollected here, honest labour what is termed as bread labour is essential in Gandhi's scheme to realize Truth. Thus, for Gandhi beautiful means 'utility objectified according to nature', and not 'pleasure objectified' as Santayana defined.[31]

Moreover, his idea of beauty or beautiful artifact is not limited to specific people who have specific and trained aesthetic sense but rather his definition of beautiful artifact attempts to include millions based on artifact's utility. Thus, the instrument that can save the starving millions, or can give some relief, is beauty. In his words:

> I must think in terms of the millions. And to the millions we cannot give that training to acquire a perception of Beauty in such a way as to see Truth in it. Show them Truth first and they will see Beauty afterwards... Whatever, can be useful to those starving millions is beautiful to my mind. Let us give today first the vital things of life and all the graces and ornaments of life will follow.[32]

Gandhi's notion of beauty might be seen in the broader socio-economic context. By enlarging the definition of beauty, like Ruskin he seems challenging the machine based civilization or modern civilization based on mass production. According to him art or beauty is possible only when there is 'living touch' of people and not by the dead 'machine designed production'. Thus, "Art can only be expressed not through inanimate power-driven machinery designed for mass-production, but only through the delicate *living touch* of the hands of men and women".[33]

In Gandhi's discourse, this idea of beauty based on *living touch* is extended further to evaluate the very nature of civilization. In his seminal text *Hind Swaraj* which is an attempt to see 'beauty in voluntary simplicity, [voluntary] poverty and slowness'.[34] Gandhi argues that Indian civilization has been 'satisfied with small villages' which is 'steady' and 'immovable' and 'This is its beauty'.[35] On the other hand, he seems arguing that modern civilization has inherent ugliness (or lack of aesthetics). His argument is: how could there be beauty in a way of life that led to exploitation of workers, increased the pauperization of the peasantry and encouraged conspicuous consumption among the few even as the majority struggled to get their basic meals? Gandhi observed:

> Now thousands of workmen meet together and for the sake of maintenance work in factories or mines. Their condition is worse than that of beasts. They are obliged to work, at the risk of their lives, at most dangerous occupations, for the sake of millionaires.[36]

Thus for Gandhi beauty is not a philosophical term but a way of life that cannot be found in cities which is emblem of modern civilization—as 'cities were a snare and a useless encumbrance' where 'gangs of thieves and robbers, prostitution and vice flourish' and 'poor are robbed by rich'.[37]

This idea can be criticized on the ground that Gandhi's idea of beauty is a very extended one as well as it seems attempting to undermine the significance of modern beautiful artifacts and their aesthetic values. Yet it might be countered by saying that Gandhi's notion of beauty is not separate from his vision of life as integrated whole and it was his ethical concern for millions that shapes his notion of beauty.

Chakrawarty rightly points out that Gandhi's notion of beauty may be seen as 'socio-aesthetics'. He argues that Gandhi's 'socio-aesthetics' incorporates careful and cautious cultivation of nobler sentiments and finer sensibilities like Truth, Goodness, Beauty and so on for endless advancement of man in the efflorescence of mysticism. The fusion of *Sarvodaya*, Non-violence, religion, education and symbolism for the desirable end-in-view of socio-aesthetics as Gandhi advocates and translates till the last day of his life, bears ample testimony to the socio-aesthetic fullness of vision of humankind.[38]

At personal level, like Plato, Gandhi does not separate beauty from ethics. Following ascetic tradition, Gandhi calls for an ethical life based on self-purification that produces harmony. This ethical dimension of Gandhi's notion of beauty is further exemplified by the art of his personal life. He says:

> As I am nearing the end of my earthly life, I can say that purity of life is the highest and truest art. The art of producing good music through a cultured voice can be achieved by many, but art of producing that music from the harmony of pure life is achieved very rarely.[39]

The purity of life as 'highest and truest art' signifies beauty in simplicity in Gandhi's world-view. This simplicity is the prime value of Gandhi's aesthetics. This simplicity is not merely outward simplicity but it comes genuinely only through 'reducing oneself to zero'. Thus Gandhi's notion of beauty finally leads one to *Moksha*—the last of the *Purusharthas*.

Thus, Gandhi's notion of beauty, on the one hand attempts to evaluate civilization, on the other, it calls for purification of the self. A man of ascetic outlook on life stands shorn of all the artificialities and make-believes. In Gandhi's view, he is nearer to life, so also nearer to beauty and truth. Thus Gandhi said, "Life is greater than all art. I would go even further and declare that the man whose life comes nearest to perfection is the greatest artist; for what is art without the sure foundation and framework of a noble life".[40]

In short, for Gandhi, beauty is not a compartment of life. But it is simple, ethical and true life that spreads beauty. In other words, Gandhi's theory of beauty like Ruskin is not divorced from morality, and he tried to demonstrate that the perception of beauty has an important relationship to man's moral and religious nature.

Gandhi's Sense of Beauty

Apart from the Gandhi's philosophical outlook on beauty, examining Gandhi's aesthetic sense and artistic feeling would not be out of context here.

One might remember that portion of autobiography in which he mentions his earliest childhood memories of two plays: *Shravan Pitribhakti Natak* and *Harischandra*. The agonized lament of the parents over Shravana's death moved him deeply and he played the melting tune on a concertina that his father had purchased for him. He also mentions in his autobiography that he acted *Harischandra* countless times. Writing some fifty years after he recorded, "still both *Harischandra* and *Shravana* are living realities for me".[41]

Furthermore in his *Autobiography*, Gandhi wrote about his visit to 'a great exhibition' at Paris in 1890. He appreciated the wonderful construction of Notre Dame and the elaborate decoration of the interior with its beautiful sculptures. Gandhi was not impressed with the fashion and frivolity of street, but inside the churches, he found a different atmosphere as he saw people kneeling and praying before the images of the Virgin that 'increases the glory of God'. On the other hand, he found no beauty in the Eiffel Tower.[42] The point is Gandhi approaches art from the ethical and moral perspective.

Later on, during his South African phase, Gandhi wrote an article "Indian Art" in the *Indian Opinion* dated 19 September, 1903. In this article, Gandhi informs his readers about a new palace being built in Mysore which was reported in *The Times of India Weekly*.[43] He reproduced certain portions of the article from the paper for the South African readers both European and Indian: "The former will be able to realize what Indian art means, and also that India, as is often believed in South Africa, is not a place dotted merely with huts inhabited by savages".[44]

Gandhi then reproduced a quotation on Indian art form William Wilson Hunter's *Indian Empire:*

> The Hindu palace-architecture of Gwalior, She [the] Indian-Muhammadan mosques and mausoleums of Agra and Delhi, with several of the older Hindu temples of Southern India, stand unrivalled for grace of outline and elaborate wealth of ornament. Of the Taj Mahal of Agra, he quoted the statement that "its builders had designed like Titans, and finished like jewellers".[45]

He would have felt happy pride at the following observations:

> The exquisite scrolls on the rock-temples at Karla and Ajanta, the delicate marble tracery and flat wood-carving of western India, the harmonious blending of forms and colours in the fabrics of Kashmir, have contributed to the restoration of taste in England. Indian art-work, when faithful to native designs, still obtains the highest honours at the international exhibitions of Europe.[46]

It points to the fact that Gandhi took interest in the beauty of colours and forms of outlines whenever, there was an object of beauty.

Gandhi distinguishes between beauty in inanimate and animate things. While he notes form, colour, and shape in inanimate objects as manifestations of beauty, he shifts this idea of beauty and its manifestation in the morality of the human beings. In his autobiography, Gandhi called Mrs. West, who came from a family of shoe-makers, a beautiful young lady. "I have called beautiful, because it was her moral beauty that at once attracted me. True beauty after all consists in purity of heart".[47]

In Gandhian philosophy of art and beauty, 'heart' occupies central space. It is the purity of means which is necessary for the attainment of truth. It is again the purity of intentions which leads to the true path. Gandhi, who attended many Khadi exhibitions and directed organizations of many of them, said that there might not be beauty in exhibits and artistic perfection in many of the items there but he never cared for these outward aspects. While delivering a speech at the opening of Khadi exhibition in Bangalore on July 3, 1927, he invited the spectators to Exhibition Court and study the Khadi Movement—through charts there. He wrote:

> I invite the candid critic also to go there and I have no doubt that he will find imperfections, he will find those charts not drawn in artistic fashion, but he will find heart put into those charts. They give you facts and figures which are compiled by students who want to serve truth nothing but the truth.[48]

In fact, Gandhi tried to encourage the native tradition of art and it was his contribution to the cause of art. As one critique points out "Gandhi did the great service for the cause of art by getting successive sessions of the Congress at Lucknow, Faijpur and Haripura artistically illuminated with the decorations of the saintly Nand Lal Bose, whom he regarded as the creative master of time".[49]

Further, one should not forget that Gandhi had a philosophical and enduring association with two of the finest literary figures of his times—Ravindranath Tagore and Romain Rolland—which was based on his deep appreciation of their multifaceted creativity.

The critics who charge against Gandhi that he had no sense of beauty, especially in the strict meaning of 'aesthetic sense', ignore the fact that Gandhi did not view *sringar* and *rasa* as generally taken by many aesthetes in terms of pleasure and sensuality but rather he interpreted *sringar* in ethical and spiritual way as discussed above. This can be illustrated by one of unnoticed examples.[50] In 1927, Gandhi visited Vishnu temple of Belur where he came across a sculptured statue of a woman on wall of temple. The sculpture showed that the woman has thrown off her *sari* because a scorpion got into. She is looking at the creature with such a fear in her eyes that moved Gandhi to praise the statue. Seemingly full of *sringar* for many aesthetes, Gandhi interpreted the symbolic meaning of this art piece from his own ethical and spiritual point of view. He explained to his companion that the scorpion is the symbol of sexuality and the lady has thrown of her *sari* in order to free herself from the scorpion of lust, i.e. *kama*.

In 1931, when he visited museums of Vatican he saw the statue of Jesus nailed to cross and said that one could not help being moved to tears. Mira, who accompanied him, gives a fascinating account of that event:

> In Vatican, Bapu's eye fell on a very striking life-size crucifix. He immediately went up to it and stood there in deep contemplation. Then he moved a little this way and that way, so as to see it from different angles, and finally went around behind it and the wall, where there was hardly room to go, and looked up at it from the back. He remained perfectly silent, and it was only when we left that he spoke and then as if still in contemplation "This was a very wonderful crucifix"—and again silence.[51]

Later on, he wrote about the visit to Rome, "If I could spend two or three months there, I would go and see the paintings and sculptures everyday and study them attentively."[52] One incident might be cited here. When Dilip Kumar Ray, a proponent of Indian music who was also the inmate of the Aurobindo Ashram, told Gandhi that he believed Gandhi to be against all arts such as music, Gandhi quickly replied: "I, opposed to arts like music! Why, I cannot even conceive of an evolution of religious life in India without music".[53] Gandhi's love for Meera (1498-1547) and Narsimha

Mehta's (15th Century) *Bhajan* (devotional song) as well as daily *Bhajan* at his prayer congregation shows Gandhi's love for music. The *Ashram Bhajnavali*, a collection of devotional hymns, is still considered one of the finest collections of devotional songs. For him, music and lyrics should have the power to lift people's ethical and spiritual level.

Further many argue that as Gandhi was concerned about practical problems of humanity in general and India in particular, he did not show academic interest and appreciation of art. This argument does not seem valid. In fact, critics ignore the fact that Gandhi in his influential text *Hind Swaraj* referred to two important works on art, Tolstoy's *What is Art* and Ruskin's *Joy For Ever* in the appendix of the text for further reading. However, it may be said here that Gandhi was not interested in theory of art but rather in the practical aspects of art. In fact it was extension of his practical idealism that he professed. As Parel points out:

> Gandhi had a serious interest in the arts. But that interest lay in the practical side of the things more than in the theoretical ones..... He did this in variety of ways: through the political symbols that he invented, through the pioneering work that he did for the revival of religious music...and above all through the effort that he made to make people aware that art was public good.[54]

Gandhi's 'serious interest in art' and 'practical side of things', what Parel observes, can be seen in Gandhi's *ashram* which was the combination of asceticism and aestheticism. In the *ashram*, Gandhi, along with his fellow workers, experimented with Truth. This experimentation with Truth also tried to demonstrate how ordinary and practical things have aesthetic aspects. Better word for this experimentation could be *tapascharya* as Gandhi and other inmates observed eleven vows (*ekadasha vrata*) to shape as well as sharpen the moral elements in their life. The inmates of the *ashram* were expected to give respect to each other and live in harmony; engage in 'bread labour' that is, the physical tasks of the *ashram's* communal life; and to adhere to strictly disciplined ethical and simple life.

As a matter of fact, Gandhi's *ashrams* are classic examples of his dialectical fusion of apparent opposites of asceticism and aesthetics. Life in the *ashram* was based on *yajna*. Gandhi defines it as an act directed to the welfare of other and done without any desire for any kind of return. Gandhi relates this *yajna* to art and joy. He cites an example of tailor Motilal, "who was a tailor at first and continued as tailor afterwards. But spirit was changed, and his work was transmuted into worship. He began to think about the welfare of the others, and his life became artistic in the real sense of the term. A life of sacrifice is the pinnacle of art, and is full of true joy".[55]

At a very personal level, his theory of aesthetics was inherent in his *khadi*, the sparse architecture of his *ashrams*, his ever-changing dress was testimony to his mastery over symbolic aspects of public life, and his life itself was a beautiful work of art.[56]

Conclusion

Gandhi's does not differentiate between asceticism and aestheticism. His understanding of beauty can be traced both to the Indian tradition as well as other Western tradition symbolized by people like Ruskin, Tolstoy and Emerson. Moreover, he enlarges the traditional notion of beauty. On the other hand, the concept of beauty which was caught in current of psychological and psycho-physical confusion, Gandhi attempted to free it from the conflicts and placed it in such a place that a layman can practice it. His notion of beauty is the extension of his metaphysics of truth and in this truth he appreciates beauty. In other words, in Gandhi's philosophy beauty comes through realization of truth. Because truth is law that binds everything, Gandhi pursues beauty in everything which is true in nature. Gandhi does not see beauty as fragmented and isolated part of life, but for him beauty may be the way of life, only if life is based on truth and goodness. Thus, truth, goodness and beauty run into one another in Gandhi's philosophy of beauty. Further, Gandhi sees beauty in the things or activities which is closer to truth/nature's law. Thus, on the one hand if he praises nature and sees beauty in heavenly body, on the other hand, he sees beauty in honest labour as it brings human being closer to nature. By this, Gandhi redefines beauty in simplicity. Contrary to many aesthetes,

Gandhi like Tolstoy does not see art in terms of beauty but defines art in terms of utility. This reflects Gandhi's practical idealism in his concept of beauty, by which he calls for art for millions. In his view, the art and beauty has no meaning if it does not help people in self-realization. Thus, Gandhi's philosophy of beauty is essentially a moral beauty. It comes from the courage of being true to one's self and being true to others. His aesthetics does not see life in fragmentation but integration of all beings. Thus according to him, greatest artist is unquestionably he who lives the purest life.

NOTES

1. Polak, M.G., *Mr. Gandhi: The Man*, Bombay: Vora, 1950, pp. 51-52.
2. Suhrud, Tridip. *Reading Gandhi in Two Tongues* and other essays, Shimla: IIAS, 2012, p. 110.
3. Pathan, B.A. *Gandhian Concept of Beauty*, Delhi: Ajanta Publication, 1989, p. 61.
4. Cited in Gandhi, *Madan: A Gandhian Aesthetics*, Chandigarh: Vikas Bharati, 1969, p. 69.
5. "I believe that we shall never know exactly why a thing is beautiful." France, Antole. *On Life and Letters*, Vol. II, New York: Garden City, p.176.
6. Durant, Will. *The Mansions of Philosophy*, New York: Garden City, 1929, p. 282.
7. *Ibid.*, 283.
8. *Ibid.*
9. *Ibid.*
10. *Op cit.*, A *Gandhian Aesthetics*, p. 26.
11. *Op cit.*, *Gandhian Concept of Beauty*. p. 15.
12. *Op cit.*, *A Gandhian Aesthetics*, p. 61.
13. Parel, Anthony J. *Gandhi's Philosophy and Quest for Harmony*, New Delhi: Cambridge University Press, 2006, p. 158.
14. *The Collected Works of Mahatma Gandhi* (Electronic Book), New Delhi, Publications Division Government of India, 1999, Vol. 25: 27 October, 1921 - 22 January, 1922, p. 79.
15. *Young India*, 20-11-1924, p. 386.
16. *Young India*, 13-11-1924. p. 377.
17. Ruskin's theory of typical beauty, www.Victorianweb.org/authors/Ruskin/atheories /2.2.html. accessed on 12-8-2012.
18. *Young India*, 13-11-1924. p. 377.

19. *Ibid.*
20. Gandhi, M.K. *From Yeravada Mandir*, Ahmedabad: Navajivan Publishing House, 1957, pp. 1-2.
21. *Ibid.*
22. *Harijan*, 13-11-1924, p. 378.
23. Emerson, Ralph. W. Selected Writings of Ralph Waldo Emerson, New York: New American Library, 1965, p. 194.
24. *Young India*, 13-11-1924, p. 377.
25. Gandhi's reading of Tolstoy's *What is Art* is evident from his letter (24-1-1916) to Valji Desai. He wanted to get translate Tolstoy's work by Valji Desai, *CWMG*, Supplementary volume 1, p. 103.
26. *Harijan*, 14-11-1936, p. 315.
27. Leo N. Tolstoy, *What is Art?* Translated by Almyer Maude, New York: MacMillan Publishing Company, 1960, p. 96.
28. *Ibid.*, p. xx.
29. *Harijan*, 7-4-1946, p. 67.
30. *Op cit.*, *A Gandhian Aesthetics*, p. 86.
31. *Op cit.*, *Mansions of Philosophy*, p. 287.
32. *Young India*, 20-11-1924, p. 386.
33. *Young India*, 14-3-1929, p. 86.
34. *CWMG* (Electronic), Vol.70, p. 242.
35. Gandhi, M.K., *Hind Swaraj or Indian Home Rule*, Ahmedabad: Navajivan Publishing House, 2008, pp. 52-3.
36. *Ibid.*, p. 32.
37. *Ibid.*, p. 54.
38. Chakrawarty, *M. Gandhian Socio-Aesthetics*, New Delhi: M.D Publications Pvt. Ltd., 1997, p. 7.
39. *Harijan*, 19-2-1938, p. 10.
40. Quoted in Rao, U.R. and R.K. Prabhu, *The Mind of Mahatma Gandhi*, Ahmedabad: Navajivan Publishing House, 2002, p. 56.
41. Gandhi, M.K. , *An Autobiography or The Story of My Experiments with Truth*, Ahmedabad: Navajivan Publishing House, 2007, p. 7.
42. *Ibid.*, pp. 71-72.
43. *CWMG* (Electronic Book), August 1, 1902- May 21, 1904. Vol. 3, pp. 248-49.
44. *Ibid.*
45. *Ibid.*
46. *Ibid.*
47. *Op cit. An Autobiography or The Story of My Experiments with Truth*, p. 284.
48. *CWMG* (Electronic Book), June 4, 1927- September 1, 1927. Vol. 39, p. 160.

49. *Triveni*, January-March, 1972, p. 24.
50. *Op cit., Gandhian Concept of Beauty*, p. 77.
51. Mirabehn, *The Spirit's Pilgrimage*. New York: Coward-McCann, 1960, p. 111.
52. *CWMG*, Vol. 49, p. 37.
53. *Ibid.*
54. *Op cit., Gandhi's Philosophy and Quest for Harmony*, p. 159.
55. www.mkgandhi.org/yeravda/chap15.htm, accessed on 5 February, p. 35.
56. *Op cit., Reading Gandhi in Two Tongues*, p. 111.

CHAPTER 5

Gandhian Alternative to Economic Development

Relevance for India Today

B.P. MATHUR

> "India's destiny lies not along the bloody way of the West, of which she shows signs of tiredness, but along the bloodless way of peace that comes from a simple and godly life. India is in danger of losing her soul. She cannot lose it and live. She must not, therefore, lazily and helplessly say, 'I cannot escape the onrush from the West.' She must be strong enough to resist it for its own sake and that of the world."
>
> —*Mahatma Gandhi*

> "Agriculture is more revolutionary than industry. In twenty-five years, Israel increased its agriculture yields seventeen times. This is amazing. People don't realise this. Agriculture is ninety-five per cent science, five per cent work."
>
> —*Shimon Peres, President of Israel*

Mahatma Gandhi's philosophy of truth, non-violence and *satyagraha* helped India get liberation from British rule and is considered a perennial philosophy to fight injustice, oppression and suppression of human rights. Martin Luther King effectively used non-violence as a weapon to secure rights and justice for the

Blacks in America. While Gandhiji's philosophy had wide acceptance to deal with political and social issues, it had not many followers in the arena of economics. He was aware of it. "Pandit Nehru wants industrialisation because he thinks that, if it is socialised, it would be free from the evils of capitalism. My own view is that evils are inherent in industrialism, and no amount of socialisation can eradicate it."[1] Gandhiji was not impressed by the two prevailing dominant systems of the management of the economy, the capitalist free-market economy and the state-bureaucratic socialism of the communist countries. Post-independence, India abandoned Gandhiji's economic philosophy and adopted a mixed economy model with the state commanding the heights of the economy. As we know, this nowhere helped solving our gigantic problems of poverty and backwardness and the economy stagnated. Post-liberalisation in 1991, we have adopted a free-market economic model, but genuine progress and development has been eluding us.

Today the global economy with the free market as its *mantra* is in a state of severe crisis. The political leadership, thinkers and intellectuals are all searching for the 'right model' of economic development but it is nowhere in sight. Does Gandhian philosophy provide an insight into how to manage the economic system?

It should be remembered that Gandhiji propounded a total philosophy of life, from which economics cannot be divorced. Gandhi's philosophy was based on truth, *ahimsa*, and service to society, particularly the poor and down-trodden. He derived inspiration from the ancient Indian philosophy of *Ramayana*, *Upanishad* and *Gita*, expounded the highest ethical standards, and felt that religion and morality are the same thing. Gandhiji did not draw distinction between economics and ethics. "Economics that hurt the moral well-being of an individual or a nation are immoral and, therefore, sinful."[2] He was not enamoured of the Western civilisation based on materialism, exploitation, competition and domination which, in his view, was responsible for India's enslavement by the British.

Gandhian Economic Philosophy

The basis of Gandhiji's economic philosophy was individual dignity and the welfare of the poorest of the poor. He felt that a man earns his dignity by working and earning his bread and livelihood. Therefore, the economic system should be organised to provide employment for everyone. "According to me, the economic Constitution of India, and for that matter of the world, should be such that no one under it should suffer from want of food and clothing. In other words, everybody should be able to get sufficient work to enable him to make two ends meet. And this ideal can be universally realised only if the means of production of the elementary necessities of life remain in control of the masses."[3] He was against mass production and industrialisation which destroyed local industry, impoverished villages and reduced man to a cog in the machine. "What I object to is the craze for machinery, not machinery as such. Men go on saving labour till thousands are without work and thrown on the open streets to die of starvation."[4] Gandhiji did not oppose all machinery, he praised the invention of Singer Sewing Machine which ended the drudgery of the housewife. His opposition to machine was particularly in the context of India as it has a huge population and unemployment. "Mechanisation is good when the hands are too few for the work intended to be accomplished. It is an evil when there are more hands than required for work as in the case of India."[5]

He was against India copying the West and its urban-centric civilisation and pleaded for *Gram-Swarajya*. "I have believed and repeated times without number that India is to be found not in its cities but in its 7,00,000 villages. But we town-dwellers have believed that India is to be found in its towns and the villages were created to minister our needs. The cities with their insolent tort are a constant menace to the life and liberty of the villages."[6] Gandhiji believed in Village Swaraj, 'independent of its neighbours for its vital needs, and yet inter-dependent for many others in which dependence is a necessity'.[7]

Gandhiji rejected a pure economic man. The modern economic theory is based on wants and not on needs and this is the source of the rat race that debases human beings by keeping them subject to their animal spirit. Want-oriented economies creates a psychology of scarcity and poverty, as all wants can never be satisfied. Prof. J.K. Mehta, a revered philosopher-economist of Allahabad University, took a Gandhian view of the science of economics which he defined 'as the science of human activities considered as an endeavour to reach the state of wantlessness'.[8] He said that a man wants to maintain mental equilibrium for which he satisfies wants, but all wants can never be satisfied. "The science of economics sets for itself the goal of removal of all wants. It is not realised, however, that the way we proceed to reach the goal is self-defeating... Economic theory developed to explain human behaviour on the fundamental postulate that man wants to satisfy his wants with least expenditure of the resources at his command. And that meant that it was assumed that in satisfying one's wants care must be taken that the fewest possible other wants were created."[9] The *Karmayoga* philosophy pleads for not wanting results of one's actions—the wider discipline of economics should pull down barriers between economics and religion. "Where the desire to satisfy wants is encouraged and efforts to raise the standard of people eulogised, man is robbed of mental peace and nations of peaceful existence." The pampering of wants is not our final desideratum, observed Prof. Mehta.

Trusteeship

Gandhiji criticised the capitalist system because it is based on ownership of the means of production and other property. He argued that unlimited wants, greed, fear, etc., arise from capitalist property relations. Gandhiji advanced a theory of trusteeship as an organisational structure under which production could be organised, instead of large industrial houses where economic power was concentrated in the hands of a few and were inherently exploitative. Socialist thinkers have for a long time been arguing that private property is at the root of the exploitative process of production and distribution and called for its abolition. Proudhon termed property as theft and Karl Marx called for a revolt by the property-less proletariat, capture of state power by the working class to be followed by a classless society. Gandhiji declared himself to be a socialist and repudiated the concept of private ownership of property. But he was opposed to the use of violence or hatred to bring about social change. He wanted to do it by moral force and persuasion. The objective is to create a non-violent non-exploitative property relationship. He equated private property in excess of basic needs of human existence with exploitation and held that private property was not a natural right but a man-made privilege, so it could be modified and altered by social action. Gandhiji simultaneously proclaimed his profound belief in the rightness of economic equality. He did not visualise a world where there will be no property but he would restrict the right of private property to what was necessary to yield an honourable livelihood, while for the excess he prescribed the principle of trusteeship. He asked those who own money to behave like trustees holding their riches on behalf of the poor.

The fundamental objective underlying trusteeship is to create a non-violent and non-exploitive property relationship. Gandhiji left a six-point programme containing his ideas about trusteeship on the basis of a draft prepared by the distinguished economist Prof. M.L. Dantewala.[10] Its salient features are: (1) Trusteeship provides a means of transforming the present capitalist order of society into an egalitarian one. (2) It does not recognise any right of private ownership of property, except inasmuch as it may be permitted by society for its own welfare. (3) It does not exclude legislative ownership and use of wealth. (4) Under state-regulated trustee-ship, an individual will not be free to hold or use his wealth for selfish satisfaction or in disregard of the interest of the society. (5) Just as it is proposed to fix a decent minimum wage, even so a limit should be fixed for the maximum income that could be allowed to any person in society. (6) The character of production will be determined by social necessity and not by personal whim or greed.

Elaborating on the concept of trusteeship, economist V.K.R.V. Rao[11] summarises it as follows: "acceptance of the principle of private ownership of property, the limit imposed upon its use for sustaining minimum living standards, the major constraints it imposes by prohibiting its use merely for selfish satisfaction or in disregard of the social interest and the inclusion of legislative regulation for determining its ownership and use in the desired direction for non-exploitive purposes". Gandhian economist J.D. Sethi[12] says that four underlying ethico-economic principles of trusteeship are: (1) non-possession; (2) non-exploitation; (3) bread labour; (4) equality of rewards. Thus trusteeship is a theory of need-based production, equitable distribution and social justice. "Philosophically, trusteeship is an economic conscience by which an individual when engaged in economic activity takes into account not only his own interests but also the interest of others."

Intermediate Technology

E.F. Schumacher,[13] the author of *Small is Beautiful*, draws inspiration from the Gandhian ideology of 'resisting the temptation of letting our luxuries become needs', and 'recognition of existence of the soul apart from the body'. He argues that man's current pursuit of profit and progress which promotes giant organisations and increased specialisation has resulted in gross economic inefficiency, environmental pollution and inhuman working conditions. He proposes a system of Intermediate Technology, based on smaller working units, communal ownership and regional workplaces utilising local labour and resources. "The technology of mass production is inherently violent, ecologically damaging, self-defeating in terms of non-renewable resources and stultifying for the human person. The technology of production by the masses, making use of the best modern knowledge and experience, is conducive to decentralisation, compatible with the laws of ecology, gentle in its use of scarce resources, and designed to serve the human person instead of making him servant of machines."[14] Intermediate technology is a technology with a human face, one that is viable and integrates the human being with his skilful hands and creative brains, into a productive process.

From the point of modern economic theory, 'labour' or 'worker' is an item of cost, to be reduced to the minimum and ensure output without employees. This approach is demeaning as work provides individual growth and fulfilment according to the Buddhist as well Vedanta (*Gita*) philosophy. However, there is need to make a distinction between mechanisation that enhances man's skill and power and one that turns the work of a man to a mechanical slave leaving man to serve the machine. "To organise work in such a manner that it becomes meaningless, boring, stultifying, or nerve racking for the worker would be little short of criminal; it would indicate a greater concern with goods than with people, an evil lack of compassion and a soul-destroying degree of attachment to the most primitive side of this worldly existence."[15] An economics which considers goods more important than people and consumption more important than creative activity, is a surrender to the forces of evil.

Schumacher faults the current philosophy of materialism under which the development of production and acquisition of wealth have become the highest goal of the modern world, to which all other goals should be subordinated. "It is of little use trying to suppress terrorism if the production of deadly devices continues to be a legitimate employment of man's creative powers. Nor can the fight against pollution be successful if the pattern of production and consumption continue to be of a scale, a complexity, and a degree of violence which, as is becoming more and more apparent, do not fit into the laws of universe, to which man is as much subject as the rest of creation."[16] Schumacher calls for guiding our actions according to the time-tested, four cardinal virtues of Christianity—prudence, justice, goodness, and beauty, if civilisation is to survive.

Building Social Business

Nobel Prize winner Muhammad Yunus has pioneered micro-credit in Bangladesh, the innovative banking programme that provides poor people—mostly women—with small loans they use to launch business and lift their families out of poverty. He has advanced the concept of social business to deal with the problems of capitalism. The existing economic theory portrays human beings in business as one-dimensional whose sole mission is maximisation of profit. As a matter of fact, human beings are multi-dimensional, their happiness comes from many sources, including selfless service to fellow human beings. This spirit of human beings combined with the powerful technology available today, offers huge opportunity to do social business. Social business has seven principles:[17] (1) The business objective is to overcome poverty, or similar problems relating to education, health, etc., not to maximise profit. (2) The company will attain financial and economic sustainability. (3) Investors will get back only their investment amount. No dividend is given beyond the original investment. (4) When the investment is paid back, profit stays with the company for expansion and improvement. (5) The company will be environmentally conscious. (6) The workforce gets market wages with better than standard working conditions. (7) Work is done with joy.

The concept of social business has been successfully experimented in Bangladesh in diverse areas such as provision of mobile phone company in rural areas, solar homes, affordable health care and modernisation of the handloom industry. Yunus, in partnership with some of the world's large business houses, such as Danone, has been producing affordable nutritious yoghart for malnourished children. Yunus says that if social business is developed and integrated into the mainstream of economic theory, it can solve many of the world's problems of poverty, hunger and ill health and 'can address the problems left behind by profit-making businesses'.

The Relevance of Gandhian Ideology Today

The Gandhian ideology, whose main focus is on welfare and dignity of the individual, provides us a broad framework into the new philosophy of economic development that we need today. We may first summarise the Gandhian principles:

- The economic system should be so organised that every individual has an opportunity of getting gainful employment, so that he can buy his own bread and essential means of living. Gandhi did not believe in the poor living on the charity or mercy of others and wanted eradication of poverty which is possible only through everyone getting employment.
- Gandhiji was opposed to mindless industrialisation as it displaces labour and causes unemployment and is the main reason for rural poverty.
- Gandhiji supported rural-centric development with agriculture and small scale industries getting pride of place, as this is the only way the unemployment problem can be solved in a labour abundant country like India.
- Gandhiji believed in the decentralised development model as this helps the fruits of development reach everyone and promotes equality and social harmony.

- Gandhiji was opposed to conspicuous consumption and luxurious living. He wanted people to have minimum needs and lead a simple life.

While Gandhiji was not opposed to private ownership of industries and business, he advocated social control of business so that the profits generated are equitably distributed so as to prevent concentration of wealth in the hands of a few people, which leads to exploitation.

We should not look towards Gandhian economics as a rigid doctrinaire framework and view with scepticism Gandhi opposing all 'machines and industrialisation' alongside the impracticability of the idea of 'rich businessmen voluntarily surrendering their wealth for social good'. Gandhiji was pragmatic and expressed views in the context of India's conditions at the time prevailing during the British Raj. If we properly understand Gandhian philosophy, we will find that it is very much relevant today, when the world is facing a severe crisis due to mass poverty and unemployment, side by side with conspicuous consumption and exploitation of natural resources. Schumacher has shown how the use of simple and intermediate technology can help micro- and small-scale industries as a rewarding and profitable occupation, in which millions of people could be employed. Muhammad Yunus, with his social business model, has demonstrated how successfully businesses can be run without the profit as the motive, and can lift people out of poverty.

Post-Second World War the pursuit of growth has been the ruling economic ideology amongst all the nations of the world, imposing a great cost on society. An economic model based on unbridled production and consumption is fundamentally flawed and responsible for the current global economic crisis, as well as the ecological and social problems that we are facing. Huge consumption fuelled by credit and corporate greed has been behind the economic crisis which the USA and West European countries are facing since 2008, and this has resulted in huge unemployment and suffering of the people.

Intellectuals, think-tanks and environmentalists all over the world are propounding a philosophy of reducing consumption and ostentatious living, to save planet Earth from destruction. The

British Sustainable Development Commission finds an inverse relationship between growth and social well-being and ecological sustainability. In the last quarter of a century, while the global economy has doubled, the increase in resource consumption has degraded an estimated 60 per cent of the world's ecosystems. The benefits of growth have been distributed very unequally, with a fifth of the world's population sharing just two per cent of the global income. The Commission observes that prosperity has to go beyond material pleasure. Two other objectives—growth-sustainability and well-being—have to move up the agenda for creating a prosperous society. A commission chaired by Nobel Prize winner economist Joseph Stiglitz has expressed severe dissatisfaction with GDP as an indicator of economic and social progress and recommended a shift from measuring economic production to measuring people's well-being. Expressing similar views, the World Watch Institute opines that we need to measure progress by improvement in well-being rather than expansion in market based economic activity and how quickly we can build a renewable energy platform, meet basic human needs, discourage wasteful consumption, and invest rather than deplete natural and cultural capital. The Club of Rome has been, for a long time, pointing out that there are ecological constraints in the existing development pattern, and has focused on the planet's physical limit in the form of depleting natural resources and the need to cut consumption. Speaking a similar language, the UNDP has been articulating the idea that GDP growth is meaningless, if it does not improve the quality of people's lives in terms of security of livelihood, freedom, empowerment and social cohesion.

Failure of the Existing Economic Model

Policy-makers all over the world are groping in the dark, trying to find a solution to the best economic model to build a stable and sustainable economy. It needs to be remembered that there is nothing like a pure capitalist or socialist path of economic development. Socialism, in its practical operation, implies control over means of production and distribution by the state, though the philosophy of socialism, when originally postulated, had its roots in the doctrine of equality and liberalism. The economists for a long time suffered from the illusion that the state acts as a platonic guardian of the people. They forgot that it is the politician and the bureaucrat who control the machinery of the state and their main aim is to exercise power and authority with scant regard to people's welfare. Due to its inherent contradiction, the socialist model, practised by the Soviet Union and its satellite East European countries, collapsed in the late 1980s.

Capitalism with its philosophy of free and unregulated markets, leads to concentration of wealth in the hands of a few causing widespread social disparity. It also encourages individual greed and avarice. For the last three decades the USA and Western countries have been unabashedly pursuing a neo-liberal economic model with liberalisation, globalisation and free play of the market forces as its *mantra*. The single most objective here is economic growth, without any thought given to its cost. This model, based on relentless consumerism, is fundamentally flawed and responsible for the current global economic crisis, mass unemployment and environmental degradation. It is time we abandon a model whose foundations rest on materialism, consumption and greed.

Eminent historian Eric Hobsbawm[18] observes that the experience of the last thirty years shows that both the socialist and free market economic systems have failed. "The twentieth century attempts to treat world history as an economic zero-sum game between private and public, pure individualism and pure collectivism, have not survived the manifest bankruptcy of the Soviet Union and the 'economy of market fundamentalism' between 1980 and 2008. Nor is a return to the one more possible than a return to the other. Since the 1980s it has been evident that the socialists, Marxist or otherwise, were left without their traditional alternative to capitalism, at least unless or until they rethought what they meant by 'socialism' and abandoned the presumption that the (manual) working class would necessarily be the chief agent of social transformation. But the believers in the 1973-2008 *reductio ad absurdum* of market society were also left helpless. A systematic alternative system may not be on the horizon, but the possibility of a disintegration, even a collapse, of the existing system is no longer to be ruled out. Neither side knows what would or could happen in that case."

The Future Direction

What we need today is to devise a new model of economic development based on the Gandhian ideology. This in practice would mean that public policy should give massive support to agriculture on which more than half the population of the country depends for their livelihood and make it a remunerative occupation on par with industry and the service sector. The state policy should also support, in a big way, thousands of micro- and small-scale industries through investment in R&D and upgradation of the capability of people working there, in terms of education, knowledge and skill, with provision of credit and other facilities. To create an egalitarian society, Big Business should be strictly regulated and converted into Social Business, so that they plough their profits back into the business for socially productive activities and are not allowed to extract surplus by way of salary, dividend, bonus and other means except what they need for a reasonable standard of living.

Mahatma Gandhi said there is enough in the world for 'everyone's need but not for his greed'. He propounded a philosophy of simple living and reducing consumption. Through his call of *Swadeshi* and *Gram Swaraj*, Gandhiji delivered a strong message for not only political independence but also economic self-reliance and inclusive growth. We should, therefore, design policy initiatives which take care of the welfare of the poorest members of the society, fulfil their basic wants and gives them a dignified and respectable living. We need a new matrix of economic development, in which progress is measured in terms of development of human capability, dignified employment for everyone, equitable distribution of income and wealth, ecological sustainability and social well-being of the community. Gandhian philosophy, properly understood, provides the solution.

NOTES

1. Rao, U.S. Mohan, *The Message of Mahatma Gandhi*, Publications Division, Government of India, 1968 (reprinted 1994), p. 54; *Harijan*, 19.9.1940.

2. Rao, U.S. Mohan, *The Message of Mahatma Gandhi*, Publications Division, Government of India, 1968 (reprinted 1994), p. 47; *Young India*, 13.10.1921.
3. *Ibid.*, p. 47, *Young India*, 15.12.1928.
4. *Ibid.*, p. 51.
5. *Ibid.*, p. 51, *Harijan*, 16.11.1934.
6. *Ibid.*, p. 73, *Young India*, 6.4.1921; 2.4.1925.
7. *Ibid.*, pp. 78, *Harijan*, 26.7.1942.
8. Mehta, J.K., *Studies in Advanced Economic Theory*, Premier Publishing Co., Delhi, 1950, p. 22.
9. Mehta, J.K., *Rhyme, Rhythm, and Truth in Economics*, Asia Publishing House, London, 1967, pp. 27-35.
10. Dantewala, M.L., 'Trusteeship: Its Value Implications' in J.D. Sethi (ed.), *Trusteeship—The Gandhian Alternative*, Gandhi Peace Foundation, New Delhi, 1986.
11. Rao, V.K.R.V., *'Trusteeship as Gandhian Instrument for Socialist Change'*, pp. 27-28 in J.D. Sethi (ed.), *ibid.*
12. Sethi, J.D., *Trusteeship and the Crisis in Economic Theory*, pp. 76-94; in J.D. Sethi (ed.), *ibid.*
13. Schumakar, E.F., *Small is Beautiful: A Study of Economics as if People Mattered*, Vintage, Random House, London, 1993.
14. *Ibid.*, p. 121.
15. *Ibid.*, pp. 39-40.
16. *Ibid.*, pp. 249-250.
17. Yunus, Muhammad, 'Building Social Business—The New Kind of Capitalism that Serves Humanity's Most Pressing Needs', *Public Affairs*, New York, 2010, p. 2; also see Muhammad Yunus, 'Creating a World Without Poverty—Social Business and the Future of Capitalism', *Public Affairs*, New York, 2007.
18. Hobsbawm, Eric, *How to Change the World*, Little Brown, London, 2011, Tales of Marx and Marxism, p. 418.

CHAPTER 6

Challenges from Violence and Terrorism

Methods and Strategies to Counter Them

Y.P. ANAND

'Gandhi had the most enlightened views of all the political men in our time. We should strive to do things in his spirit; not to use violence in fighting for our cause and to refrain from taking part in anything we believe is evil.'

—*Albert Einstein* (June 18, 1950), in the UNO broadcast on 'The Pursuit of Peace'

A. Challenges from Violence and Terrorism

Mahatma Gandhi was martyred on January 30, 1948, after his lifelong struggle against violence and terrorism, and for his philosophy of non-violence and *satyagraha*, of brotherhood of humankind and of unity of all lives. United Nations General Assembly has unanimously resolved on June 14, 2007, henceforth, to observe Gandhiji's birthday, October 2, as the 'International Day of Non-violence'. Hence, this is an opportune occasion to hold this meet on 'Challenges from Violence and Terrorism: Methods and Strategies to Counter Them'.

The Second World War ended in 1945, and formation of the United Nations, international interdependence, and the gathering process of decolonization by the imperial powers, should have ensured peace in the world. But the reality has been the opposite and Gandhiji's criticism of the 'modern' civilization for "its adoration of the brute in us, its adoration of the matter and its unmixed materialism" has proved to be prophetic. The Berlin Wall has fallen, apartheid as well as the old forms of colonial rule have ended, science and technology had made unprecedented progress, material wealth has grown enormously, the process of globalization has moved apace, and the reach of media, travel and communications has grown fast, but so also have been the growth in lethality and quantum of weapons of mass destruction, pervasive violence, disparities and exploitation in newer forms, and alienation. These have led to worldwide spread of terrorist activities, intolerance, violent conflicts on political, religious, ethnic, economic grounds, increasingly compounded by issues of environmental degradation, finite nature of energy and material resources, and global warming. Now violence, and terrorism too are global, both internal and external. War and enmity are both within and with other societies and nation-states.

Violence spreads also through glorification in the media and cinema, religious fundamentalism, and a chauvinistic sense of 'nationalism'. Modern state has been an instrument of both violence and welfare, however, with its growing power of violence, its welfare functions have tended to weaken. Western model of development does not accept that the opposite of poverty and deprivation is not just higher GDP and indulgent consumerism, but it means meeting the basic needs for a decent living, self-sufficiency and a non-violent, egalitarian, humane, happy and sustainable social order, and that growing greed and aggrandizement tend to generate, and hence cannot redress, socially unacceptable inequalities and inequities.

Some of the salient issues constituting 'Challenges from Violence and Terrorism' are briefly discussed under the sub-headings of 'Direct Violence', 'Direct Violence as Terrorism', and 'Violence: Social, Economic, Environmental' in the following paras A.2, A.3, and A.4.

A.2 Direct Violence

Direct violence may take the form of external and internal wars involving the military, insurgencies and terrorist activities (*see* A.3), organized crime, ethnic or communal riots, drug mafias and gang wars, and common crime.

Even though the Cold War has ended, military spending in 2004 in the world was the ever highest at $1.035 trillion, or $162/person; the US share being $455 billion, and the largest growth over that in 2003 having been in South Asia, especially in India. The prospects of a ban on nuclear weapons are receding and their proliferation seems to be now a matter of national achievement. Legal and illegal trade in arms is a growing global phenomenon. In India, the availability of licensed and unlicensed arms is a common feature. Easy availability of arms itself fuels local wars and conflicts. The LTTE led murderous war in Sri Lanka is continuing for two decades primarily due to easy access to all categories of arms. Developed countries are the main international arms exporters and they are not willing to control this global menace because of the influence of the industrial-military interests and mafias.

Twentieth century was the bloodiest in human history. First and Second World Wars and wars in Vietnam and the Gulf alone killed 86 million people, bulk of them innocent non-combatants. Over a hundred million unexploded land-mines are buried in a large number of countries leading to civilian deaths long after the wars are over. Since 1945 itself over 20 million have died and nearly three times wounded in the numerous local wars. 'Nationalism', industrial production, the bureaucratic state, and science and technology have been harnessed to the cause of war more and more.

Various warlords in Afghanistan, supported by USA arms and funds, channelled through Pakistan, fought the Cold War on behalf of the USA. The war in Afghanistan has continued with changing allies and opponents; it has ravaged the whole country, made millions into internal and external refugees, killed a million or two in this game of neo-colonialism. USA was an ally of Iraq when Iraq was fighting against Iran in a bloody war, but attacked it when Iraq attacked Kuwait in 1991—the first Gulf War. Under the USA imposed sanctions, Iraq's economy was destroyed and nearly 500,000 children died for want of food and medicines. These sanctions were continuing when USA directly attacked Iraq in 2003. Until June 2006, according to a recent report 151,000 Iraqi civilians have been killed (earlier the US researchers in 2006 had estimated the figure as 601,027). Since March 2003 USA has lost about 4,000 military personnel, the number of wounded being nearly eight times. But the other consequences are far more pervasive and long-lasting: the country has been decimated.

There are ethnic genocides still going on in parts of Africa. Communal riots are a well-known feature in India, the most telling examples in recent years being the riots in Delhi (1984) and Gujarat (2002) in which the Governments remained mute spectators. In India, armed police, paramilitary forces and even military are called upon to control riots and insurgencies by the very people whom they are supposed to protect. Murders of political leaders, and other political violence, such as, during elections, are not so rare in the subcontinent. The statistics of general crime, rapes and killings are a usual phenomenon in varying degrees in different countries.

A.3 Direct Violence as Terrorism

It is not easy to define 'Terrorism' which is an organized form of extreme violence in human thinking and conduct prevailing on national or international scales. It arises basically out of political-economic issues driven by religious, ethnic or similar motivations, and is related to the access to weapon systems, funds, technology, and institutional support. It is driven by extreme views on issues of faith, identity, a deep-rooted sense of injustice, oppression, inequality, deprivation, frustration, hurt, desperation, search for a purpose in life.

United Nations Security Council passed Resolution 1373 (September 28, 2001) dealing with the 'How' of terrorism: it noted the close connection between international terrorism and transnational organized crime, illicit drugs, money laundering and illegal movement of nuclear, chemical and biological and other deadly materials. But it did not deal with the 'Why' of it.

In the discussion that followed in the General Assembly, views varied on the definition of 'Terrorism'; such as: "Acts of pure terrorism, involving attacks against innocent civilian populations—which cannot be justified under any circumstances—should be differentiated from the legitimate struggles of people under colonial or alien domination and foreign occupation for self-determination and national liberation."/"It will continue to haunt us if the roots of terrorism, which lie in the inequality of societies, in the exploitation of down-trodden, in the denial of fundamental rights and in the sense of injustice, are not addressed."/"Such an attempt [to classify resistance to occupation as a terrorist act] will turn concepts topsy turvy, and only hatred can be engendered from this kind of oppression."/"Legitimacy as well as sustainability of the global struggle against terrorism rests on applying a single set of standards to all."

India has experienced a series of terrorist attacks in recent years. The issue of terrorism became truly international after September 11, 2001, the Black Tuesday, when organized terrorism hijacked civilian planes in the USA and hit the only superpower of the world in its homeland at its most potent symbols of economic and military supremacy. Nearly 4000 dead and $100 (?) billion destroyed. In reply, the USA and its allies have occupied Afghanistan and Iraq.

Terrorism is anti-human and seeks to resolve conflicts with maximum violence. It kills the innocent. It feeds on human susceptibilities and frailties even while seeking redress of the genuine or otherwise perceived wrongs. It breeds hatred and barbaric satisfaction over destruction of life and property. It is secretive and cowardly. It employs evil even while ostensibly fighting against it. It makes devils out of ordinary, particularly the impressionable, human beings. Yet, the question of 'motivation', particularly in the case of 'suicide' squads remains a complex issue. Different views [in Palestine] include: "The easiest thing is to find a martyr. In our nation we have thousands who want to be martyrs."/"What the rank-and file [of Hamas] seemed to live and die for, in the end, was neither hospitals, nor politics nor ideology nor religion nor the Apocalypse, but rather an ecstatic camaraderie in the face of death on the path of Allah." All need to think why such otherwise normal youth come forth to destroy themselves and others, unless they nurture a sense of extreme injustice against which they feel helpless and without hope.

But, terrorism may not arise only from underground outfits or individuals, nor is it a new phenomenon. Wiping out the indigenous populations in the Americas or Australia, Hitler's holocaust of six million Jews, the 'collectivization' programme in the USSR and the Great Leap Forward/Cultural Revolution in Communist China which eliminated millions, dropping of atom bombs on Hiroshima and Nagasaki civilian populations, carpet bombing of Vietnam, and blockade of Iraq after the first Gulf War were all examples of terrorist acts. Sustenance of the industrial-military complexes and profiteering from supply of arms to oppressive regimes, mafias and terrorists too are acts of terrorism. Insurgency, such as in India, is another form of terrorism. Nearly 1 in 6 Indians now live under its shadow. The 'Naxalite' corridor now extends from Bihar to Jharkhand, Orissa, Chhattisgarh, Andhra Pradesh, and Maharashtra. In fact, it extends into Nepal also. In Pakistan, insurgent-terrorist groups and strongholds are also well-known.

Among the consequences of terrorist activities have been: (a) An ever-increasing 'security' being provided for even minor public figures (in India 'Z' category security is taken as a measure of political importance) at public cost; and (b) Proliferation of private security agencies particularly to serve the well-off class in their places of residence, shopping and pleasure. In India, such business is worth ₹ 25,000 crore, and is growing at the rate of 25 per cent annually.

A.4 Violence: Social, Economic and Environmental

Direct violence and terrorism are many times a reflection of the politico-socio-economic violence. In developing countries, chances of death from malnutrition and preventable diseases are many times more than from direct aggression. For example, out of 33.2 million cases of HIV/AIDS by end 2007, 22.5 were in Sub-Saharan Africa. An environment of pervasive disparities and exploitation tends to brutalize the society and engender insensitivity towards the weak and poor, corruption, and arrogance of power and wealth. Criminalization of politics, state and society, religious fundamentalism, and modern media cultures catering to the market also tend to make the struggle for equity more difficult.

Downsides of unbridled capitalism have not vanished simply because those of state socialism became apparent. Both central planning and emaciated welfare state structures have failed to address the issues of 'war within'. Socio-economic goals of 'development', viz., economic growth, equity, democracy, and stability are not inherently coincident. Triumphant globalism with its stress on profit and consumerism lacks social or ethical concerns. Transmission of power, education and wealth is mostly dynastic, and concern for the entitlements and capabilities is largely an academic exercise. While India has been 'shining', disparities have grown and even now 26.1 per cent of Indians are below even a dismal 'Poverty Line'. According to a more humane PL, providing for minimum nutrition, basic needs of health, water and sanitation, shelter and clothing, energy for lighting and cooking, education and other unavoidable basic needs, 68.6 per cent Indians are estimated to be below PL [*Economic and Political Weekly*, 24.6.2006:2534-40]. As Gandhiji said: "The hungry millions ask for one poem, the invigorating food".

A recent study by National Commission for Enterprises in Unorganized Sector (India) concludes that there is congruence of the poor and vulnerable groups with the deprived and discriminated social groups, and with very poor educational achievement. These groups constitute the unorganized workforce of 39.6 crore (93% of total workforce) with poor working conditions, no social security and lack of regular employment. There are 3 million workers in brick kilns around Delhi, who work mostly along with other family members who are not even counted.

Out of 27 million bonded labours in the world, nearly 15-20 million are in South Asia. Trafficking in human beings is the third largest illicit trade in the world after arms and drugs. Illegal trade in human organs of the poor, particularly kidneys, is a well-organized racket in India. The National Rural Employment Guarantee Act (NREGA) is meant to provide employment for only 100 days in a year to one member of a family at the rate of a meagre ₹ 60 to 100 per day, even then it is not applicable all over. Not only 87.6 per cent of India's 10.127 crore farm-holders are 'marginal' (owning less than 1 ha) and 'small' (1-2 ha), but there is a growing population of landless rural labourers. They desperately need some employment to meet their survival needs. As against this, the number of millionaires and billionaires is rising fast in India, the fast growing luxury goods market is now worth over ₹ 600 crore, and even the wealth and lifestyles of many political figures have risen fast without any ostensible sources of such income.

Environment related damage too has mostly affected the poor and weaker sections. Those dependent for survival on local resource base in a symbiotic existence, such as tribal populations, forest dwellers, hill people, and fishing communities have suffered severe deprivations since independence because the 'development' projects have made them *refugees* in large numbers, damaged, polluted and obliterated their habitats, and even taken away their tradition rights to land, water, and forests in the name of environment protection. In rural areas of India, about 5 lakh die per year due to internal smoke pollution in the rural homes. Resources are being concentrated in urban areas whereas still 70 per cent population is in rural areas. A recent UN Development Report shows that 40 million of the world's poor will bear the brunt of anticipated climate change while they contribute relatively the least to it. There is a wide disparity between the rich and the poor in per head consumption of energy and other resources as also in generation of pollution and wastes, which itself is a cause of violence and terrorism today in the world.

The condition of youth, women and children deserves a special mention. The youth when devoid of adequate education or employable skills and reasonable employment, but witness to conspicuous consumption around them, fall prey to fundamentalism, terrorism, crime, and social disaffection. The condition of women in the Indian society is one of suppression and exploitation. With nearly one million cases of female foeticide per year, high rates of maternal mortality, child marriage and the institution of dowry, and prevalent male domination in the society at large as also seen by poor representation in legislatures, and higher professions, large number of cases of rape, and prostitution, it is a long list of discrimination, prejudice and open violence.

Children are the weakest part of the society. In India, their deprivation and exploitation is seen most by the following indicators:

- According to 2001 Census, there are 12.7 million child labour (5-14 years old) and 28.4 million adolescent labour (5-17 years old)—unofficial estimates would be much higher. Children work in agriculture, in fire works and match factories, in restaurants, as hawkers, as beggars, polishing shoes, and so on. Child labour have no protection as no trade union is allowed for those below 15.

- Three-fourths of the children are anaemic, nearly half (under 5) are under-weight, child mortality (under 5) is 96/1000 live births (2.1 million died in 2006), two-thirds of street children are physically abused, 0.3-0.5 million children are in prostitution.
- Sixteen per cent children are out of school and the drop-out rate is very high. Article 45 of the Constitution, requiring state to 'endeavour' to have every child up to the age of 14 provided with 'free and compulsory' schooling by 1960 has been totally ignored. The Constitution (86th Amendment) Act 2002 has had little effect so far.

1.2 million children per year are trafficked worldwide.

B. Methods and Strategies to Counter them

> 'Violence can only be met by non-violence.'
>
> — Mahatma Gandhi

First World War was fought ostensibly "to make the world safe for democracy", and Second World War to protect the four freedoms—of speech, of worship, from want, and from fear. Post-Second World War era was marred by antagonistic competition between 'democratic' capitalism and collectivist communism. Now even that is behind us, but violence and terrorism continue to have their sway in even more virulent and pervasive forms.

Eric Hobsbawm in his recent book *Globalization, Democracy, Terrorism* [Little Brown, 2007] rightly points out that even after the *Nine-Eleven* (2001), international power structures have remained unaffected: "None of this diminishes the scale of the genuine global crisis of which transformations of political violence are expressions. They seem to reflect the profound social dislocations brought about at all levels of society by the most rapid and dramatic transformation in human life and society ever witnessed". Global crises are exacerbated by failures of decolonization in parts of the world and the end of a stable, or any, international order.

Many persons may be ready to die or even more so to kill—for money and for something smaller or larger. The colonial rule was maintained through reliance on local intermediaries, apparent legitimacy of its effective power, and simple device of 'divide and rule'. The present situation in Afghanistan, Iraq and other such cases shows the difficulties that even the most powerful occupier faces when any of these conditions fail to exist. Even within countries, armed power of the state has failed to ensure effective control in territories such as Sri Lanka and Palestine.

Various effects of globalization include vast migrations forced by political, religious, economic and environmental grounds. Urbanization itself—today nearly half of world's population lives in urban areas as against a sixth in 1900—is a process of internal and external globalization. These processes generate situations that both liberalize and generate resistance and violence. The issues of control over finite resources of energy, materials, food and water too have exacerbated to a point where either the rich lower their standards of consumption or the situation becomes even more divisive and violent. Mere good words fill no stomach.

While on one hand there is a race for the GDP growth and possession of military might as the twin measures of elitist 'national' power, on the other, world's main 'development' challenges were rightly defined through the eight Goals drawn from the Millennium Declaration adopted by 189 nations in the Millennium Summit in September 2000. These Goals, to be achieved by 2015, indicate the other end of the stark human reality: (i) Eradicate extreme poverty and hunger; (ii) Achieve universal primary education; (iii) Promote gender equality and empower women; (iv) Reduce child mortality; (v) Improve maternal health; (vi) Combat HIV/AIDS, malaria; and other diseases; (vii) Ensure environmental sustainability; (viii) Develop a global partnership for development. Even here the world powers pay only lip service, though these deprivations underlie much of the violence, terrorism, genocides (as in Africa) and riots. Such deprivations and injustices affect women and children relatively more harshly, and incite the youth who are just starting their adult lives much more towards violence, terrorism and crime.

In its report titled 'The Limits of Growth' (1972), the Club of Rome had observed: "If the present growth trends in world population, industrialization, pollution, food production and resource depletion continue unchanged, the limits to growth on this planet will be reached sometime during next 100 years". It gave a charter for "a society that is materially sufficient, socially equitable and ecologically sustainable, and also more satisfying in human terms than the growth-obsessed society of today". The report titled 'Beyond the Limits: Sequel to the Limits of Growth' (1992) by D.H. Meadows *et al.* then warns: "The most telling indicator of disequilibrium in the world today is the mad state of environment and the increasing misery it has brought to all—especially the down-trodden and the marginalized whose livelihood is directly dependent on a healthy environment". Developed countries, instead of controlling their consumption rates of the world resources, are spending enormous sums on clean-up operations and partly exporting hazardous industries and toxic wastes to developing countries. As Barry Commoner has written in 'Making Peace with the Planet': "Survival depends equally on ending war with the nature and—wars among ourselves". Gandhiji has summed it up well: "Earth provides enough to satisfy every man's needs but not for every man's greed".

Gandhiji had written: "By patriotism I mean the welfare of the whole state"—and not a nationalistic penchant for violence and counter-violence. On January 27, 1948, he had reiterated his concern for welfare thus: "The Congress has won political freedom but it has yet to win economic freedom, social and moral freedom.—All-embracing constructive work evokes the energy of all the units of the millions". Then, on November 25, 1949, during the course of his speech summing up the work of the Constituent Assembly, Dr. B.R. Ambedkar warned not to be content with "mere political democracy". He said that on January 26, 1950, India was "going to enter a life of contradictions. In politics we will be recognizing the principle of one man one vote and one vote one value. In our social and economic life, we shall...continue to deny the principle of one man one value....How long shall we continue to deny equality in our social and economic life? If...for long, we shall do so only by putting our political democracy in peril".

It is in these contexts that we must think about appropriate methods and strategies to counter violence and terrorism. Even as the means of violence grow and become global and the ability of those in power to control violence shows its limits, there is also inherent in humankind a tremendous urge for peace and brotherhood. With this as general background it is proposed to further indicate some of the critical issues constituting methods and strategies to counter violence and terrorism under the sub-headings covering: B.2 Gandhian Non-violent Approaches—The Only Way to Resist Violence; B.3 Roles of Politicians, State Agencies, and Judiciary; B.4 Role of Educationists, Scientists and other Professionals and Spiritual and Religious Leaders; B.5 Role of Business and Industry, Media and Cinema, and Artists; B.6 Role of Civil Society and Issues of Youth, Women and Children; and B.7 Relevance of (i) 'Shanti Sena', and (ii) Global Initiative for Department/Ministry of Peace.

B.2 Gandhian Non-violent Approaches – The Only Way to Resist Violence

> 'Violence is bred by inequality, non-violence by equality.'
> 'Non-violence is the law of our species as violence is the law of the brute.'
> 'The first step in non-violence is that we cultivate in our daily life—truthfulness, humility, tolerance, loving kindness.'
> —Mahatma Gandhi

The Gandhian non-violent approaches to resist violence and terrorism may be considered in two parts: (a) Conflict resolution by non-violent resistance to all forms of perceived injustice and oppression, or, his philosophy and technique of *satyagraha* for conflict resolution, and (b) observance of non-violence in all human conduct.

It was on September 11, 1906—Gandhi's *Nine-Eleven*—that he first propounded his philosophy of non-violent resistance, later named by him as *Satyagraha* ('holding on to Truth'), in his address to 3000 Indians assembled in Johannesburg to protest against racial discrimination. This was followed by a series of *Satyagrahas* over next eight years. From 1915 till his martyrdom on January 30,1948, he led the largest mass of people in human history in *Satyagrahas* for India's freedom struggle and for a series of socio-economic reforms, covering practically all aspects of human existence in pursuit of establishing a non-violent, egalitarian and sustainable social order. He has become a role model and guide for all such movements in the world. He defined *Satyagraha* as Truth-force, Love-force, and Soul-force. It is based on principles of Truth and Non-violence as exemplified in ethics of Right Means for Right Ends, Primacy of Duty over Right, and Resist Evil and not the Evil-doer. As Martin Luther King, Jr., wrote: "Gandhi was probably the first person in history to lift the love ethic of Jesus above mere interaction between individuals to a powerful and effective force on a large-scale."

Extensive literature is available on philosophy and practice of Gandhian *satyagraha*. Here only a few key ideas are being given in his own words as indicators:

- "Non-cooperation with evil is as much a duty as cooperation with good."
- "Those who seek to destroy men rather than manners adopt the latter and become worse. They do not know the root of evil."
- "That action alone is just that does not harm either party to a dispute."
- *Satyagraha* "excludes every form of violence, direct or indirect—in thought, word or deed—never be the result of anger or malice—as a complete substitute for violence".
- "The *Satyagrahi*, whilst he is everready for fight, must be equally eager for peace."
- "The *Satyagrahi* bids goodbye to fear. He is never afraid of trusting the opponent."
- "[P]ursuit of truth did not admit of violence being inflicted on one's opponent, but—he must be weaned from error by patience and sympathy. For what appears to be truth to one may appear to be error to the other."
- "Man lived freely by his readiness to die, if need be, at the hands of his brother, never by killing him."

Gandhiji never supported underground activity or the secrecy that goes with terrorist activities:

- "I do not appreciate underground activity. Only open challenge and open activity is for all to follow. Real *Swaraj must* be felt by all—man, woman and child. To labour for that consummation is true revolution."
- "Even violence has its code of ethics. For instance to butcher helpless old men, women and children is not bravery but rank cowardice. Chivalry requires that they should be protected even at the cost of one's life."

B.3 Role of Politicians, State Agencies and Judiciary

The conduct of political, state, and judicial structures is the key to the conduct of a society and the nation as these together control instruments of social and economic power and welfare as well as instruments of organized violence.

Political systems must be seen to deliver true democracy—political, economic, social, and moral, to look after more specifically the interests of the poor, the weak, and the deprived, to ensure provision of basic needs of all, to ensure equitable entitlements in fields of education, health and employment, to particularly look after the rural areas which are routinely neglected in development programmes, to secure a non-violent social order based on non-discrimination on religious, caste, gender or other grounds, and to involve even 'the last' person in the social stream. Similarly, the whole judicial process and its associated functions, intermediaries such as lawyers, authorities, and procedures must be seen to be accessible to all within their capacity, equitable, accountable, non-dilatory and to deliver justice.

Here too, the best guidance even today comes from the Gandhian thought and practice. Gandhian political economy, and his concept of *sarvodaya* as opposed to the utilitarian concepts of market capitalism, are vast subjects. Here only a few of his ideas are given as examples:

- Democracy means "mobilizing entire physical, economic and spiritual resources of all—people in the common service of all".
- "The spirit of democracy cannot be established—in the

midst of terrorism, whether governmental or popular." It "requires the inculcation of the spirit of brotherhood".

- "Democracy, disciplined and enlightened, is the finest thing in the world. A democracy prejudiced, ignorant, superstitious—may be self-destroyed."
- If we are intolerant of difference of opinion, we "run the risk of missing truth".
- The State must be secular: "The State would look after your secular welfare, health, communications, foreign relations, currency and so on, but not your or my religion. That is everybody's personal concern".
- The corrupt deserved "to be blotted out of public life".
- "The structure of the world federation can be raised only on a foundation of non-violence".

He wanted a decentralized and participatory polity because the State "represents violence in a concentrated and organized form and cannot be sustained and defended without adequate force".

Just as India became independent he gave a *talisman* to the new rulers: "Whenever, you are in doubt, or when the self becomes too much with you.... Recall the face of the poorest and the weakest man...and ask yourself if the step you contemplate is going to be of any use to him. Will...it restore him to a control over his own life and destiny? In other words, will it lead to *swaraj* for the hungry and spiritually starving millions? Then you will find your doubts and yourself melting away". In today's India, the spread of Naxalite violence is one result of the Indian rulers having ignored this *talisman*. The Recognition of Forest Rights Act 2006, which has been notified on January 1, 2008, is a small step towards redressing the century old exploitation of Scheduled Tribes and other traditional forest dwellers.

B.4 Role of Educationists, Scientists and other Professionals and Spiritual and Religious Leaders

Education is that which liberates us from want, ignorance, untruth and violence. As Gandhiji said, "True education should be easily accessible to all" and be "of use to every villager in his life".

That society will have least violence where all children get equal opportunity for education and imbibe right social values in common neighbourhood schools. The provision under Article 45 of the Constitution, had been subverted by all governments till now because it was put as a non-binding 'Directive Principles of State Policy' and not as a 'Fundamental Right'. Hence, even now, millions of children remain illiterate and work as child labour, many of those who go to school, drop out *en route*, and further a social apartheid has been institutionalized in free India with expensive 'Public' schools coming up for the upper classes and as a result the aided and government schools further deteriorating by neglect in their quality of education. This is a classic case of what Dr. Ambedkar had warned that with this Constitution, India was "going to enter a life of contradictions". This is also a source of social alienation, poverty, and social violence.

The Government has apparently tried to rectify the situation through the 86th Amendment to the Constitution in 2002, whereby the provisions under Article 45 has been scattered into three components and the responsibility of the State has been diluted and instead poor parents made responsible if the children do not go to a school: (1) Under Art. 21A (Fundamental Rights): "The State shall provide free and compulsory education to all children of the age of 6 to 14 years *in such manner as the State may, by law, determine*". (2) Art. 51A (k) (Fundamental Duties): "who is a parent or guardian to provide opportunities for education to his child or, as the case may be,...the age of 6 and 14 years." (3) Revised Art. 45: "The State shall endeavour to provide early childhood care and education for all children until they complete the age of 6 years".

Educationists, professionals and religious leaders also need to ponder how to make the whole process of school and higher education much more conducive to establishment of a non-violent social order, how to link educational institutions with the surrounding communities, inculcate right values in students and youth, develop spirit of co-operation, tolerance, dialogue and compassion in the increasingly competitive market economy and derooted societies, and help identify tensions, anxieties, frustrations, alienation, and conflicts and work out structures for conflict management and resolution. Finally, in universities, it is essential to introduce courses in Peace Studies so that the academic environment is duly sensitized against growing violence and terrorism in the society.

Similarly, in the realm of science a bias needs to be built up against use of science for destructive purposes and development of instruments of violence and war. The tradition that grew in this direction in mid-20th century and then waned needs to be revived. Gandhiji had said: "Science of war leads one to dictatorship pure and simple. Science of non-violence can alone lead one to pure democracy". He also declared: "I hold he who invented the atom bomb, committed the greatest sin in the world of science".

The role of spiritual and religious leaders is very important as much of the violence and even terrorism in today's world takes its inspiration from a fundamentalist view of religion. Religious persecution and intolerance have been a source of mass violence in human history and of communal riots and even Partition in India. Here again we need to take lesson from the Gandhian approach to true religion: "Indeed religion should pervade everyone of our actions. Here religion does not mean sectarianism. It means a belief in ordered moral government of the universe....This religion transcends Hinduism, Islam, Christianity, etc. It does not supersede them. It harmonizes them and gives them reality".

B.5 Role of Business and Industry, Media and Cinema and Artists

> 'True economics—promotes the good of all including—the weakest and is indispensable for decent living.'
> 'Tens of millions go about begging while a hundred or two become millionaires. The true economics is that by which every man or woman gets a living by physical labour.'
>
> — Mahatma Gandhi

Business and industry, media and entertainment industry, and art, all these are among the expressions of different facets of economic-cultural activity in modern societies. These are driven, directly or indirectly, by financial motives. However, these are, simultaneously, very vital social activities today and must, therefore, subserve social objectives even while retaining their urge for financial gains and professional success. How, in these days of market capitalism, these sectors may still contribute towards the growth of a non-violent and egalitarian social order is the primary issue and hence the duty of their leaders.

Business and industry, in search for higher profits, today are involved in production and distribution—both legal and illegal—of instruments of war including armaments, explosives, small arms and land-mines, hazardous materials, drugs and narcotics, spurious medicines and other consumables, and other such goods and services which amount to loss and damage to human life and health. The issue of Special Economic Zones (SEZs) in India is a typical example how the money power of business and industry and the political power can collude to abuse the provision of 'public purpose' allowed to the Government in the case of compulsory land acquisition in order to favour the rich at the cost of the poor, thus leading to widespread violence.

Fortunately, in recent years, the concept of 'Corporate Social Responsibility' (CSR) has received large-scale acceptance in organized business and industry. It is necessary to work much more on it to see how the community at large can be made an effective stakeholder in this sector and how its socially negative aspects can be minimized and controlled. In this direction, Gandhian concepts of 'Trusteeship' can provide many leads and workable ideas.

Media and entertainment industry play an ever-growing role in modern society. However, in order to 'sell' their services under growing competition, these sectors have at times tended to pander to the baser instincts and violent and divisive tendencies among human groups. In the name of freedom of expression they even at times tend to subvert social peace and good. Their leadership needs to seriously think how to prevent such negative tendencies from flourishing.

Journalism is a noble profession. Mahatma Gandhi has been one of the greatest journalists and writers in history. It is instructive to understand how he ran various journals from 1903 (when he started the weekly newspaper *Indian Opinion*) till his martyrdom. A few of his observations in this regard are given below as a guide:

- "To be true to my faith, therefore, I may not write in anger or malice. I may not write idly. I may not write merely to excite passion."

- "The reader can have no idea of the restraint I have to exercise—in the choice of topics and my vocabulary.—Often my vanity dictates a smart expression or my anger a harsh adjective. It is a terrible ordeal but a fine exercise to remove these weeds."
- To his son, Manilal: "You write what is the truth in *Indian Opinion*."
- "And the true function of journalism is to educate the public mind, not to stock the public mind with wanted and unwanted impressions. A journalist has, therefore, to use his discretion, as to what to report and when."
- "The press was called the Fourth Estate....but to misuse that power was criminal....he would appeal to fellow journalists to realize their responsibility and to carry on their work with no idea other than that of upholding the truth."

In the case of artists, the primary issue appears to be their approach of "art for art's sake", as if they are not accountable towards the society in which they enrich themselves. In any social activity, broad interests of the society remain relevant. This does not mean any undue constraints on creativity. As Gandhiji had said: "Whenever men begin to see Beauty in Truth, then true Art will arise". Secondly, "Any activity in which the masses cannot participate is not true art, but a kind of self-indulgence, whether it concerns the voice or clothes or stone". Thirdly, "I believe firmly that both religion and art have to serve the identical aims of moral and spiritual elevation".

We must have art in all facets of our life. Artists also need freedom to create. At the same time art must concern the masses, must not cater to the baser instincts, or sectarianism, nor hurt the feelings of large groups as these tend to generate social isolation or violence. We must also encourage on a large-scale rural and folk arts and crafts and artistic skills of ordinary people.

B.6 Role of Civil Society and Issues of Youth, Women and Children

> "The good of the individual is contained in the good of all."

> "I shall work for an India in which the poorest shall feel that it is their country in whose making they have an effective voice; an India in which there shall be no high class and low class of people; an India in which all communities shall live in perfect harmony. There can be no room in such an India for the curse of untouchability or the curse of intoxicating drinks or drugs. Women will enjoy the same rights as men. Since we shall be at peace with all the rest of the world, neither exploiting nor being exploited, we shall have the smallest army imaginable.— This is the India of my dreams." — Mahatma Gandhi

Civil society covers the society at large and its activities, particularly the activities of the growing number and sizes of 'non-government' or 'voluntary' or 'non-profit' or 'social' organizations and groups which are today contributing enormously to the 'constructive work' being done. Of course, there are also some groups which tend to encourage sectarian interests and even violent and terrorist activities, but their memberships, sources of funds and other support, and cadre training, are usually less open and are even secretive. But these are exceptions and it is the duty of governments as well as civil society to ensure that such organizations are not able to flourish.

The largest vulnerable sections in a society are youth, women, and children. Of course, there are also other vulnerable sections, such as the very poor and deprived, the old and infirm, and the handicapped. The civil society, functioning through its 'constructive work' organizations and other socially conscious groups and individuals, must ensure that these and other vulnerable sections are protected and allowed to grow to their full potential irrespective of their socio-economic or religious or caste backgrounds. The State can be truly democratic and secular only if the civil society consciously acts as a watchdog to ensure this not only in the functioning of the State and its various agencies but also in the conduct of the various sections of the society itself.

Youth are the future of a society. In India they constitute nearly 30 per cent of the population. They are victims of the prevalent wide disparities and the inequalities imposed by inheritance of means, education and skills, and power. This leads to frustration, anger, alienation and violence. It is mostly the youth who function as foot-soldiers of terrorist activities. It is for each civil society to ponder and decide how to give a constructive future to each youth. Otherwise they may become an enemy within. Societies also need to encourage youth activities, apart from studies, such as sports, social work, arts, and skill-building pursuits. In a market economy, one thing that the youth needs is employment as a means of livelihood. It is for both the State and the civil society to ensure that each youth, irrespective of his/her endowments, can develop capabilities to their full potential, and have the opportunity to function according to these.

Gender equality needs to be brought about by both legal and extra-legal efforts. At present in India there are major deficits in gender equity in school education, in political representation and in the economic sector. Traditional social norms and mind-sets too need to be reformed. Civil society has to work much harder than it is doing at present to ensure gender justice. Some specific suggestions in this regard are:

- Punishment for 'murder' for all those involved in female foeticide.
- All primary and secondary schools to have girl students equal in number to boy students.
- All political parties to put up women as at least 40 per cent of their candidates.

As Gandhiji said: "Of all the evils for which man has made himself responsible, none is so degrading, so shocking or so brutal as his abuse of the better half of humanity".

Children are the weakest and most dependent section of a society. They are also its foundation. The issues of most serious concern in India which have remained largely unattended by both the state and the society since independence include non-provision of universal 'free and compulsory' school education, undernourishment, high child mortality, large-scale child labour, and child-begging. These constitute the most serious and inexcusable policy and institutional failure of the Indian State and society.

There have been the World Summit of Children, the International Convention on 'Rights of Child' adopted by the UN in 1989, and other such documents of intention. But children have no votes and no power. Only when a society understands how such a neglect of its children jeopardizes its own future, will these maladies be remedied. As Gandhiji said: "If we are to reach real peace in this world—we shall have to begin with children, and if they grow in the natural innocence—we shall go from love to love and peace to peace".

B.7 *Relevance of (i) 'Shanti Sena' (Peace Army) and (ii) Global Initiative for Department/Ministry of Peace (DoP)*

> 'Just as one must learn the art of killing in the training for violence, so one must learn the art of dying in the training for non-violence. It is a bad outlook for the world if this spirit of violence takes hold of the mass mind.'
>
> — Mahatma Gandhi

While various agencies, sectors and groups constituting the State and the society have vital roles to play in countering violence and terrorism, as indicated in paras B.2 to B.6 above, it may also be necessary to establish special institutional structures to pursue and strengthen the effort. It is proposed to consider two such measures here, Shanti Sena (Peace Army) and Department or Ministry of Peace.

(i) 'Shanti Sena' (Peace Army)

Gandhiji has written extensively on qualifications, training and functioning of such a 'Peace Brigade' or 'Non-violent Volunteer Corps'. During the freedom struggle itself he had constituted 'Seva Dal' (Service Corps) and volunteer groups to work in the villages and for other 'constructive work' and for *satyagraha*. For example, he had prescribed following 'Qualifications of a Peace Brigade':

"1. He or she must have a living faith in non-violence. This is impossible without a living faith in God....means respect for the lives of even those who may be called opponents or *goondas*....a process of stilling the fury of man when the brute in him gets the mastery over him.

2. This messenger of peace must have equal regard for all the principal religions of the earth....
3. Generally speaking this work of peace can only be done by local men....
4. This work can be done singly or in groups. Therefore, no one needs to wait for companions.
5. This messenger of peace will cultivate, through personal service, contacts with the people in his locality or chosen circle....
6. ....a peace bringer must have a character beyond reproach and...strict impartiality.
7. ....will not wait till the conflagration breaks out, but will try to handle the situation in anticipation.
8. Whilst....well if there are some whole-time workers, it is not absolutely necessary....
9. There should be a distinctive dress....

These are but general suggestions.

Regarding 'Training' of such a corps, Gandhiji wrote: "A very small part of the preliminary training received by the military is common to the non-violent army. These are discipline, drill, singing in chorus, flag hoisting, signalling and the like. Even this is not absolutely necessary and the basis is different. The positively necessary training for non-violent army is an immovable faith in God, willing and perfect obedience to the chief of the non-violent army and perfect inward and outward cooperation between the units of the army".

During the freedom struggle itself, Khan Abdul Ghaffar Khan too had set a corps of "*Khudai Khidmatgars*" (Servants of God; also called 'Red Shirts'). Under him, one who aspired to become a *Khudai Khidmatgar*, declared on solemn oath: "I am a *Khudai Khidmatgar*, and as God needs no service I shall serve Him by serving His creatures selflessly. I shall never use violence, I shall not retaliate or take revenge, and I shall forgive anyone who indulges in oppression and excesses against me. I shall treat every Pakhtun as my brother and comrade. I shall give up evil customs and practices. I shall lead a simple life, do good and refrain from wrong-doing. I shall develop good character and cultivate good habits. I shall not lead an idle life. I shall expect no reward for my services. I shall be fearless and be prepared for any sacrifice".

After independence, Vinoba Bhave had instituted and written much about such 'non-violent organizations'. A number of other such attempts have also been made since then. Thus, there is a rich literature of views and experience available on the subject.

In today's environment, it may be necessary to consider establishing a permanent institution of 'Shanti Sena' (Peace Army) which will have an appropriately trained set of members to deal with the situations of social violence such as communal riots and other sectarian violence. It is necessary to carefully consider the structure of such an 'army', the role of the trainers, of part-time and whole-time members in it, of 'volunteers' and paid members, and various other issues such as those of funding, accommodation and other requirements. As for any new organization, its functioning, type of training, and 'rules' may also change with experience.

(ii) Global Initiatives for Department/Ministry of Peace (DoP)

All over the world peace groups, organizations and activists have been pressing for the need to set up a Department or Ministry of 'Peace' just as every State has a Department or Ministry of 'Defence' which controls an armed military organization as well as departments and ministries for internal 'Law and Order', namely, various categories of police and paramilitary forces. Just as the conventional military, paramilitary and police forces under present departments/ministries counter external and internal violence and terrorism through armed and violent methods and strategies, the proposed department/Ministry of 'Peace' will develop, train and utilize non-violent 'forces' to handle at least the issues of internal law and order, riots and insurgencies to the extent possible. They will complement the roles of existing armed forces and shall progressively replace them as far as possible. It is obvious that the requirement of funds and other inputs for the 'Peace' forces will be less than those required for the corresponding armed units since the expenditures on arms and their associated systems will be obviated. It will also lead to the people at large looking at these 'forces' more as their comrades and not as a body to be feared.

It is a subject which needs a serious consideration by the Government of India. At least a small beginning could be made by having such a Peace Force in J & K area, in 'Naxalite' affected areas, and in the North-East region under the Government itself.

Conclusion

This chapter attempts to provide some preliminary ideas on the subject of 'Challenges from Violence and Terrorism and Methods and Strategies to Counter Them'. These are meant to initiate wide-ranging serious discussions on the subject during the Meet being held on the subject on January 27/28, 2008, at New Delhi.

Non-violence is a way of life and in order to adopt if we need to continuously cultivate the 'divine' qualities, as opposed to the 'devilish' qualities, as enunciated in the *Gita* [ch. XVI, verse 1-3]: Truth, non-violence, fearlessness, purity of heart, *shanti*, forgiveness, avoidance of anger, tenderness towards all life, uprightness, non-slander, self-restraint, spiritual study, steadfastness in knowledge and *yoga*, sacrifice, alms giving, austerity, renunciation, freedom from greed, gentleness, modesty, gravity, spiritedness, absence of hatred, fortitude, non-arrogance, and purity. The *Gita* also counts non-violence as an essential ingredient of Knowledge.

No doubt that the path of non-violence is the ideal way of life for human society. However, it may not be always seem easy to follow unless we consciously strive for it. How may we prepare and train ourselves for practicing true non-violence in word, thought and deed? We may do so by continuous studying the thought and life of Mahatma Gandhi and other leaders who have set the path and shown the way. Gandhiji had written: "I know the path. It is straight and narrow. It is like the edge of a sword. I rejoice to walk on it. I weep when I slip. God's word is: 'He who strives never perishes'. I have implicit faith in that promise". Let all us resolve to follow Gandhiji on the path of non-violence !

CHAPTER 7

Gandhian Economic Doctrines

RAM BINOD SINGH

Science of economics is in crisis. Rarely would an economist not talk about the crisis while dealing with contemporary issues. When a science is in crises, it begins to question its own philosophical assumptions and methods and begins a search for alternative paradigms. Unfortunately, the century-old reign of positivist economics, which included famous models and their numerous versions such as neo-classical, Keynesian, and even Marxian economics, lost track of its philosophical assumptions. Indeed, the main reason for the crisis is that modern economics has no philosophy whatsoever. The diseases of economic science have spread to other social sciences also.

The crisis has to be first seen in a historical perspective. About more than two centuries ago, right at a time when science of Economics was discovered, it was called a dismal science. There were two reasons for this. First, economics was torn away from moral philosophy of which it was a part in the curricula of the universities. Second, the economic situation, which was translated into economic laws, was one of unrelieved misery on the one hand and garish riches on the other. But a century later, the science of economics became a matter of great optimism as it opened up tremendous vistas for the production of goods and services. Paradoxically, as life became more and more complex, holistic analysis gave way to compartmentalization and specialization, which increasingly rested on pure economic analysis. Then was born the economic man in whose name the economists played game with one another in terms of fancy theories unconcerned with the problem of relationship between facts and values. Wherever, the question of values was brought in, economists rejected the challenge and pushed out values as belonging to some other fields of analysis. Even earlier, Adam Smith, the father of modern economics, desperately tried to deal with both but could not link the two. The question that he asked in his Moral Sentiments were left out in his Wealth of Nations, despite the fact that he waited for years to publish the latter in order to find in it a place for ethical issue.

We find a certain parallel between developments in philosophy and those in economics. Just as philosophy moved from rationalism to empiricism and logical positivism, economics also shed its non-economic contents and concentrated on the so-called economic man. Whenever, the economic man was found to be inconsistent in his behaviour or gave preference to non-economic considerations or seemed to violate every economic law, this was all explained by the non-operation of the phrase "other things remaining the same". The difference between Gandhi and all other theorists is that he begins with the *ceteris paribus*.

Gandhian Economics has assumed significance on account of deficiencies and inconsistencies of existing economic theories all over the world. For long there has existed a wide chasm between professional economics and Gandhian economics. Economists for long smugly dismissed Gandhi as anti-technology and anti-growth, as an advocate of return to the simple and non-competitive pre-industrial economy. The recent contributions by eminent social scientists like M.L. Dantwala,[1] B.N. Ganguli,[2] Bhabtosh Dutta,[3] J.K. Mehta,[4] Raj Krishna,[5] J.D. Sethi,[6] and others have initiated discussion and rethinking on Gandhi's economic ideas. Bhabtosh Dutta regarded Gandhian Economics as an important part of Indian economic thought. He also called for a serious attempt to find out how far Gandhian prescriptions could be integrated into a broader programme of economic development. Further, interest in Gandhian thought has been reinforced by new problems of the world economy, the ecological and over exhaustion of non-renewable resources, the ecological and environmental imbalances affecting the quality of life, the widening gap between rich and poor nations, the consequences of consumerism, and above all, the growth of violence and the threat of nuclear holocaust troubling the entire mankind. Acquisitive social order has become the compulsive motivation for the mankind leading to cut throat competition and rat race.

In India itself economists have become increasingly aware of Gandhi's insight into phenomena of mass poverty and economic dependence, into the causal relationship between elite prosperity and mass poverty. Again, economic science has been moving away from moral discord towards rediscovering the unity of means and ends, the moral order and economic order and the moral problems and economic problems. Here also the disorientations created by the disjunction between means and ends, values and interests, and by modes of thought predominantly centred on pursuits of economic growth almost as an end in itself, have led to rediscovery of Gandhi as both a moral and an economic philosopher still very relevant in the contemporary context.

Academic discussion on Gandhian economics, however, poses certain difficulties. Gandhi, was neither academic economist himself nor was he, like his predecessors Dadabhai Naoroji or Ranade, familiar with the concepts and categories of modern economics. It becomes, naturally, very difficult for academic circle to understand Gandhi's thought and its subtle meanings and implications. Further, Gandhi was establishing communication primarily with the masses rather than with the sophisticated experts and specialist and this fact influenced the choice of his idioms, his phraseology and his symbolism.

It may be noted that Gandhi tried his economic policy experiment at a point of history when the option of utilizing the nation-state was denied to the Indian people as an instrument of policy. Moreover, India was the victim of the First Industrial Revolution and of modern technology, suited to conditions in England, which promoted this Industrial Revolution. Gandhi's critique of technology and industrialism were evolved in this historical context when India had no opportunity to adapt modern technology to Indian conditions and to create an Indian variant of the Industrial Revolution as was done by Japan.

Gandhian economics must be viewed, therefore, not in static terms. Gandhian economics creatively adapted to the period after independence must be neither anti-state nor anti-technology and anti-growth. It must help to explore new forms of technology and economic growth suited to Indian conditions and to the goals of self-reliance and mass uplift. His writings and speeches show that Gandhi was not at all fundamentalist, he was all the time interested in finding solutions to people's problems. Any technology, traditional or modern and any pattern of economic growth based on the utilization of this technology, which is in accord with the criteria of self-reliance, mass uplift and a non-acquisitive orientation is acceptable to Gandhi. Whatever was beneficial for the masses was welcomed by Gandhi.

In this background Gandhian economics must be tapped for a blending of social and physical engineering to set the small producer on the path of growth. Decentralised and mass-participatory institutional framework from village level onwards, technological innovations for raising the productivity of land and labour and for extending the scope for diversification of the rural economy, and introduction of community organization, community spirit and orientation as a corrective to corrosive individualism and class acquisitiveness, it is in these fields that new opportunities and scope have arisen for operationalising Gandhian concepts and insights.

Distortions have been created in the world order. The consciousness of the people in general has been raised that large majority of the population consider nuclear war both probable and a serious threat. In democratic countries government policy remains completely opposite to the interest of the large majority. Like a dark cloud, there is constant spectre of nuclear holocaust, depressing personalities and distorting policies in addition to the armament competition between the East and West, the world is divided between Rich North and Poor South. The logic of development policy with its emphasis on industrialisation has promoted infrastructure in these countries that encourage a miniscule minority to live luxuriously in a sea of mass poverty where malnutrition, hunger, non-existence of shelter and medical care is the rule. UNICEF estimates that 5 millions children die every year for lack of food in a world where food production far outstrips its need. The process of development divides the country into dual society of rich and poor and recent globalisation has further exacerbated the situation. The dynamics of dual society and compulsion of international relations between rich and poor countries bring to power authoritarian governments that rule by police state mentality where the institutions created to uphold law and order are themselves involved in murdering their own citizens, euphemism for the now common term disappearance. The countries in the south thus are in continuous turmoil and on the edge of a violent revolution successful or otherwise.

The existing world order in the name of affluence in rich and development in poor countries are involved in the extraction of continuously depleting non-renewable resources so that it is now reaching the limits of mother earth. The Limits to Grow Study[7] by The Club of Rome, Social Limits to Growths[8], by Fred Hirch and other studies confirmed this alarming situation. The impact of all this on the world economic system is profound. The visible effects are on the world monetary system and international liquidity. A large number of countries in the South are already heavily burdened by foreign debt. India had to save its face by mortgaging its gold to Swiss Bank. As much as 100 per cent of export of a number of countries are already mortgaged to the payment of interest on debt and the total debt is increasing.

The various instabilities of the international order is telling upon the economic and political health of various countries, rich, poor, East or West. In the rich countries the quality of life is deteriorating even if the standard of living has increased. In the poor countries, poverty stalks one in the face. The size of poor population is unbelievably large. The growth in poverty, deterioration in the quality of life, instability in the international monetary system, depletion of non-renewable global resource, murder by police, and production of weapons of mass destruction have been rationalised by the policies of economic growth and economic development. When the advice of the elite economists has been sought as to how these trends can be reversed they have argued for the acceleration of the rates of economic growth and development, i.e., more of the same. The high priests have lost their authority. There is questioning of the existing, return to old and search for new ideas. The state of economic science is in flux.[9]

Not only are people in general losing faith in the effectiveness of economic policies and the consistencies as well as capacity of economic ideas to explain such reality, even economists themselves are recognizing the deficiencies of economic theories and ideas. One of the major effects is to make relevant some of the cultural and religious issues that rationalist ideology had discarded completely. The public perceptions about failures of economics arise from such phenomena as high deficits, high wages, high inflation, high interest rates, high unemployment and visible decline in the standard of living. Even economists agree that there is something wrong with economics.

Deficiencies in Economic Theories

The loss of faith in economics by economist is of a different kind. There are three basic areas in economics: microeconomics, macroeconomics and international economics. Microeconomics deals with the process of decision-making regarding supply, demand, price, etc., at the individual and firm level. Macroeconomics relates to the decision of government. It involves monetary and fiscal policies. The objective is to develop a process of high growth rate of the economy. The major school of thought has been Keynesian. International economics attempts to understand the growth and composition in the global economy as it is affected by the interplay of various countries and economies. It deals with such issues as North-South dialogue, exchange rate, tariff, balance of payment, international debt, capital flow and transfers.

There are three things wrong with economics. There is no accepted or consistent body of knowledge in international economics. Opposite conclusions can be obtained from the same theoretical ideas: gains from trade or immuring growth, depending upon the curvature of the curves. It has no predictive power and there is no consensus. As presently constituted, it is a hotchpotch of some macroeconomics with many other things thrown in. For sometime in 1950s and 1960s, thanks to war efforts, macroeconomics seemed to have predictive value even if it had no elegant theory. In 1970s and onward, with stagflation, deepening recession, it lost its only defence. And finally, microeconomics is absolutely irrelevant. Its greatest strength is in its mathematical elegance. This is also a source of economists' illusion. The reality is, however, catching up. Virtually all assumptions in microeconomics are unrealistic and untenable. Utility functions are neither dependent nor transitive. Production functions are conceptually impossible to define and wholly unknown to business involved in production. There is little flexibility in prices; full mobility of factors is not compatible with production. Factor prices have no relationship with productivity; it is rationalized after the fact. As the experience of excellent companies of Japan confirms, marginal productivity is indefinable, much less quantifiable. Productivity and efficiency follow from teamwork. Culture, motivation is far more important than economic reward. As a result, microeconomics has no predictive value.

In view of the irrelevance of microeconomics, theoretical deficiencies of macroeconomics and incoherence of international economics, there is a need to reformulate the structure of economic thought. Such a reformulation, would involve the development of microeconomics based on realistic assumptions, grounding of macro economics in microeconomics and extension of such macro economics to international economics taking into considerations the realities of the world order. In view of the diversity and variations in cultures, ecologies, environment, plus people and production, this is perhaps an impossible task. However, because of the failure of economics and the deficiencies of existing economic ideas, a search for a reformulation is important.

Part of the problem with the conventional economics is that it is based on unrealistic assumptions. To start with, it assumes the world is made up of economic beings, not of flesh and blood, but cool, calculative, rational persons motivated by self-interest, a fancy term for greed and selfishness. These economic beings are all knowing. They know themselves fully about what they desire and what they do not. Furthermore, these economic beings have no relation with one another, except narrow economic relationship. They do not get satisfaction from loving, from caring, from sharing or from work. Sufficient to say that it does point out towards the untenability of the assumptions implied in economic analysis when compared with the real world.

Gandhian Economics

The real world is full of real people: people of flesh and blood, people who have good nature and bad nature, people who care for others and cooperate. Families are bound by ties of love. So are groups of people, tribes and nations. In Gandhi's words, "I claim that even now, though the social structure is not based on a conscious acceptance of non-violence, all over the world mankind lives and men retain their possessions on the sufferance of one another. If they had not done so only the fewest and the most ferocious would survive.[10] Why more people make sacrifices; just the opposites of self-interest. It is common for parents to make sacrifices for their children and *vice versa*. Hardly a day passes when people do not discover, even in the urban ghettos and jungles human kindness. Conventional economics misses this reality, no wonder it is out of touch.

What is needed is to formulate a different economics—an economics based on love, sharing and truth instead of the conventional economics based on greed, envy, hatred and falsehood. Gandhi laid the basic ideas for such an economics of love, truth and non-violence. It starts from the fundamental assumption that human beings are good, decent, moral, cooperative and non-violent. The objective of such economics is to build on brotherly and sisterly love for each other, to extend the love of the family to the love of the humanity.

Gandhian economics is thus based, fundamentally on different ethical and moral principles. "I must confess that I do not draw a sharp or any distinction between economics and ethics. Economics that hurts the moral well-being of an individual or a nation is immoral and, therefore sinful.[11]

Now there is no dearth of literature on Gandhian economics. This literature is based on the idea that thought and practices of Gandhi provide a complete, if not fully articulated basis for economic theory. Two points need to be made at this stage. First, Gandhian economics and thought in spite of its emphasis on the local level, relate to the global economy. It is universal. Global issues are highly related to the local issues. This interrelationship follows from a Gandhian propositions regarding the existing reality, namely (i) there is an elite-mass contradiction in every society, and (ii) in this elite-mass division, the national elites exploit the national masses and international elites exploit masses all over the world. The elite-mass contradiction is fundamental to Gandhian thought and analysis. So long this contradiction exists anywhere, it can disrupt, and destroy, a Gandhian economy and society. Secondly, analysis in Gandhian Economy is based on a theoretical construct. This theoretical construct is an "idealized Gandhian Society". This theoretical construct is similar to theoretical construct in neo-classical economics; such as "equilibrium", "Pareto-optimality" that do not relate directly to existing reality. In view of the general lack of familiarity with the ideal in Gandhian Economics, one might argue that the theoretical construct of an idealized Gandhian Society is an unrealistic assumption. The argument, however, would be similar if one were to say that equilibrium; perfect competition, etc., are unrealistic assumptions. Yet in neo-classical economics, one would hardly go very far without these assumptions.[12]

From the elite-mass contradiction, it follows that any society is divided into two sub-societies; (i) the elite society, and (ii) the mass society.[13] The elite society is made up of a small part of the population. Its members are elites, economically rich, politically powerful, urbanized, educated in elite institutions, etc. The society defines its own class. The elite society has the control of these instruments of decision-making at virtually all levels. It is the control of these instruments that gives this society the power to make all sorts of decisions, economic and non-economic; such as to arm some groups and disarm others, to prosecute certain crimes while ignoring others, to produce certain goods and not others, to invest, to tax, to subsidise, etc. Even though the elite society controls the instruments of decision making power, it cannot exist by itself. In this regard it is a parasite. It needs the other, mass-society, fundamentally.

The mass-society is made up of the bulk of the population. These are politically powerless, economically poor and mostly exploited. Yet this is the society, which provides manpower for the production of all goods and services for military, police, etc. Generally, this mass-society is divided on various emotional issues such as race, religion, etc. The mass-society suffers from a lack of all sorts of goods, services, and opportunities.

These two sub-societies are distinguished by four characteristics: economic, political, elitism, and exploitation. These may also be distinguished by the possession or lack of privilege; the elite society is the privileged society. Obviously, there are a lot of interactions between these two sub-societies. These interactions promote its own dynamics, which further sharpens the elite-mass contradiction.

The objectives of Gandhian economics is to understand the forces of interrelationships, that would lead to a society or economy towards the idealised Gandhian society. The idealized Gandhian society is one in which the mass-elite contradiction is ultimately resolved. In other words, in the idealised Gandhian society there are no elites and no masses. Furthermore, social and economic institutions promote the movement towards the idealised society and help maintain it in its idealised form.

It is a fact that Gandhi was not an economist in the narrow sense of the term. In fact, economics is becoming so much specialized and complex that even trained economists feel hesitant in claiming such a title for themselves. But there is much in Gandhian thought which is relevant to this subject. Gandhi was not interested in economic science as such but as it attempts to study certain aspects of human beings and he was intensely interested in problems of living, many of his views are of interest to economists. On occasions, Gandhi had wandered much inside the realm of economics. This does not imply that Gandhi could be categorised as an economists, in fact, that would be reducing his stature as a man interested in the welfare of his fellow beings. Yet, to ignore his contribution to economic Science may impoverish this expanding branch of human knowledge.[14]

On 22 December, 1916, Mohandas Karamchand Gandhi spoke before an economic society in Allahabad. The title of his address was "Does Economic Progress Clash with Real Progress?" right at the onset he felt it necessary to warn his audience, explaining:

> "Frankly and truly, I know little of economics, as you naturally understand it. Only the other day, sitting at an evening meal, a civilian friend deluged me with a series of questions on my crankism. As he proceeded in his cross-examination, I being a willing victim, he found no difficulty in discovering my gross ignorance of the matter. I appeared to him to be handling with a cocksureness worthy only of a man who knows not that he knows not. To his horror and even indignation, I suppose, he found that I had not even read books on economics by such well-known authorities as Mill, Marshall, Adam Smith, and a host of other such authors. In despair, he ended by advising me to read these books before experimenting in matters economic at the expense of trusting friends. But there came to us moments in life when about something we need no proof from without. A little voice within us tells us, "You are on the right track, turn neither to your left nor right, but keep to the straight and narrow away. With such help we march forward, slowly indeed, but surely and steadily. That is my position."

In the major part of his address, Gandhi first argued that material advance has a strong tendency to lead to moral decay. Then he proposed: "you cannot serve God and Mammon' for an economic truth of the highest value. We have to make a choice. Western nations are groaning under the heels of the monster-God of materialism." He pleaded for an ideal economy where there is more truth than gold, and greater charity than love of the self. Concluding his address, he admonished his audience: "let us seek first the kingdom of God and his righteousness, and the irrevocable promise is that everything will be added onto us. These are real economics. May you and I treasure them and enforce them in our daily life."

As far it is known, this short lecture which took place relatively early in Gandhi's long career, marks the only occasion where he focused directly on the subject of economics and did so before an educated audience on a college campus. Not surprisingly, Gandhi is known more as the father of Indian independence and as an advocate and practitioner of the technique of the non-violent civil disobedience than as a celebrated economist in any real sense of the term. An examination of his lecture clearly points to what he knew rather than what he did not know. He was not interested in the scope and method of economic science as the economists normally understand it. Rather he worked for a whole life time on articulating the principles of an alternative and "more real" human economy centring on the very themes outlined in his lecture: the task of correlation between material expansion and genuine process, and need for an economics-*cum*-ethics that will enable moral growth and dignity for all, the fallacy of seeking happiness in individual acquisitive behaviour, and the need for encouraging people to seek a life rich in self-esteem and genuine meaning.

An attempt to understand the Gandhian perspective in general, and also his economics in particular, will have to be fully appreciated. The two books that so profoundly influenced his world view and continue to shape his ideas throughout his life, one is *Bhagavad Gita*. To him, the *Gita* was not a description of real battle scene but the struggle between the two natures in us: the good and the evils." It is the description of the central duel going on within ourselves given so vividly as to make us think for the time being that the deeds therein were actually done by human beings, in the eyes of Gandhi, the text provides a complete and reasoned moral code which satisfies the intellect as well as the heart. The other book that deeply influenced Gandhi was *Unto This Last* by John Ruskin. In Gandhi's own words this book brought about an instantaneous and practical transformation in his life. Ruskin was a humanistic critic of John Stuart Mill, whose utilitarian orientation Ruskin relentlessly attacked. The exact nature of the influence of Ruskin on Gandhi is somewhat controversial. Yet it is undisputable that most of Gandhi's primary concepts, including the sanctity of labour, truth in self-sacrifice, justice based on fellow-feeling, trusteeship, priority of care for the poor, importance of a moral political economy, and emphasis on human needs can all be found in one form or another in *Unto This Last*.[15]

The Gandhi perspective on economics can be divided into four basic domains. There is the emphasis on economics as a moral science, there is reconstruction of the economic foundations, there is novel contributions to economic theory, and finally, there are the more practical insights into economic policy.

Many conventional economists rooted either in neoclassical or the Marxist traditions still take pride that economic is a positive science, meaning that it observes and describes what is rather than engaging in supposedly unscientific judgments of what ought to be. Today most experts in scientific method have learnt to question this traditional doctrine and readily grant the meaninglessness and impossibility of presenting a supposedly value-free science. Whether we like it or not, values are always present, either in an explicit or in an implicit form. Good science, therefore, needs to operate with good values. Gandhi deserves credit for having been one of the first to burst out of the straitjacket of positivism and involve himself with the construction of a normative economics. At one time he claimed, "That economics is untrue which ignores or disregards moral values". A normative economics of Gandhian style, that intertwines economics and ethics into one inseparable whole, reflects a vertical, multidimensional image of man where both material and spiritual forces need to embrace each other in the human quest for unity and wholeness. The integrated and holistic perspective in economics boils down to this simple injunction: never advocate actions or policies that lead to material advancement at the cost of social, moral, or spiritual impoverishment. Instead, the economists, as a holistic economists, should ascertain that his organizational principles and policies enable, possibly even encourage, a higher or overall quality of life for all.

When Edgeworth, one of the founders of modern economics, averred the first principle of economics that every agent is actuated only by self-interest. This dogma is sustained in all the texts of economic theory as the principle of maximising behaviour. Any action, regardless of how altruistic it may seem is ultimately explainable by the maximization of use value, or utility, of it is in our rational self-interest. Only recently have philosophers rigorously come to see the falsity of this claim.[16] The Gandhian theme of limitations to maximization behaviour is not only the theme but a novelty in itself. Economic welfare is discussed in duality of satisfying versus maximising behaviour. Gandhi sees non-possession needing to be grounded in commitment to truth (*dharma*), not self-interest (*artha*). Once it is recognised that the public good is at times not secured by maximisation of private self-restraint or even self-sacrifice. Adam Smith's invisible hand loses much of its glamour. Now economist are entertaining new thoughts in what kind of action does lead to social welfare.

Just as building economic theory around the notion of utilitarian self-interest puts much emphasis on the twin aspects of individualistic mobility and competition, so does a non-self-interest economics emphasises the social virtues of loyalty and cooperation. No other Gandhian concept illustrates this better than that of *Swadeshi*, the spirit in us which restricts us to the use and service of our immediate surrounding to the exclusion of the more remote. Clearly, then Gandhian economics is not built around the abstract notion of atomistic rational economic man who ceaselessly calculates the pros and cons of action to determine when his own advantage is maximised. *Sarvodaya* is a full-fledged alternative to the utilitarian goal of using an existing resource base for output of goods available for consumption. Rather it seeks to develop resource to enable a decent life for everyone. No doubt, deep in Gandhian economics, we find an implicit notion that every human being has the right to live decently. Gandhian concept of justice is opposed to Rawlsian theory of justice. To Gandhi, pure justice is never attained by fear, but is inspired by fellow feeling or compassion for another and that way of justice which has no place in it for fellow-feeling or compassion for another, and that way of justice which has no place in it for fellow-feeling or compassion is known as satanic, western or modern justice. Moreover, such care for the less privileged does not limit itself to assuring them material sufficiency, but also the kind of individual dignity arising out of a more adequate provision of socially and morally meaningful work.

This Gandhi effort to reorient economic thought away from self-interest-centred maximisation and away from the long ingrained utilitarian conception of social welfare as an aggregation of individual welfare, towards a perspective that has room for moral actions, and towards *Sarvodaya*, the welfare of all indicated by the well-being of the poor can be seem as a shift away from an economics based on individual desires and wants towards an economics of human needs. Much of what we want we do not really need and *vice versa*. We all have an inborn need to be whole and we need a holistic economics to acknowledge this and enable us to work towards that end.

Self-realisation, as against self-aggrandisement, is the ultimate human need. As such, it not only relates to material survival but also to a life rich in social dignity and spiritual meaning. Increasingly, many conventional economists have been pointing to this most elementary type of market failure. It shows in a logically tight argument how the market tends to erode the non-economic framework that is absolutely essential to its functioning.[17]

The special foundational feature of Gandhian economics to promote higher human capacities was also eloquently recognised by E.F. Schumacher, the author of *Small is Beautiful*, when he wrote in a foreword to a book on trusteeship. If you want a good society you must appeal to the goodness that is in people, provoke it, stimulate it, take it for granted, and claim it. The more we assume that economics and politics are about nothing other than gain and power, the more this becomes true, and the better instincts of the people are being suppressed instead of encouraged.

Construction of Gandhian Economics

A focus on the basic transformation that economics undergoes with the fresh metaphysical outlook of Gandhi clearly indicates his vision of economics. Among various Gandhian elements, *swadeshi* attracts the greatest attention. The altered metaphysical framework casts serious doubt on the conventional theorists strong preference for free markets, competition, and their collective role of the price system.

As far his practical insight into macroeconomic issues, more specifically the economics of employment and growth, development and international trade, as well as his insight into the intrinsic limitation of the Marxian alternative, much of Gandhian economics is only thoroughly understandable once its metaphysical and spiritual ground is fully appreciated. This is especially the case with his concepts of *Swadeshi*, non-possession, trusteeship, non-violence, and *Sarvodaya*. The same is generally true of his rejection of Marx as well. But at the same time, several of Gandhi's other contributions can also be understood and found meaningful without a direct reference to this spiritual and ethical outlook. This is particularly true of his economic theory of growth and development as well as his theory of structural unemployment.

The conventional development strategy takes it for granted that development is to occur by means of capital-intensive technologies replacing the traditional labour-intensive activities and with it gradual elimination of the limited exchange system of traditional village economics. It is here that Gandhian perspective differs radically and sheds much additional light. Rather than focusing on the growth of the urban sector, he foresaw the central and ever-worsening problem of stagnation and decay of the traditional sector resulting directly from such modernisation and single-minded stress of urban capital-intensive development. On account of the "backwash effect", much of the indigenous skill and crafts get destroyed by new market competition of mass produced consumption goods. By giving priority to investment in the labour-intensive occupations, production by the masses replaces mass production. Here Gandhi's advocacy of "appropriate technology" "as distinct from least cost technology" is understandable.

As a relentless champion of the cause of the poor, Gandhi saw capitalism as an order of institutional violence and exploitation inhibiting social justice and individual self-realisation. This is the common meeting point of Gandhi and Marx, but they differ on the means and procedure for bringing about socio-economic transformation. In short contrast, conflicts, exploitation and war, according to Gandhi, have their roots in the acquisitive nature of our lower self. It is all struggle between ego and self. If we yield to violence by partaking in the class struggle, capitalism may eventually collapse but in the process we have bred more, not less, violence in the social system. All this could scarcely be better expressed than by Gandhi himself:

> "It would destroy the system if I believed that the use of the most deadly weapons could only perpetuate the system, though it may destroy men rather than manners, adopt latter and become worse than those whom they destroy under the mistaken belief that the manner will die with the men. They do not know the roots of evil."

It may be said that Gandhian economics is tantamount to an economics of non-violence (*ahimsa*). By understanding the implied meaning of *Ahimsa*, one can appreciate the Gandhian legacy for economists. This legacy is nothing less than a coherent outline of a brand new economics of love waiting to be realised. Gandhi left for us a guide to non-violent economic action:

> "I will give you a talisman. Whenever you are in doubt or when the self become too much for you, apply the following test. Recall the face of the poorest and the weakest man whom you have seen and ask yourself is the step that you contemplate is going to be of any use to him. Will he gain anything by it? Will it restore him to a control over his own life and destiny? In other words, will it lead to *Swaraj* for the hungry and spiritually starving millions? Then, you will find your doubt and self melting away."

Basic Concepts of Gandhian Economics

There are six basic concepts that are essential in Gandhian Economics. These are all related to each other. There is no hierarchy among them. They are all equally important. They are (1) *Swadeshi*, (ii) bread-labour, (iii) *aprigraha* or non-possession, (iv) trusteeship, (v) non-exploitation, and (vi) equality.[18]

The basic elements in the *Swadeshi* principle can be started in the following propositions. One, an individual consumer will reduce his/her wants and reorder the preference function such that is made up mostly of goods produced in the neighbourhood defined in terms of a community. Two, the consumer will cooperate with neighbour producer/worker to produce the goods efficiently. The emphasis is on cooperation between the producer and consumer. Contrary to the existing situation where efficiency is determined by competition between producers, in *swadeshi* efficiency is ensured *via* the cooperation between the producer and consumer neighbours. The *Swadeshi* principle leads to a downward shift in the cost function.[19]

The concept of bread-labour involves a union of two basic principles: (i) the expenditure of energy through body work, and (ii) the moral values enjoined to such energy use. Not only must work produce something, this production must also be ethical in itself. Work involved in the production of war goods, to entrap, hurt and torture people, etc., do not satisfy the criteria of bread-labour. On the other hand, work performed in the service of other human beings is bread-labour. In another language, it may he similar to high-entropy work.[20] In Gandhian economics and society, major part of the production of goods and services arise from bread-labour. In view of the ethical dimension in bread-labour, it is also voluntary work. Generally speaking, people will not produce unethical goods except under force; wage payment can be, and many a time, are source of force. J.D. Sethi distinguished four components of labour, namely: (i) minimum physically necessary labour, (ii) instrument of self-actualisation, (iii) method of service, and (iv) means to earn livelihood.[21]

The concept of bread-labour provides an important tool for analysing the composition of total output. The total output may be divided into three categories: (i) value-in-use; (ii) value-in-exchange; and (iii) value-in-threat. Bread-labour implies that production will be weighted heavily in favour of (i) and against (ii).

Aprigraha or non-possession means "possession by all." The principles implied in the concept of *aprigraha* are as follow:

(i) The welfare of an individual person depends not on the consumption of commodities but also on service to other fellow human beings; service being at least as important as consumption;
(ii) The utility space, defined by consumption of goods alone, is limited on the other hand, welfare obtainable from service is unlimited; and
(iii) The object is not to maximize utility or consumption of goods.

Being limited, maximization of utility is not a meaningful objective. The objective instead is to obtain a certain level of utility. The underlying principle is contentment or "enough" as against "greed" and more and more. Accordingly, *aprigraha* or non-possession defines a demand relationship between price and consumption. However, this demand function is somewhat different from that are two limits given by a maximum and minimum of consumption. There is certain level, beyond which consumption of a commodity will not increase. There is certain level of consumption that everyone will obtain; whether the person has income or not.[22]

Non-possession follows from truth and non-violence. It involves that person should not possess anything that one does not need. The Gandhian concept of theft is based on *aprigraha*. Accordingly, anyone who possesses things and objects not needed by oneself but needed by others is a theft. This is an essential concept in *swaraj*, because it brings to the most coveted state: "to each according to one's need". This also implies institutional forms. The whole concept of private ownership of property where property is distinguished from tools, comes under sharp questioning. Non-possession is not compatible with capitalism. Here Gandhi has been misunderstood or misinterpreted by Marxists as a defender of private property and as being soft on capitalism. Clearly, the concept of *aprigraha* is the strongest denunciation of capitalistic forms.

The craving of possession is an artificial one, it goes on unceasingly and is never fully satisfied. Desire is never satisfied by enjoyment of the objects of desires, it grows more and more as does the fire to which fuel is added.[23]

The concept of trusteeship follows from the highest moral principles of service to others. In Gandhi's own words, "what belongs to me is the right to an honourable livelihood, no better than enjoyed by millions of others. The rest of my wealth belongs to the community and must be used for the welfare of the community. In other words, the endowments of better abilities and larger resources do not allow the person the privilege of using these for personal gain. Instead, there are obligations to the community. The ethical proposition is that these endowments are given to a person as a trust and these have to be used for the benefit of all. As can be appreciated, this principle is contrary to the principle of incentive and places major limitation on property rights. In view of this, trusteeship implies decentralization.[24] Decentralisation follows from the fact that trusteeship imposes a negative relationship between economic privilege and political or other power. Trusteeship thus poses a limit to power and its use. By trusteeship is meant that all those people who possess things as well as "capabilities, abilities, or other natural gifts" must hold these possessions as trustees for all other. They should not derive the benefits from these possessions for themselves. On the contrary, the possession brings immediately an obligation. Possession is a burden if it is defined as a negative relationship between privilege and the decision making power.

Non-exploitation involves the reduction, and eventual elimination of privileges. Three types of privileges may be distinguished: (i) privilege of non-accountability, (ii) privilege of easy opportunities, and (iii) economic privilege. These three privileges though analytically distinct, are not independent of each other. On the contrary, these are highly interrelated; one promoting the other. The basis of elite-mass contradiction lies in the concept of exploitation. Non-exploitation thus, involves the reduction in this elite-mass contradiction. Non-exploitation follows straightforwardly from the concept and principle of non-violence. One cannot exploit the others without doing violence. It is both a simple and a complex concept. The complexity arises particularly from the nature of the society all the world over today. Some thinkers maintain that both Marxist and capitalistic societies, as constituted today, have institutionalized exploitation, particularly in the production of goods and services. In view of the inequalities and the prevalence of alienation, the very concept of market may be exploitative.

The concept of equality involves a redistribution of assets in favour of the poor and away from the rich. In a way, the Weak Equity Axiom, follows from the principle of equality.[25] The effect of such a redistribution is to change prices, lowering the prices of necessities consumed and needed by both the elite and mass society, and raising those of luxuries; consumed only by the elite-society.

On macro-economic consideration the community as a whole is able to produce virtually all the goods needed by it; unless, of course, such production is not possible for either technical or resource reasons. As far trade is concerned, we find that *swadeshi*, at the macroeconomic level, implies two propositions. One, the country needs to import little. It imports only those goods it cannot produce. Two, it has an exportable surplus. Similarly, bread-labour defines a particular composition of the production in the country. It will consist of value-in-use only and there will be little, if any, value-in-threat. The poor producers who produce values-in-use only are the most vulnerable in the modern society.

In view of the limits to consumption, the economy will have high rate of savings. Thus growth will lead to more saving than consumption. This principle of *aprigraha* will lead to a redistribution of total output between public and private consumption. Private consumption based on primarily material goods will reach a limit while public consumption would grow. The effect is to create a society where there will be private poverty and public affluence instead of private affluence and public poverty as talked about by J.K. Galbraith.[26] This is the central crises of the developed capitalist system.

Equality is an objective of social policy. Not only do principles of *swadeshi*, bread-labour and *aprigraha* promotes equality, the society itself formulates redistribution policies that bring about equality. The concept of non-exploitation and trusteeship determine the nature of institutions that generate the environment conducive to Gandhian economic principles. Non-exploitation involves elimination of all kinds of privileges. Trusteeship refers to management techniques and style. The Japanese management seems to incorporate some of the principles of trusteeship. Japanese management is based on the concept of joint family system where the senior members consider it a trust rather than a source of income and privilege. The level of hierarchy is less, the job in the corporation is secure, the emphasis is on team and cooperative work and seniority is respected. The Gandhian economics is far more relevant even today. The policies of the Maoist government in China followed the path which was very close to Gandhian patch.[27] As a result China was able to feed, clothe, educate and provide minimum health care of all of its more than one billion people.

In neo-classical and neo-Marxian economies, consumption is a source of utility. The classical economists distinguished between "basic" and "non-basic" goods. Adam Smith differentiated between productive and non-productive labour. In Marx, it is derived from distinction between "Value-in-use" and "Value-in-exchange". Neo-classical and neo-Marxian economists obliterated these distinction between "basic" and "non-basic" goods. In Gandhian economics this distinction between "basic" and "non-basic" goods is fundamental. Gandhian economics will accept the hierarchy of "needs" defined by Maslow. In these hierarchies, there is the necessary consumption that satisfied physiological and security needs on the one hand and "self-actualisation" on the other. The former group of needs is socially determined. While the latter group is necessary for the creative needs of an individual. Along with material goods to satisfy these needs must come the possibility to satisfy love, respect, and a sense of belonging.

Work in Gandhian Society is a source of utility while in neo-classical economics it is full of disutility. There is radical difference between the basic propositions of consumption between neo-classical and Gandhian approach. In the industrial society, non-basic goods form the major part in the total output as the income elasticity of "non-basic-goods" is far greater than that of "basic-goods". Hence, it is always more profitable to produce "non-basic-goods". In Gandhian societies—parts of China, perhaps are the only example where the emphasis is on the production of basic goods. Some non-basic goods are also produced but they are small parts of the total output.

In Gandhian system the mode of production cannot be exploitative by their very nature. The technology must satisfy the three major conditions:

(i) Technology must increase the productivity of the worker.
(ii) Technology must not replace the workers.
(iii) The worker must have complete control of the technology.

Thus, the very purpose, goal and measure of production are different in Gandhian order, similarly distribution is also guided by different criteria under Gandhian order. They are to facilitate the consumer to increase their satisfaction and thereby their welfare rather than exploiting the masses on the plea of creating additional value through trade and transaction.

The interesting thing about this new production and distribution system is that it requires a different type of relationship in the work place; cooperation and collaboration instead of competition. In the emerging era of productivity, social justice is not incompatible with economic growth but essential to it. A social organization premised on equity, security and participation will generate greater productivity than one premised on greed and fear.

Collaboration and collective adaptation are becoming more important to an industrialized nation's well-being than are personal ambition. And at an even more fundamental level, the goals of prosperity and social justices cannot validly be separated.[28] To a large extent, the ideas of social justice, equity, participation, security, etc., are the very essence of Gandhian economics. Finally, Gandhi does not stand for the out of date policy of free trade and *laissez faire*, planning for a balanced and rational economy is of prime importance.[29] We need to look up on humanity not as a mere organism but as a living organism united from within by those values which are inseparable from human dignity and freedom. When the sense of human community is absent, society becomes riotous and mob. Gandhian values alone can save the society and humanity.

NOTES

1. Dantwala, M.L. (1944), *Gandhian Reconsidered*, Padma Publication, Bombay.
2. Ganguli, B.N., (1973), *Gandhi's Social Philosophy: Perspective and Relevance*, Vikas, Delhi.
3. Bhabtosh Dutta (1978), *Indian Economic Thought*, Tata McGraw Hill, New Delhi.
4. Mehta, J.K. (1985), *Gandhian Thought*, Ashish Publishing House, New Delhi.
5. Raj Krishna (1979) "The Nehru-Gandhi Polarity and Economic Policy" in B.R. Nanda *et al.*, *Gandhi and Nehru*, Oxford University Press, Delhi.
6. Sethi, J.D. (1978) *Gandhi Today*, Viaks, Delhi.
7. The Limits to Growth (1972), A Report for the Club of Rome Project on Predicament of Mankind.
8. Fred Hirsch, *The Social Limits to Growth.*
9. Thurrow, Lester (1984), *Dangerous Currents: The State of Economics*, New York, Vintage Books.
10. Gandhi, Mahatma (1966), *Socialism of My Conception*, Bhartiya Vidya Bhawan.
11. Ramesh Diwan (1985), *Essays in Gandhian Economics*, Gandhi Peace Foundation, New Delhi.
12. Diwan, Ramesh and Marks Lutz (1985), Essays in Gandhian Economics, Gandhi Peace Foundation.

13. Diwan, Ramesh and Dennnis Livingston (1979), *Alternative Development Strategies and Appropriates Technology, Science Policy for Equitable World Order*, New York, Pergamon Press.
14. Bepin Behari, *Gandhian Economic Philosophy*, Vora & Company Publishers, Bombay.
15. M.C. Langhlin, Elizabeth, T. (1974), *Ruskin and Gandhi*, London.
16. D.P. Gandhier (1967), "Morality and Advantage", *The Philosophical Review*, October, p. 1 - 460-75.
17. Fred Hirrch (1976), *op cit.*
18. Diwan and Shushila Gidwani (1979), "Elements in Gandhian Economics", *Gandhi Marg*, 1 August, pp. 248-258.
19. Diwan, Ramesh (1981), "Toward an Economics of Human Development and the Gandhian Concept of Swadeshi", *Gandhi Marg*. 3 April 1999, 5-15.
20. Diwan and Mark Lutz (1985), *op. cit.* p. 119.
21. J.D. Sethi (1978), *op. cit.*
22. Diwan, Ramesh (1982), "The Economics of Love, or An Attempt at Gandhian Economics", *Journal of Economics Issues*, Vol. XVI, No. 2, June, pp. 413-433.
23. S. Radha Krishnan, *The Emerging World Society*, Orient Paperback, 1980, p. 54.
24. Diwan, Ramesh "Trusteeship and Decentralisation", *Gandhi Marg*, 1 January, pp. 625-659.
25. Sen, Amartya (1973), *On Economic Inequality*, Oxford, Clarendon Press.
26. J.K. Galbraith (1987), *A History of Economics*, Hamis, Hamilton, London.
27. Gurley, John G. (1976), *China's Economy and the Maoist Strategy*, New York, Monthly Review Press.
28. Reich, Robert (1993), *The New American Frontiers*, New York, The Times Books.
29. Narayan, Shriman (1960), *Principles of Gandhian Planning*, Kitab Mahal, Allahabad.

CHAPTER 8

Gandhian Idea of Economic Independence

A.N. PANDA

Very few individuals are born in this world with the capability to influence the destiny of nations long after they leave this world for their heavenly abode. They put forward such powerful ideas and make such contributions during their lifetime that they continue to motivate the people even after they are no longer there to regulate and direct their followers. Mahatma Gandhi was one of such few great personalities who forwarded ideas which continue to provide guidance to the people of the world in general and those of India in particular for all time to come. His ideas and opinions are still relevant to the people as these continue to create hope in a period in which there is an atmosphere of despair and resentment throughout the world. He still invokes creative and positive thoughts in the minds of people to face various worldly challenges.

Mahatma Gandhi was a multifaceted personality. During his lifetime he has advanced ideas and opinions on multifarious issues and given suggestions on how to deal with heterogeneous questions. He has expressed his opinions on a variety of topics and made recommendations to tackle the prevailing problems faced by mankind. As he has delved into different aspects he has not developed any carefully organised viewpoint which can be presented as Gandhian philosophy and he has been often criticised by his critics that he has not contributed any systematic concept. However, if one goes deeper into his writings and speeches one can find many useful and discernible prescriptions with regard to various difficulties faced in life. More significantly, the most glaring difference Gandhi has from many other great personalities of the world is that he propagated only such opinions which he had already experimented during his lifetime.

Mahatma Gandhi is generally credited with the freedom of India and regarded as the most successful political leader of the country to guide the common mass to their independence. He took charge of the freedom struggle at a critical stage and fruitfully led it to its desirable end. He played an instrumental role to galvanise the passive Indians to a dynamic state and inspired them to actively oppose the colonisers; he was responsible for ultimately driving away the British from India. He was truly a leader of the common man and he was able to dismantle the British Rule in India by transforming the elite freedom movement into a mass movement.

Mahatma Gandhi considered the individual as the centre of the social system and the goal of a man was to realise his moral being. Gandhiji laid emphasis on the performance of duty by the individual. He proposed that society should provide maximum opportunity to the individual to attain his personal development which included his ability to perform selfless service for others and willing fulfilment of his social obligations. An individual should be free so that he would carry out his obligations to the best of his ability. Gandhi believed that no country should be subjugated by another because freedom was necessary for the citizens to discharge their duties efficiently.

According to Gandhi, an individual should be free from all limitations to pursue his best personality which was attainment of a moral self. The best moral self could not be achieved if an individual suffered from economic hindrances. Therefore, Gandhi also focused on economic independence of the individual. He was in favour of evolving an economic system which would allow freedom to the individual from economic point of view and would make him economically free by satisfying his basic material needs. As per him, if the bare necessities of an individual remained unfulfilled he could not be in a position to enjoy his political freedom. An economically enslaved man could not be expected to take political decisions independently.

Before going into the economic system as prescribed by Mahatma Gandhi it is necessary to understand the few economic premises on which Gandhi lays specific significance. Gandhi believes that 'increase of material comforts generally does not in any way whatsoever conduce to moral growth'. It means Gandhi attaches priority to the growth of the moral personality of the individual as he regards the individual as a moral being; a moral being does not seek worldly pleasure and is not after the material aggrandizements and possessions, as his aim in life is attaining moral perfection.

Gandhi always gave equal importance to both the means and the ends. To him, means was like the root and the goal was the fruit. As said by him, "The means may be likened to a seed, the end to a tree; and there is just the same inviolable connection between the means and the end as there is between the seed and the tree".[1] Therefore, he asserted, "there is no connection between the means and the end is a great mistake".[2] He authoritatively told that if a bad method was applied for a good cause then neither the means could be justified nor the outcome would be a good one and ultimately, the consequence would be dreadful and he said, "We reap exactly as we sow".[3] So, according to him, the means and ends could never be separated from each other like the fruit and the root. Hence, all activities of the individual must have an ethical basis. Unless an action had an ethical foundation it became immoral and undesirable.

The economic activity of a man must have an ethical foundation and without a moral basis it became an undesirable act on the part of the individual. Thus, unlike many economists who gave importance to the increase of production of goods and services so that the profit could be maximized and the possessions of the possessor could be increased, Gandhi laid emphasis on the final utilization of the products for the betterment of humanity. Even he propagated for applying the moral principles in the conduct of international relations so that the entire mankind was benefited. In his words, "That economics is untrue which ignores or disregards moral values. The extension of law of non-violence in the domain of economics means nothing less than the introduction of moral values as a factor to be considered in regulating international commerce. And I must confess that my ambition is nothing less than to see international relations placed on a moral basis through India's efforts".[4]

Mahatma Gandhi was against injustice of any kind. He was opposed to the exploitation of one by another. He was a champion of equality of individuals. He considered all human beings as the sons of God and all were entitled to enjoy the basic facilities of life. In the economic field, according to the Mahatma, the bare necessities of all must be fulfilled because without such contentment no individual could lead a life of dignity and self-respect. Hence, in the economic field, there should not be a gap between the haves and the havenots and the haves were only the custodians of the resources of society. He assumed that the rich were not given the licence to exploit the poor and become richer at the cost of the latter.

Gandhi was out and out a peace loving person and he abhorred violence of any kind. He regarded violence as the weapon of a beast. For him, the display of violence was a demonstration of the destructive nature of an actor. Only when a man became controlled by his animal instincts he became violent. But he had a strong conviction that non-violence was consonant with the true nature of human beings which was basically noble. He strongly affirmed, "It is the only true force of life".[5] He criticized the use of violent means in any human conduct. He did not prescribe for hurting an individual in any manner. It had been commented, "Gandhi's non-violence is based on the higher aspects of human nature, which rebel against tyranny, injustice and authoritarianism".[6] According to the Mahatma, the supreme law of the universe must be respected and he said, "Non-violence is the supreme law"[7]. Even in economic activities he did not want an individual to be hurt to the minimum extent. So to him, the purpose and economic activity was to fulfil a material need of an individual and that too not at the cost of hurting another individual in any way. Therefore, the economic system should be such that the needs of all would be satisfied but nobody would suffer.

Village Economy and Rural Development

Mahatma Gandhi had a clear understanding of the Indian economy. He had realised the importance of village in India. While Gandhi advocated for freedom of the country from the foreign rulers he craved for freedom not only in the political sense but also in its totality. He had an integral view of freedom. To Gandhi, every individual and every part of the country must be free from all forms of hindrances and even a unit at the lowest level must have freedom. He said, "Independence must begin at the bottom. Thus every village will be a republic or Panchayat having full powers. It follows, therefore, that every village has to be self-sustained and capable of managing its affairs even to the extent of defending itself against the whole world".[8] He was of the opinion that village was the core unit of Indian democracy and said, "In the true democracy of India, the unit is the village".[9] He continued, "I have believed and repeated times without number that India is to be found not in its few cities, but in its 70,00,000 villages...."[10]

As India is a country of villages where 80 per cent of people inhabit in villages, the economy of the country should be so decided that the requirements of the rural people should be met. Underlining, the importance of villages in India he has said, "if village perishes, India will perish too".[11] The villages should be self-sufficient; to make them self-reliant, it is necessary to produce goods and create services which would be useful for the people of villages. Every village should be a self-contained economic unit where all the basic needs of the people are to be fulfilled by the village itself.

Mahatma Gandhi opposed hegemony of any kind and wanted that people of India must be free; he fought for '*Swaraj*'. He said, "It is *Swaraj* when we learn to rule ourselves".[12] He used the term '*Swaraj*' to denote self-government and preferred *Swaraj* for everybody; even for the lowest of the low should have *Swaraj*. He proclaimed, "the *Swaraj* of my dream is the poor man's *Swaraj*".[3] Unless the poorest of the poor had access to the highest authority and the right to exercise decision-making power, independence had no value; everybody must have the prerogative to decide for himself. Mahatma Gandhi stated, "That *Swaraj* is the poor man's *Swaraj* or *Rama Raj*. Ram symbolized justice and equity, Rama symbolized truth and charity. Justice and equity mean the establishment of just and equitable relations between capital and labour, between the landlord and the tenant. The land and the capitalist will cease to exploit the tenant and the labourer, but studiously protect his interests".[14]

Gandhiji believed that the responsibility of the state was to provide opportunity to the individual to attain perfection in his life; so an individual must be free in the state to develop his moral self. He announced, "The real question is how to bring about man's highest intellectual, economic, political and moral development".[15] All persons residing in the state must have the prospect of leading a life towards their goals and there should not be any discrimination between the people of urban areas and those of rural areas. In his opinion "there should be equality between the town dwellers and villagers in the standard of food and drink, clothing and other living conditions. In order to realise this equality today, people should be able to produce their own necessities of life, i.e., clothing, foodstuffs, dwellings and lighting and water".[16] Therefore, there must be village *Swaraj*. He clarified, "My idea of village *Swaraj* is that it is a complete republic, independent of its neighbours for its own vital wants and yet interdependent for many others in which dependence is necessity".[17]

Gandhiji feels that the essential needs of all must be fulfilled by the goods produced in the village itself. The distribution system in the village should be so managed that all get their vital necessities fulfilled. He proposes that if the surplus goods are distributed among the needy and poor villagers there would not be any person in the village who would be hungry and helpless and at the mercy of others. If poverty can be eradicated from the rural areas, there would not be any starvation in the rural areas and in the country. So the prerequisite is to end the problems of the people of rural India and to do so, it is necessary to give importance to the rural economy and remove poverty of the rural people. Therefore, Gandhi gave importance to village economy and enriching the village life.

Concept of *Swadeshi*

To revitalise the Indian economy Gandhi suggested adoption of *Swadeshi*. He narrated that *Swadeshi* meant using of locally produced goods and acceptance of the indigenous talent in preference to imported goods and alien genius. In his words, "*Swadeshi* is that spirit in us which restricts us of the use and service of our immediate surroundings to the exclusion of the more remote".[18] He observed,

"Much of the deep poverty of the masses is due to the ruinous departure from *Swadeshi* in the economic and industrial life."[19] He remarked that the departure from traditional economic life was the cause of suffering for the masses in India. Because India had ruined its village economy the country was on the verge of destruction. To negate the damaging trend of Indian economy the most imperative step was to resuscitate the rural economy in the country. He commented, "Every village in India will almost be a self-supporting and self-contained unit, exchanging only such necessary commodities with other villages where they are not locally producible".[20]

He linked the country's loss of freedom with the ruin of village economy and end of self-sufficiency of the villagers. He firmly believed that the people of India had developed a slave mentality as they were dependent upon the supply from foreign lands and unless this mind set was changed India could not be free in true sense of the term. So he advised, "It is a world-known maxim that the removal of the cause of a disease results in the removal of the disease itself. Similarly, if the cause of India's slavery be removed, India can become free".[21]

Explaining the comprehensive meaning of *Swadeshi* Gandhiji continued, "I have never considered the exclusion of everything foreign under every conceivable circumstance as a part of *Swadeshi*. The broad definition of *Swadeshi* is the use of all home-made things to the exclusion of foreign things in so far as such use is necessary for the protection of home-industry, more especially those industries without which India will become pauperised... *Swadeshi* which excludes the use of everything foreign, no matter how beneficent it may be and irrespective of the fact that it impoverishes nobody, is a narrow interpretation of *Swadeshi*".[22] The idea of *Swadeshi* was not narrow in its interpretation. It did not mean rejection of anything foreign just for the sake of rejection. It was, for Gandhiji, a justification for survival of the local talent and its growth. But if necessary, something foreign could be utilised for one's own growth and he said, "for I shall buy from every part of the world that is needed for my growth. But by the same token, I refuse to buy from anybody anything however nice or beautiful if, it interferes with my growth or injures those whom nature has made my first care".[23]

He maintained, "I have never considered the exclusion of everything foreign under every conceivable circumstance as a part of *Swadeshi*. The broad definition of *swadeshi* is the use of all home-made things to the exclusion of foreign things, in so far as such use is necessary for the protection of some industry".[24] He further stated, "To reject foreign manufacturers because they are foreign and go on wasting national time and money in the promotion in one's country of manufacture for which it is not suited would be a criminal folly and a negation of *swadeshi* spirit".[25]

Propagation of Cottage Industry

Mahatma Gandhi condemned the predisposition to earn money for the sake of earning it.[26] He criticized the inclination to maximize profit by remaining engaged in different economic activities. He disapproved the profit making tendency of people which was making the people slaves of money and reflected, "Formerly, men were made slaves under physical compulsion. Now they are enslaved by temptation of money and of the luxuries that money can buy".[27]

In Gandhi's view, the goal of economic activities is to fulfil the material needs of mankind and he wants that the basic needs of all should be satisfied and all must lead a life with dignity. All these will be possible only if all are provided with a means of livelihood. To do so, there must be end of unemployment. In a capitalist system, big industries are established for large scale production and to generate wealth for the rich; in this system, the rich becomes richer as the purpose of all such economic activities is to increase production so that profit can be maximized and the owners of capitalist establishments get scope to increase their property. It also becomes easier for the capitalists to control the workers in a more stringent manner as the industries can be established at limited number of places and very often it leads to exploitation of workers at the hands of the mill owners. Further, due to use of heavy machineries many workers lose their means of livelihood. It results in increasing the number of poor people in the society on the one hand and increasing the degree of their poverty on the other hand.

Gandhiji was against centralised production and he opposed concentration of economic power in the hands of a few persons.

He was for intensive, small scale and cooperative farming and development of cottage industry. He propagated for social justice and economic opportunities for all and mentioned, "What do I resent is the wanton and wicked destruction of the one cottage industry of India that kept the wolf from the doors of thousands of homes scattered over a surface 1,900 miles long and 1,500 miles broad".[28] Mahatma Gandhi supported organisation of economy through decentralisation and village Panchayats. He objected to the use of machines to produce goods which led to destruction of cottage industry. He gave preference to decentralization of economic power of the society because according to him, centralization was generally associated with coercion which was unethical.

Giving the example of weavers and the important role they can play in the economy of the country he presented the view, "If the weavers wake up and decide exclusively to weave hand spun yarn, not only would million earn a little by spinning but, along with them, thousands of others employed in ginning, carding and starching would get more work to do. The daily earnings of thousands of carpenters and blacksmiths would go up".[29]

If cottage industry is given importance then large number of workers can be employed in different economic units. It will not only end concentration of wealth in the hands of fewer individuals and end exploitation of many at the hands of a few but also help ending unemployment problem in the society and transforming the economy into a need based economic system as the people of different parts of the country would produce goods necessary for the people of those areas. Ultimately, it would lead to economic self-reliance of the people.

Rejecting the modern way of industrialisation Gandhi gave the opinion that modern form of industrialisation was detrimental to the country's economy as it resulted in destroying local talent, creating unemployment and making the people of India poor. So he concluded, "India does not need to be industrialised in the modern sense of the term".[30]

Especially he was in favour of producing cloth by the native weavers and gave his idea in these words, "I have nothing to say against the development of any other industry in India by means of machinery, but I do say that to supply India with cloth, manufactured either outside or inside through gigantic mills, is an economic blunder of the first magnitude, just as it would be to supply cheap bread through huge bakeries established in chief centres of India and to destroy the family stove".[31]

Criticising the profit motive of the mill owners and advising people not to use mill-made clothes Gandhiji said, "Those of us, therefore, who have accepted *swadeshi* as a religious duty should not use mill-made clothes".[32]

Gandhi had understood that Indian economy in the past had a glorious history and it was capable of meeting the needs of all people in the country. Every village in the country was a self-sufficient and self-reliant economic unit. The villagers used to fulfil all their basic needs in the village itself. But when the British came, they changed the need-based economy of India into a profit-based economy as their main motive was to earn profit for themselves and they were concerned neither for the Indian people in general nor for the Indian workers. As a result, the Indian economy got destroyed and was replaced by a system which catered to the desires of the colonizers. The aboriginal talent was ignored and the native workers became unemployed. The people of the country got habituated to use foreign goods and became party to the destruction of the economy of their own motherland.

Gandhiji dreamt of an ideal village and expressed his dream in these words, "It will produce its own grains, vegetables and fruits and its own Khadi".[33]

Advising the boycott of foreign cloth and engaging the peasants in spinning he said, "The plan, therefore, is not merely to induce the peasant to refuse to buy the cheap and nice-looking foreign fabric but also by teaching him to utilize his spare hours in carding and spinning cotton and getting it woven by the village weavers, to dress himself in *Khaddar* so woven and thus to save him the cost of buying foreign and, for that matter, even Indian mill-made cloth. Thus, boycott of foreign cloth by means of hand-spinning and hand-weaving, i.e., *Khaddar*, not only saves the peasant's money, but it enables us workers to render social service of a first class order. It brings us into direct touch with the villagers. It enables us to give them real political education and teach them to become self-sustained and self-reliant".[34]

He relied on the premise that *Swaraj* was dependent of *swadeshi*. If a country had self-sufficiency to generate and meet its economic needs indigenously and detested using foreign product it was bound to retain its independence. He claimed, "I am convinced that, if the country understands the idea of complete *swadeshi*, she will secure *swaraj* without having to resort to civil disobedience or non-violent revolt".[35]

Rejecting the much quoted economic principle that demand determined supply and controlled the market, he strongly contended, "I do not endorse the proposition that supply follows demand. On the contrary, demand is often artificially created by unscrupulous vendors. And if a nation is bound, as I hold it is, like individuals to comply with a code of moral conduct, then it must consider the welfare of those whose wants it seeks to supply. It is wrong and immoral for a nation to supply for instance intoxicating liquor to those who are addicted to drink."[36]

He viewed hand-spinning as an expression of self-reliance and assertion of one's self-dependency. Supporting the use of hand-spinning he firmly believed on the utility of it and opined, "Attacks on hand-spinning notwithstanding, I cling to the belief, that *Swaraj* is unattainable without the beautiful art becoming universal in India. The reasoning applied to the proposition is incredibly simple. India cannot live unless her homes become self-supporting. They cannot become so, unless they have a supplementary occupation. It will, therefore, not avail if all our cloth was manufactured in our mills. If hand-spinning became universal, every home would get a share of the crores and without any complicated machinery being necessary. And India is able to manufacture all her cloth. It is understood, that when spinning becomes universal, the millions of weavers and lakhs of carders will revert to their original occupation".[37]

Trusteeship System

Though Gandhi was not against private property of an individual and did not object to material possessions by individuals after their achievement, he never permitted the possessors to misuse their possessions for private pleasure. He regarded private possessions as the trust of whole society which belonged to the entire humanity and were to be used for the benefit of the needy ones. Mahatma Gandhi was against concentration of wealth in the hands of a few. In his opinion, concentration of economic power in the hands of a few created an economic class and it exploited those who were without material possessions. The rich people, because of their wealth became privileged and got the additional advantages in other fields and tightened their grips in deciding the fates of the unfortunates; as a result, the underprivileged people remained at the mercy of the rich people and became susceptible to be exploited. At the same time, Gandhi believed that the rich people had no right over the property created by the labour of other people and whatever was generated by the society must belong to members of the entire society. Therefore, he thought the owners of property as the custodians of those possessions.

He concurred with the age old Indian precept of renunciation of material possessions and comfort and acknowledged its value in life. According to him, one should lead a simple life and should not be over indulgent in worldly pleasures. He conceded, "The spirit of renunciation should rule all activities of life. A house holder does not cease to be one, if he regards life as a duty rather than as indulgence. A merchant, who operates in the sacrificial spirit, will have crores passing through his hands, but he will, if he follows the law, use his abilities for service. He will, therefore, not cheat or speculate, will lead a simple life, will not injure a living soul and will lose millions rather than harm anybody".[38] He further added, "Self-indulgence leads to destruction, and renunciation to immortality".[39]

If one was engaged in the futile exercise of creating material possessions, then it was inconsequential for Gandhi. Gandhiji subscribed to the view that the ultimate goal of riches was to serve humanity and if it was not in the interest of the poor then it had no justification. Accumulation of property for self-satisfaction was a criminal act for him and it was a matter of shame and thus, he revolted against the ridiculous yearning to increase material assets and declared, "We should bury our heads in shame if we add to our wealth. Indeed, we may possess wealth for service. But some people accumulate wealth, regarding their greed as their religion. This is not proper".[40]

The Mahatma always highlighted self-control in individual conduct and he emphatically stated all human beings must possess this attribute while dealing with their fellow human beings. According to him, all the capability of an individual was to be utilised for the betterment of society and the ultimate goal of an individual was to serve others by making self-sacrifice. Therefore, the proprietor of material possessions should regard the more unfortunate ones as his brothers and be helpful to them at the time of need. The rich and the poor were not adversaries but partners in the society and both should behave accordingly. If the rich failed in their duty to come to the help of poor they would denigrate themselves before their superior-self, the self which stood for the ultimate moral precept of selfless service. Thus he opined, "If capital is not to fall into utter discredit, it behoves capitalists voluntarily to exercize self-restraint and make common cause with labour".[41]

He commended the members of the ancient Indian business class who were known as *Vaisyas*; their profession was production and distribution of material goods for other members of the society. Praising their role in society he recalled, "If we analyze the functions of the *Vaisya* of the ancient times, we find that he was assigned the duty of production and distribution not for personal gain but for common good. All the wealth that he amassed, he held as a trustee for the nation. Capitalists, if they are to fulfil their real function, must exist not as exploiters, but as servants of society".[42] He counselled the rich, "I want the rich to hold their riches in trust for the poor or to give them up for them".[43]

He insisted on the cooperative relationship between the rich and the poor. Unlike other philosophers such as Marx, Mahatma Gandhi did not propagate for a class war between the capitalists and the labourer because he believed a class war perpetuated the differences between the competing groups. He opined in these words, "To inflame labour against moneyed men is to perpetuate class hatred and all the evil consequences flowing from it. The strife is a vicious circle to be avoided at any cost. It is an admission of weakness, a sign of inferiority complex. The moment labour recognizes its dignity, money will find its rightful place, i.e., it will be held in trust for labour. For, labour is more than money".[44] He further explained that the rich should voluntarily relinquish their indulgence on their possessions. He left the choice to the rich to take a voluntary renunciation of their riches and advised them in this manner, "Similarly would all rejoice if a capitalist were to divest himself of exclusive ownership and declare himself to be in possession as a trustee for the people".[45]

He believed that the objective of capital was to serve the interests of the poor and if the worldly possessions were spent otherwise it could be considered as their misuse. Therefore, capital should have the target of fulfilling the interests of the poor in society. In Gandhi's view, "Capital should be labour's servant, not its master".[46] The capitalists must regard themselves as the caretakers of the property they owned and Gandhi advised them to act as the trustees of their worldly possessions.

Praising the trusteeship system he opined, "It is an attempt to secure the best use of property for the people by competent hands".[47]

The Gandhian concept of trusteeship was based on the premise that one could not appropriate wealth without violence and Gandhi was against use of violence for any purpose. But if property was regarded as a trust to be used for the benefit of all then the possessors of property would not misuse their resources to aggrandize more riches by using force and exploiting others; they would not accumulate wealth for the benefit of others through improper methods. Thus, to end the perversities of human beings he did not give them license to misuse their property for self-appeasement though he gave right to property to private individuals.

The trusteeship system was not based on superior-subordinate relationship; neither the rich were superior nor the poor were subordinate. The whole system was based on mutual cooperation and give and take principle. In Gandhi's opinion, "The trusteeship theory is not unilateral, and does not in the least imply superiority of the trustee. It is, as I have shown, a perfectly mutual affair, and each believes that his own interest is best safeguarded by safeguarding the interest of the other".[48]

Mahatma Gandhi was against the use of property as an instrument of exploitation and he favoured the end of exploitation through a non-violent way. He advised those who had property must regard it as a trust and must not use it for oppressing others. All property should be held in trust, no matter who owned it and what its nature or quantity was. No one should have property more than what one needed.

Conclusion

According to Gandhi, the economic system should be such that the bare needs of all can be met, economy should grow in a peaceful manner and the means of production and distribution should be based on ethical basis. There should not be paucity of material goods for anybody and the requirements of all should be fulfilled. The economic benefits of the society should be shared by all persons living in the society as the means of production and distribution belong to the society as a whole; whatever things are created by the economic system are the trusts of the entire society put at the trusteeship of the rich people.

Thus, Gandhi visualized an economic system in which there should be no capitalist class with the power to control all economic activities for increasing their wealth at the cost of the economic needs of the needy and poor people. To him, the economic system should be a need based system and all economic activities must be carried on to fulfil the requirements of the people. He asserted this by giving an example, "At one time our national economics was this that just as we produced our own corn and consumed it so did we produce our own cotton, spin it in our homes and wear the clothes spun by our weavers from our own yarn. The first part of this description is still true while the latter part has almost ceased to hold good. A man generally spends upon his clothing a tenth of what he spends upon his food; hence instead of distributing ten per cent of our income among ourselves we now send it to England or to our own mills".[49]

In an ideal economic system, production should not be made for purely profit motive. It has a social purpose and it must serve the interests of the people in society. If anything is created solely to earn profit then, to Gandhi, it was unethical.

Gandhi advocated *Swadeshi* should be the principle of economic independence. The people must use whatever was locally available and should not depend on foreign supply. He championed for the cause of the native workers. He propagated for the enhancement of the locally known skill. According to him, the native workers should be encouraged to produce things which were needed for the people of the locality. *Swadeshi* would serve the twin purpose of ending dependence on foreign supply and encouraging the local talents. It would also end the unemployment problem in the country. So he opposed the use of foreign goods as he was aware that the British had come to India to earn profit and they were keeping the Indians as slaves because they wanted to continue increasing their profit. Moreover, they were utilizing that earning to suppress the Indians and colonize the whole country. He propagated for the revival of village economy in India to revive the whole country against the British. Mahatma Gandhi wanted the adoption of *Khadi* as a symbol of self-reliance. Therefore, Gandhi pays special importance to the rural economic activities such as *Khadi*, handlooms and handicraft. The principles of *Swadeshi* and trusteeship, according to Gandhi, would provide economic independence and establish a sound economic system where the needs of all would be fulfilled and all would lead a life of dignity.

NOTES

1. Gandhi, M.K., *Hind Swaraj*, Navajivan Publishing House, Ahmedabad, 1938, p. 51.
2. *Ibid.*, p. 51.
3. *Ibid.*, p. 52.
4. *Collected Works of Mahatma Gandhi*, XXV, The Publications Division, Ministry of Information and Broadcasting, New Delhi, 1967, p. 475.
5. Gandhi, M.K., *Non-violence in War and Peace*, Vol. I, Navajivan Publishing House, Ahmedabad, 1948, p. 114.
6. Radhakrishnan, S. "Introduction" in Radhakrishnan, S. ed. *Mahatma Gandhi 100 Years*, Gandhi Peace Foundation, New Delhi, 1968, p. 9.
7. Gandhi, M.K., *Non-violence in War and Peace*, Vol. I, Navajivan Publishing House, Ahmedabad, 1948, p. 172.
8. Gandhi, M.K., *The Village Reconstruction*, edited and published by A.T. Hingorani, Bharatiya Vidhya Bhawan, Bombay, 1966, p. 117.
9. *Ibid.*, p. 119.
10. *Ibid.*, p. 105.
11. *Ibid.*, p. 43.
12. Gandhi, M.K., *Hind Swaraj*, Navajivan Publishing House,

Ahmedabad, 1938, p. 47.

13. Gandhi, M.K., *Capital and Labour*, edited and published by A.T. Hingorani, Bharatiya Vidhya Bhawan, Bombay, 1970, p. 53.
14. *Young India*, May 28, 1931.
15. Gandhi, M.K., *The Village Reconstruction*, edited and published by A.T. Hingorani, Bharatiya Vidhya Bhawan, Bombay, 1966, p. 42.
16. *Ibid.*, p. 42.
17. *Ibid.*, p. 115.
18. Gandhi, M.K., *The Gospel of Swadeshi*, edited and published by A.T. Hingorani, Bharatiya Vidhya Bhawan, Bombay, 1967, p. 1.
19. *Ibid.*, p. 4.
20. *Ibid.*, p. 5.
21. Gandhi, M.K., *Hind Swaraj*, Navajivan Publishing House, Ahmedabad, 1938, p. 47.
22. *Young India*, 17.2.1926, p. 218.
23. *Young India*, 12.3.1925, p. 88.
24. *Young India*, 17.2.1926, p. 213.
25. Gandhi, M.K., *From Yervada Mandir*, Allahabad, Navjivan Publishing House, 1957, p. 51.
26. Gandhi, M.K., *Hind Swaraj*, Navajivan Publishing House, Ahmedabad, 1938, p. 30.
27. *Collected Works of Mahatma Gandhi*, XXV, The Publications Division, Ministry of Information and Broadcasting, New Delhi, 1967, p. 476.
28. *Ibid.*, p. 476.
29. *Collected Works of Mahatma Gandhi*, XXI, The Publications Division, Ministry of Information and Broadcasting, New Delhi, 1966, p. 329.
30. Gandhi, M.K., *The Village Reconstruction*, edited and published by A.T. Hingorani, Bharatiya Vidhya Bhawan, Bombay, 1966, p. 13.
31. *Ibid.*, p. 14.
32. *Collected Works of Mahatma Gandhi*, XXI, The Publications Division, Ministry of Information and Broadcasting, New Delhi, 1966, p. 255.
33. Gandhi, M.K., *The Village Reconstruction*, edited and published by A.T. Hingorani, Bharatiya Vidhya Bhawan, Bombay, 1966, p. 111.
34. *Collected Works of Mahatma Gandhi*, XXV, The Publications Division, Ministry of Information and Broadcasting, New Delhi, 1967, p. 474.
35. *Collected Works of Mahatma Gandhi*, XXI, The Publications Division, Ministry of Information and Broadcasting, New Delhi, 1966, p. 293.
36. *Collected Works of Mahatma Gandhi*, XXV, The Publications Division, Ministry of Information and Broadcasting, New Delhi, 1967, p. 474.
37. *Collected Works of Mahatma Gandhi*, XXI, The Publications Division, Ministry of Information and Broadcasting, New Delhi, 1966, pp. 178-179.

38. Gandhi, M.K., *Service Before Self*, edited and published by A.T. Hingorani, Bharatiya Vidhya Bhawan, Bombay, 1971, pp. 5-6.
39. *Ibid.*, p. 6.
40. *Ibid.*, p. 95.
41. *Young India*, July 25, 1929.
42. *Young India*, December 19, 1929.
43. *Young India*, April, 2, 1931.
44. *Harijan*, October 19, 1935.
45. *Harijan*, February 20, 1937.
46. Gandhi, M.K., *Capital and Labour*, edited and published by A.T. Hingorani, Bharatiya Vidhya Bhawan, Bombay, 1970, p. 79.
47. *Harijan*, February 20, 1937.
48. *Harijan*, June 25, 1938.
49. *Collected Works of Mahatma Gandhi*, XXV, The Publications Division, Ministry of Information and Broadcasting, New Delhi, 1967, p. 556.

CHAPTER 9

Gandhian Perspective of Human Rights

D. VENKATESWARA RAO

Mahatma Gandhi has now been acclaimed by the world as twentieth century's greatest man of peace and human rights. He symbolizes Truth and Non-violence and if the world would ever be without war, it would have to go the Gandhian way. He fought for the human rights of the oppressed all through his life, first in South Africa and then in India. While leading nationwide campaigns to ease poverty, expand women's rights, build religious and ethnic harmony and eliminate the injustices of the caste system, Gandhi supremely applied the principles of non-violent civil disobedience, playing a key role in freeing India from foreign domination. The United Nations has declared October 2, his birth day as the International day of non-violence. This year, UNESCO has decided to launch Mahatma Gandhi Institute of Education for Peace and Sustainable Development in India. Above all, the Mahatma has inspired many a peace prize winner of the world—Martin Luther King, Dalai Lama, and Aung San Suu Kyi, included have credited Gandhi as a source of inspiration in their struggles to achieve equal rights for their people.

Mahatma Gandhi was a simple soul and son of the soil in true sense of the words. He gave message of non-violence and peace to the people who were struggling to get rid of the British Rule. He laid down the golden principles regarding politics, business and even the religion which always show us the light of peace at the end of every tunnel of dismay. Gandhi has been attributed as being the inspiration or model for various rights struggles around the world.

Universal Declaration of Human Rights

While some dictionaries define the word right as "a privilege", when used in the context of "human rights", we are talking about something more basic. Every person is entitled to certain fundamental rights, simply by the fact of being human. These are called "human rights", rather than a privilege, which can be taken away at someone's whim. Every person is entitled to certain rights—simply by the fact that they are a human being. They are "rights" because they are things you are allowed to be, to do or to have. These rights are there for your protection against people who might want to harm or hurt you. They are also there to help us get along with each other and live in peace.

Many people know something about their rights. Generally they know they have the right to food and a safe place to stay. They know they have a right to be paid for the work they do. But there are many other rights. When human rights are not well-known by people, abuses such as discrimination, intolerance, injustice, oppression and slavery can arise. Born out of the atrocities and enormous loss of life during Second World War, the United Nations Universal Declaration of Human Rights was signed in 1948 to provide a common understanding of what everyone's rights are. It forms the basis for a world built on freedom, justice and peace.

Recognition of the inherent dignity and of the equal and inalienable rights of all members of the human family is the foundation of freedom, justice and peace in the world. Whereas, disregard and contempt for human rights have resulted in barbarous acts which have outraged the conscience of mankind, and the advent of a world in which human beings shall enjoy freedom of speech and belief and freedom from fear and want has been proclaimed as the highest aspiration of the common people. It is essential, if man is not to be compelled to have recourse, as a last resort, to rebellion against tyranny and oppression, that human rights should be protected by the rule of law. It is also essential to promote the development of friendly relations between nations.

The peoples of the United Nations have in the Charter reaffirmed their faith in fundamental human rights, in the dignity and worth of the human person and in the equal rights of men and women and have determined to promote social progress and better standards of life in larger freedom.

The protection of fundamental human rights was a foundation stone in the establishment of the United States over 200 years ago. Since then, a central goal of U.S. foreign policy has been the promotion of respect for human rights, as embodied in the Universal Declaration of Human Rights. The United States understands that the existence of human rights helps secure the peace, deter aggression, promote the rule of law, combat crime and corruption, strengthen democracies, and prevent humanitarian crises. The Member States have pledged themselves to achieve, in cooperation with the United Nations, the promotion of universal respect for and observance of human rights and fundamental freedoms. A common understanding of these rights and freedoms is of the greatest importance for the full realization of this pledge. Therefore, the General Assembly proclaims this Universal Declaration of Human Rights as a common standard of achievement for all peoples and all nations, to the end that every individual and every organ of society, keeping this declaration constantly in mind, shall strive by teaching and education to promote respect for these rights and freedoms and by progressive measures, national and international, to secure their universal and effective recognition and observance, both among the peoples of Member States themselves and among the peoples of territories under their jurisdiction.

Human Rights

True democracy must recognize the dignity of each member of the society, irrespective of position and wealth he commands and ensure that nothing unjust is done to anyone. Rights of individuals are inalienable because they ensure freedom, which is the birth right of each human being. But freedom cannot be boundless; it cannot be used to take away the freedom of others. Freedom and rights have to be shared equally by all, including women, children, physically challenged, and poor. All human rights must be guaranteed by law and a stage may come when even duties have to be guaranteed by law. The sharing of rights had the sanction of not only law but also the civil society.

Human rights are rights inherent to all human beings, whatever our nationality, place of residence, sex, national or ethnic origin, colour, religion, language, or any other status. We are all equally entitled to our human rights without discrimination. These rights are all interrelated, interdependent and indivisible. Universal human rights are often expressed and guaranteed by law, in the form of treaties, customary international law, general principles and other sources of international law. International human rights law lays down obligations on governments to act in certain ways or to refrain from certain acts, in order to promote and protect human rights and fundamental freedoms of individuals or groups.

The term "human rights" has been made familiar by its use in today's international political discourse, and the prominence accorded to it by the media. However, its meaning is not always apparent or indisputable. Without going into abstract philosophical debates, it would suffice to say that a right is something to which we are entitled. This word in ordinary English usage not only means a "lawful entitlement"; it also means a "just entitlement".[1]

The idea of human rights or the rights of the individual is commonly associated with the various forms of liberal individualism as they developed in the West. While most authors believe that human rights are vital, they disagree about the nature and source of authority of human rights. They argue that without a legal status, rights cannot be enforced. In this context it is important to note that where human rights are upheld by laws, they can be both moral as well as legal rights.

According to a moral or philosophical approach, human rights are necessary to human dignity.[2] Some of the sources of legitimacy identified are religion or morality modified by medieval philosophers, and later espoused by political thinkers who saw human rights as derived from the principles of the law of nature-contending that human rights stem from a higher law than the state. The positivists, on the other hand, contend that all authority stems from what the state and officials have prescribed.[3]

In the modern Indian context, Manoranjan Mohanty contends

that "Rights have been conceptualized not as claims recognized by the state but as political affirmations pursued through struggles. This is not to say that rights need no sanction of the state. It is to assert that even if they do not have the state sanction they are rights because they are accepted by the current stage of the human civilization as basic conditions deserved for every human being. The struggle for rights seeks state recognition but pursues it in society and culture to further realize it in practice.[4]

Universal and Inalienable

The principle of universality of human rights is the cornerstone of international human rights law. This principle, as first emphasized in the Universal Declaration on Human Rights in 1948, has been reiterated in numerous international human rights conventions, declarations, and resolutions. The 1993 Vienna World Conference on Human Rights, for example, noted that it is the duty of states to promote and protect all human rights and fundamental freedoms, regardless of their political, economic and cultural systems. All states have ratified at least one, and 80 per cent of states have ratified four or more, of the core human rights treaties, reflecting consent of states which creates legal obligations for them and giving concrete expression to universality. Some fundamental human rights norms enjoy universal protection by customary international law across all boundaries and civilizations. Human rights are inalienable. They should not be taken away, except in specific situations and according to due process. For example, the right to liberty may be restricted if a person is found guilty of a crime by a court of law.

Interdependent and Indivisible

All human rights are indivisible, whether they are civil and political rights, such as the right to life, equality before the law and freedom of expression; economic, social and cultural rights, such as the rights to work, social security and education, or collective rights, such as the rights to development and self-determination, are indivisible, interrelated and interdependent. The improvement of one right facilitates advancement of the others. Likewise, the deprivation of one right adversely affects the others.

Equal and Non-discriminatory

Non-discrimination is a cross-cutting principle in international human rights law. The principle is present in all the major human rights treaties and provides the central theme of some of international human rights conventions such as the International Convention on the Elimination of All Forms of Racial Discrimination and the Convention on the Elimination of All Forms of Discrimination against Women. The principle applies to everyone in relation to all human rights and freedoms and it prohibits discrimination on the basis of a list of non-exhaustive categories such as sex, race, colour and so on. The principle of non-discrimination is complemented by the principle of equality, as stated in Article 1 of the Universal Declaration of Human Rights: "All human beings are born free and equal in dignity and rights".

Both Rights and Obligations

Human rights entail both rights and obligations. States assume obligations and duties under international law to respect, to protect and to fulfil human rights. The obligation to respect means that States must refrain from interfering with or curtailing the enjoyment of human rights. The obligation to protect requires States to protect individuals and groups against human rights abuses. The obligation to fulfil means that states must take positive action to facilitate the enjoyment of basic human rights. At the individual level, while we are entitled our human rights, we should also respect the human rights of others.

Gandhian Perspective of Human Rights

Gandhi's objective was to attain independence, but his other objective was to save Indian society, and more specifically, Hinduism. He insisted that India should show her capacity to reform herself even while asking for freedom. His method of integrating nationalist aspirations within the framework of social reform explains his extraordinary tactics, for example, his manner of suddenly calling off a movement when the nature of the movement turned violent.[5] His thrust was that of a social reformer campaigning amongst the higher castes of the Hindu community, propagating social acceptance of the untouchables by the community. In this process, he renamed the untouchables "*Harijans*" (sons of God).

Gandhi takes the attitude of a social reformer calling upon the higher castes to accept the Untouchables. He does not say that the Untouchables have rights, but says that upper castes have a duty towards them. When he advocates resistance, he adds that it must be done in the manner of *Satyagraha*—that is, not by asking for rights, but by showing the other person what his duty is. It is obvious that Gandhian notions are not sympathetic to human rights unless they are products of duties well-performed.

Gandhi's programme of social reform was based on duties rather than on rights. He said very clearly that he did not care for rights, but for duties. If all simply insist on rights and no duties, there will be utter confusion and chaos. If instead of insisting on rights everyone does his duty, there will immediately be the rule of order established among mankind.[6] One of the prime duties of the citizen is to protect the rights of others. This involves sacrifice of certain rights which impinge on the rights of other. That is why Gandhi cautioned the people of India just before independence: "the great evil that is afflicting our society today" of everyone calming to have rights but not duties.

He argued that if there were any rights at all, it could only be the result of well-performed duties: It is, therefore, necessary to understand the correlation between rights and duties. I venture to suggest that rights that do not flow directly from duty well performed are not worth having. They will be usurpations sooner discarded the better.[7] While fighting for the human rights of the people, Gandhi impressed on them that rights and duties were two sides of the same coin. Those who want to enjoy rights must be prepared to perform their duties. Duties well perform by all will automatically protect the rights of all. He considers insistence on rights without corresponding duties as a great evil afflicting the society.

According to him: "real rights are a result of performance of duty; and, where everybody wants right, who shall give them to whom? "If man will only realize that it is unmanly to obey laws that are unjust, no man's tyranny will enslave him. This is the key to self-rule or home rule."

When Gandhi returned to India from South Africa in 1916, he challenged the trampling of human rights of the weaker sections of Indian society and the first thing he did was to educate the people and organize them to fight against it. While he prepared the country to fight against the British Rule, he made frontal attack on some of the society's, evils such as gender inequality, oppression of the untouchables (*dalits*), and exploitation of the peasantry.

Gandhi considered education as the most powerful process to make people aware of their rights and duties and to prepare them to fight for their right. What is the meaning of education? It simply means knowledge of letters. It is merely an instrument, and an instrument may be well used or abused. Therefore, whether you take elementary education, it is not required for the main thing. It does not make men of us. It does not enable us to do our duty. In its place it can be of use and it has place when we have brought our senses under subjection and our ethics on a firm foundation. Our ancient school system is enough. Character building has the first place in primary education. A building erected on that foundation will last.

Similarly, Gandhi was committed to justice for all. For the establishment of justice he not only called on people time and again, but launched non-violent actions and some of them remained exemplary from the success viewpoint. Through them he introduced an adaptable and effective way to the world. How could he minimize the importance of people's rights? He categorically spoke of social, political and economic growth and prosperity of all. He led the way to *Sarvodaya* through his worth mentioning ideas of decentralization of power and Trusteeship. Hence, for us it is beyond imagination that a person like Gandhi could overlook the question of fundamental rights of the people?

Undoubtedly, along with freedom and justice, Gandhi wished equal rights for all. As it is known to us, Gandhi not only accepted the importance of fundamental rights of citizens, but made the issue of people's rights indispensable in all of his non-violent actions he carried out for the freedom of India. Prior to it in his actions in South Africa equality of rights of the people was a vital issue. Therefore, those who are of the opinion that Gandhi ever overlooked human rights, or he preferred duties over rights, are not correct.

Ninth Annual Human Rights Youth Summit

The Ninth Annual International Human Rights Summit, September 7–9, 2012, was held at the International Auditorium in the heart of Brussels. The Summit was attended by youth delegates from 30 countries. Although the Universal Declaration of Human Rights was ratified in 1948, human rights remains an urgent issue in the world today. According to the United Nations World Food Programme, under nutrition contributes to five million deaths of children under five in developing countries each year. UNICEF estimates 150 million children aged 5–14 in developing countries are engaged in child labour. The International Labour Organization (ILO) estimates 2.4 million people were victims of human trafficking in the decade from 1995–2005.

Youth for Human Rights International (YHRI) was founded on the principle of increasing awareness of human rights through education as the first step towards accomplishing meaningful human rights reforms, and educational ideals and programmes were emphasized in the three-day summit. YHRI also raises awareness through distribution of human rights education materials, and human rights world tours. In recent years, the summit has been held at the United Nations in New York and Geneva. This year's summit was held in Brussels, the official seat of the European Commission, Council of the European Union, European Council, and one of the two seats of the European Parliament. Delegates were selected from some 1,000 applicants based on their record of contribution to the cause of human rights, and the three day event afforded many opportunities to expand the scope of their work. Youth delegates met and networked with their counterparts from other countries and with adult leaders in human rights. They honed skills necessary to accomplish their purposes, including communication, organization and public speaking, and they planned their activities for the coming years.

Conclusion

In fact, Mahatma Gandhi has his own refined, exemplary and adaptable view about people's rights. His views regarding rights of citizens, besides proving their merit as per the standards set through various contemporary and modern concepts related to them, are connected with morality. As democracy of Gandhi's imagination is not possible without high morality, therefore, morality occupies the central place in it. Moreover, morality develops a sense of responsibility in human beings on the strength of which they go forward to protect, respect and honour the rights of each other. Gandhi practised human rights as no man or woman has before or after. On the scores of advocacy of the rights of gender, race, religion, age and disability he is unique.

The importance given to duty in Indian culture has been so blatantly misused by those in power and authority to deny the legitimate rights of the weaker sections of the society that the majority of people the world over insist on rights and rights alone. Gandhi too, all through his life fought for the political rights of all those countries which were denied of their right to govern themselves; and the socio-economic and political rights of the poor, *dalits*, women, and other weaker sections of the society. No wonder then, that Gandhi has become a symbol of Human Rights the world over. He stands for justice for all but we know that law alone cannot ensure justice: we need a strong moral force that Gandhi used to defend the weak and throw the British out. That is why he laid equal emphasis on duties.

Constitution of India lists all human rights but no duties. The current situation in India, more than six and half decades after independence, clearly points that so long as rights alone are insisted upon and the duties that each individual, community, society and nation must perform to make rights meaningful are neglected, no one can enjoy his rights peacefully. In fact the rights that people can claim today are only the legally enforceable rights. The education system neither prepares the people to claim their rights, nor sensitizes them to perform their duties.

NOTES

1. David Selby, *Human Rights*, Cambridge: Cambridge University Press, 1987, p. 7.

2. Jack Donnelly, *International Human Rights*, p. 21.
3. Jerome J. Shestack, "The Jurisprudence of Human Rights", in Theodor Meron (ed.), *Human Rights in International Law: Legal and Policy Issues,* Oxford: Clarendon Press, 1984, Vol. 1, pp. 75-83.
4. Manoranjan Mohanty, "The Changing Definition of Rights in India", in Sujata Patel, Jasodhara Bagchi, and Krishna Raj (eds.), *Thinking Social Sciences in India: Essays in Honour of Alice Thorner*, New Delhi: Sage, 2002, p. 437.
5. An excellent example is calling of the Non-co-operation movement in February 1922 after a crowd attacked a police station in Chauri Chaura, killing 22 policemen. See A.R. Desai *Social Background of Indian Nationalism*, Bombay: Popular Prakashan, 1976, p. 352.
6. M.K. Gandhi, "Rights and Duties", in Raghvan Iyer (ed.), *The Moral and Political Writings of Mahatma Gandhi*, Oxford: Clarendon Press, 1986, Vol. 3, p. 496. (First published in *Harijan*, 6 July, 1947).
7. *Ibid.*

CHAPTER 10

Gandhian Roadmap to World Peace

JOSEPH BENJAMIN

Introduction

Mahatma Gandhi the tallest Indian of the twentieth century has shown to the world that non-violence is a path of peace and a potent means of conflict resolution. His strategy of peace can be understood in the framework of European history.

For the preservation of peace many treaties and meetings were held in post-Westphalia Europe like Vienna Conference, Hague Peace Conference of 1899 and 1907. It was in order of things as Hugo Grotius, Machiavelli were Europeans. Then the geographic sweep widened and we see League of Nations and United Nations were fashioned to maintain peace in the world. Disarmament, obverse side of peace coin, too, reared its head for establishing the elusive mirage of peace.

After Second World War, the world leaders made an effort to form a group of nations to control the arms race. After the World Wars, there has been arms race by many nations especially by Super Powers (USA and USSR). There has been a series of meetings between the leaders of Super Powers on disarmament.[1]

On October 25, 1945 the UNO (United Nations of Organization) was established. The Charter of United Nations took up a solution where the Covenant of League of Nations had left off. According to Article 11, paragraph 1, of the Charter, "The General Assembly may consider the general principles of cooperation in the maintenance of international peace and security, including the principles governing disarmament and the regulation of armaments......."

Today, the whole world is bothered about the increase of terrorism. In some ways, the event of September 11, 2002 was an important landmark if not a turning point in the history of the world. At the same time, 26/11 was the dreaded events of 21st century.

Defining Peace

Peace is a state of existence without communal disharmony, conflicts arising out of caste, creed, colour, race, gender discrimination, region, religion, ethnicity, inequality of status and opportunity, disparity between the 'rich and poor', regional imbalance, human rights violation and maintaining the concept of 'unity in diversity' and the harmony with nature.[2]

Peace is not merely the absence of war and hatred (negative peace) but also the presence of cooperation, compassion and worldwide justice (positive peace). In the global context, Peace signifies the state of 'No war' status, absence of intolerable economic dominance by some countries, no expansionist intentions, good neighbourly relations, respect for freedom, no ideological overtones, absence of religious fundamentalism, terrorism, human rights violations, discrimination and ecological imbalance.

As the physical distance between community and community, nation and nation is closing consequent upon modern communication network, popularly known as 'globalization', interpersonal, intercommunity, international understanding are increasingly becoming necessary to avoid conflict of all forms. So there is a search for world peace.

It is believed that this search would provide congenial ground for peaceful co-existence and usher in a new era of co-development. There is also a fear, particularly in the developing countries that indiscrete developmental efforts may create disparities, environmental degradation, and depletion of non-renewable resources. Therefore, it is obvious that search for Peace and need for Development should be taken together.

In this context, the role of a world body, like the UNO and other international bodies becomes increasingly crucial. If humanity is to survive, this body should emerge as an autonomous and the strongest organization that human beings have ever created for selfprotection and survival. However, the UNO needs a Gandhi to keep its strong and weak members in reasonable symbiotic relationships.

Peace never means just the absence of trouble: rather it means total well-being; everything that makes for a person's highest good. This peace always has to do with personal relationship: a person's relationship to self, fellow human beings and to the Lord of all. It is the peace that is born of the reconciliation of people estranged, whether by commission or by omission, both from God and others. Only when people can live in peace with their Maker can a durable peace exist in human relations. Peace with God, peace with oneself, peace in one's own heart, peace in the family and peace in humankind, all belong together. Peace is both a God's gift and a human work.

Peace is a state of being calm, quiet, and free of the disturbance. From a military and political point of view peace means freedom from such violent disturbances as wars and riots. It does not mean total harmony among people.[3]

Throughout the history, most people have wanted lasting peace. Religions and philosophers have called for the peaceful settlement of disagreements. Yet since earliest times, the world has seldom had a long period of unbroken peace. Through the centuries, people have probably spent at least as much time at war as at peace.

Gandhian Path of Peace

First and foremost, we must find it within ourselves. By sharing our inner peace with others, peace will spread. Gandhi experienced and promoted peace in India and the whole world. Today we need Gandhi model of peace. Gandhiji was one of the most outstanding men that the twentieth century has produced. He made the technique of non-violence as the powerful weapon in his fight against Imperialism and experienced the power of non-violence in various fields of human life and activity with wider dimension resulting in for reaching consequences. In academic seminars, today

Gandhi's principles are seldom treated as a topic of serious discussion. But the whole world knows and acknowledges that Gandhiji was a great revolutionary of 20th century. One of the greatest admirers of Gandhi was Albert Einstein, who saw Gandhiji's non-violence a possible antidote to the massive violence unleashed by the fission of atom. Once he said, "It is unbelievable that a human like Mahatma Gandhi walked in flesh on this earth". Gunnar Myrdal, the Swedish economist and a Nobel laureate in Economics, after his survey of socio-economic problems of the underdeveloped world pronounced Gandhi "in practically all fields an enlightened liberal". Today, when we experience the terrorism, which is like a virus spreading throughout the whole world, Gandhian model of peace is the need of the hour.

Gandhiji preached non-violence. He was impressed by this famous line from *Mahabharat, Ahimsa Parmodharma*: meaning non-violence is the supreme virtue. He was highly impressed by the *Sermon on the Mount* of Jesus Christ. He admitted that he did not invent the virtue of non-violence rather it was as old as mountains. Not only Gandhiji preached non-violence but also he practiced this principle in his life. His non-violent freedom struggle against colonialism could drive the mighty British from the Indian soil. Whether, it was his struggle against the racial discrimination in South Africa in the last decade of 19th century and first decade of the 20th century or his struggle against colonialism, he often emphasized on the principle of non-violence. This was the greatest weapon that world has ever produced. Gandhiji was of the firm belief that with the practice of non-violence the worst enemy could be conquered. He even suggested, during the Second World War, to make a huge human wall against the forces of Hitler and his allies, which could quell their violent spirit.

The violence that dehumanizes has many names and many faces. It can take the form of a continued violence against the girl child and all women, the violence of child labour and of bonded labour; the violence of displacement of tribes and *dalits* made internal refugees by the mega-dams and mega-projects of industries, national or multinational, the ideologies of exclusion in the name of gender, caste, religion, culture, language, ethnicity—all these forms of violence negate that peace is the harvest of justice.

To build peace on the foundation of justice, we need to tap and draw upon the reserves of hope that are ecumenical, cultural and religious. From this discovery of the multiple resources of peoples for the elimination of violence and the building of a culture of peace, we need to learn a new model of cooperation and networking and solidarity as embodiments of the culture of peace. As the Argentinian Nobel laureate for peace, Perez Esquivel said, "with closed fists we cannot sow seeds. We sow seeds with open hands. We need the open hands of cooperation and solidarity to sow seeds of peace". This is possible when there is purity of link between means and ends as it is between the seed and the tree.[4]

What is Ahimsa?

The Indian concept of *ahimsa* (non-violence) concerns not only non-violence between humans but also non-violence between humans and nature. We can also reflect on the tradition of *ahimsa* in relation to the culture of peace. Gandhiji interpreted it as the political agenda for the Independence struggle. Grammatically speaking, *ahimsa* is a desiderative noun and it is a negative concept. As a desiderative, it points to radical renunciation of violence from the heart. In this sense *ahimsa* calls for a fundamental option against violence and at the same time a fundamental option for a culture of peace and a civilization of love. The negative form hides a positive content. Gandhiji rightly interpreted *ahimsa* in the sense of love and faithfulness to truth, which he calls *Satyagraha*. The culture of peace and the civilization of love demand that we are committed to praxis and a life-style that embody these values. For Gandhiji, non-violence was the means to achieve the ends, that is truth. He never believed in war as a means. He was strong critic of nuclear weapons. He believed that practitioner of non-violence must be moved by the spirit of sacrifice, service and suffering.

According to Indian tradition one of the fine symbols embodying divine benevolence is the *abhaya mudra*, which very meaningfully relates to the culture of peace and the civilization of love. *Abhaya* (fearlessness) is the negation of all threats to life and humanity. *Abhaya* and peace go together. Freedom from threats and the well-being of people are constitutive elements of the culture of peace. The *abhaya mudra* should be a significant mark and symbol of social harmony and peace. Authentic peace is tested by the freedom from threats to the powerless of society. If the culture of peace is a relational enterprise built by the diverse subaltern solidarities of the powerless it will prepare the way of peace for all. *Antyodaya* leads to *Sarvodaya*[5].

Gandhian Way of World Peace

In 1942, Gandhi reluctantly endorsed the Quit India Plan, calling on London for Indian independence "before dawn, if it could be had". He and the Congress leaders were arrested and jailed. Huge demonstrations soon flared into rioting and revolt. Mobs attacked any symbol of British power, and the disorder cut off British communications to its armies at the frontier. Government forces struck back hard and nearly 1,000 Indians were killed before the uprising flamed out. Gandhi was finally freed on May 5, 1944. He had spent several days in jail in his life.

By end of war, Britain was ready to let India go. But the moment of Gandhi's greatest triumph, on August 15, 1947, was also the hour of his defeat. India gained freedom but lost unity when Britain granted independence on the same day it created the new Muslim state of Pakistan. Partition dishonoured Gandhi's sect-blind creed. The killing before partition made it inevitable, and the slaughter afterward trampled on his appeals to tolerance and trust. All the village pilgrimages he made in 1946 and 1947 could not stop Muslims and Hindus from killing one another. He blamed himself when Indians rejected the non-violence he had made a way of life.

Assassination made a martyr of the apostle of non-violence. The Hindu fanatic who fired three bullets into Gandhi at point-blank range on January 30, 1948, blamed him for letting Muslims steal part of the Hindu nation, or not hating Muslims. Not long before, Gandhi had noted his new irrelevance. "Everybody is eager to garland my photos", he said, "But nobody wants to follow my advice". The world reveres the Mahatma while ignoring half of what he taught. His backward, romantic vision of a simple society seems woolly minded. Much of his ascetic personal philosophy has lost meaning for later generations. Global politics has little place today for his absolute pacifism or gentle tolerance.

Yet, Gandhi is that rare great man held in universal esteem, a figure lifted from history to moral icon. The fundamental message of his transcendent personality persists. He stamped his ideas on history, igniting three of the century's great revolutions—against colonialism, racism, and violence. His concept of non-violent resistance liberated one nation and spread the end of colonial empires around the world. His marches and fasts fired the imagination of oppressed people everywhere. Like the millions of Indians who pressed around his funeral cortège seeking *darshan*—contact with his sanctity—millions more have sought freedom and justice under Mahatma's guiding light. He shines as a conscience for the world. The saint and the politician go hand in hand, proclaiming the power of love, peace and freedom.

Gandhi: An Ambassador of Peace and Non-Violence

We are living today in an age of conflicts—conflicts within each nation and in the international world. Within the nations there are the problems of castes and economic classes, of the haves and the havenots, which some people feel can be solved only through violence. In the international level there are the problems of imperialism and colonialism and arms race which will destroy all the progress that humanity has made through the centuries and even destroy mankind overnight. For these and many other national and international problems, which keep coming up there, seems to be no solutions in sight. There is such a new method which humanity can try without annihilating itself through nuclear weapons—the method of diminishing national and international tensions and avoiding strife and violence, which was tried in India with some success under the leadership of Gandhi, whom in affection and reverence we call the Father of Indian Nation.[6]

How is it then that today these optimistic hopes of a brighter future have almost disappeared and everywhere there is apprehension and fear for the future. This is chiefly due to the unprecedented cruelty, inhumanity and immorality of the last two world wars. Even when there is no war, its tensions and threats continue, resulting in the stockpiling of weapons of a kind which if used are sure to destroy the world. But the tragedy is that with all that knowledge they assiduously go on piling these destructive weapons and inventing new ones more destructive and demonic.

For the people of India, Gandhi is primarily, and naturally, the Father of the Nation, the man who did more than any other one person to gain India's freedom from foreign rule. No one can know the truth without being the truth. And it may in a sense be said of one whose God was truth: No one can know Gandhi without being Gandhi. For to be Gandhi in any degree must involve the acceptance of his three disciplines: *Brahmacharya, Ahimsa and Satyagraha.*

Even as Jesus relied on the Truth—the truth that, will of God was wholly good, that he manifested that will and could only do what the Father willed and did—for healing the sick, suffering and sinning; so Gandhi relied upon the same truth for purifying his inner life and for establishing peace and friendly relations between men and nations. Truth has in his opinion the great and, finally, the only power or the end.

Those who speak casually of 'adopting Gandhi's' method would do well to study these exacting conditions for they alone make the policy of *ahimsa*—universal compassionate love, mercy and harmlessness—possible and effective.

Therefore, in a world dedicated to science worship it is not going to be an easy matter to adopt the methods of Gandhi, for these put the curb of *Ahimsa* on scientific experimentation as on all other forms of violence and cruelty, even as the golden rule from the *Sermon on the Mount* was originally intended to do so.

No useful purpose can be served by hiding from us the fact that really to adopt the methods of Gandhi is to accept a completely different way of life from that led by humanity today and that nothing less radical will solve the problems of the present age. According to Gandhi the moral principles, which guide the conduct of individuals in the social field, must also guide their conduct in the political and the international fields. Gandhi conceives of man as a social individual. His individuality comes out best when he works for social ends. The basic moral principles as Gandhi conceives them are truth, non-violence and scrupulous regard for the means to bring about desirable ends.

Gandhi believed that a peaceful and just world could be established through what he has called *Satyagraha*. *Satyagraha* is a movement intended to replace methods of violence and is entirely based upon truth and non-violence.

Gandhi considers that truth in this world cannot be discovered except through non-violence. Gandhi's philosophy of life for the individual as well as for groups and nations in all their activities was, as we have seen, based upon the idea of the supremacy of moral law. This means that we have to follow the moral laws and one cannot injure others. This law can only be fulfilled through voluntary and unyielding self-suffering. *Satyagraha*, therefore, implies readiness to suffer for a cause one holds to be just and right. The testimony of history is eloquent on this point. No advance in any field of human activity, spiritual, moral, artistic, intellectual, or scientific has ever taken place without the unyielding suffering and even martyrdom of man.

Gandhi's death at the hands of an assassin added to the number of disguised martyrs for noble causes. As Gandhi worked for national independence, his scope of activity in the international field was limited. But he held that *Satyagraha* could equally work in the entire field of international politics. However, *Satyagraha*, it will have to be made in his spirit of non-violence and truth and readiness to suffer for a cause. According to Gandhi, "We have to make truth and non-violence, matters not merely of individual practice, but for practice by groups, communities and nations".

Something great, in the true sense of the word, happened in the first half of the twentieth century. When the greater part of the world had chosen the way of war and bloodshed, atrocity and genocide, Mahatma Gandhi, the martyr of peace chose the way of love and non-violence, peace and forgiveness. If the greater number of world leaders believed in victory and glory through the destruction of their fellow brethren, he recognized self-sacrifice and self-giving as the true-glory and the only way to victory. No one was more convinced about the progress of humankind in the first half of this century than the prophet of peace himself, Mahatma Gandhi.

Peace: From Individual to Universal Level

Gandhi put the individual at the centre of the society and made him the prime agent of social transformation. Man, who is intrinsically good, has to be animated to believe in the divine in Him. He focused on the transformation of the individual through self-discipline and "constructive programme". His unique method of *Satyagraha* was aimed at self-purification as well as conversion of the oppressor. This will result in systematic transformation of the socio-economic and political system. In this transformed society every individual will have due place, inviolable rights and inalienable responsibility.

A new world order would emerge; a civilization of love would be built up when the transformation of the society takes place through the reformation of the individual. Transcendent values will take hold; and a global village, are one world; a federation of independent and yet interdependent states will become a reality. Though *ahimsa* was proposed as an ideal, Gandhi realized that it is impossible to eschew violence completely. Gandhi wanted non-violence to become a living creed to believe in and to practice a living sermon.

Satyagraha: A Tool for Peace

Some people assert their privileges aggressively, regardless of moral rights and wrongs. They do so at the expense of others and eventually their own, since privileges are acquired through violence, difficult to maintain and, therefore, less profitable in the long-run, than those everyone agrees to share peacefully. These aggressive self-promoters recognize each other and compete viciously among themselves. The survivors of this struggle bond together to form even more vicious elites. In most cases, the rest of us submit to their brutal demands in order to maintain the peace. Just because the meek often reject violence, that does not disqualify their legitimate demands. On the contrary, they benefit more people; including the most powerful. Meanwhile arbitrary and violent demands induce more costs, conflicts and social contradictions. This is the basic paradox. Totalitarian societies may seem mighty. But in truth, they are rigid, friable and unstable. Eventually, they become hollow husks, only seemingly mighty, that collapse spontaneously. Today totalitarian societies have almost collapsed in the world.

On the other hand, the more turbulent a society's information flow, the more dialogue commotion it permits, the stronger and more flexible it becomes. Turbulent, apparently shaky societies may submit to foreign aggression. However, they can overcome long-term challenges with greater ease. They may even assimilate successful invaders and thrive in the long run.

The basis of Gandhian struggle is *Satyagraha* which he considered as a fundamental peace management tool. Gandhi coined the term "passive resistance" during his first social experiments in South Africa, and then shunned it.

Gandhi's Principles of *Satyagraha*

- *Satya* (Truth)
- *Ahimsa* (Non-violence)
- *Tapasya* (Voluntary suffering for the good of others)
- *Sarvodaya* (Common welfare).

According to Gandhi we are not only supposed to love our enemy. We are also supposed to seduce him through our truth and non-violence. If we are error-free (a difficult and demanding task), our enemy will become our loyal friend—no matter what he used to think about us—and act accordingly. The process is voluntary on both sides. It should be fearless from the start in your case. It will be fearless in the end for your fear-freed enemy. We may judge the act of our opponent. However, we may only respect or pity him for himself, as we would a beloved family member who's shined or strayed. Our shield must be *Tapasya*: our willingness to accept self-suffering in order to reduce the suffering of others but not our own. Suffering in our own cause is not a part of *Satyagraha*.

Mahatma Gandhi prescribed following code[7] for volunteers, who dream a better world based on truth, love and peace:

- Harbour no anger but suffer the anger of the opponent. Refuse to return the assault of the opponent.
- Do not submit to any order given in anger, even though severe punishment is threatened for disobeying.
- Refrain from insults and swearing.
- Protect opponents from insult or attack, even at the risk of life.

- Do not resist arrest nor the attachment of property, unless holding property as a trustee.
- Refuse to surrender any property held in trust at the risk of life.
- If taken prisoner, behave in an examplary manner.
- As a member of a *Satyagraha* unit obey the orders of *Satyagraha* leaders, and resign from the unit in the event of serious disagreement.
- Do not expect guarantees for maintenance of dependents.

The potent legacy Gandhi left to India was the Technique of *Satyagraha*. There was in this instrument of action, power to effect change. *Satyagraha* had become the cry of all those who felt aggrieved, and popular agitations, however organized and whenever their objective, were widely described as "*Satyagraha* movements". Informed, responsible, and concerned people today reflect upon the hope; with fond memories, and yet with anxiety for the future.

Charity begins at home; so also the practice of non-violence. From home, it should spread to society and then to the country and to the world at large. Individuals and nations should be trained to follow the path of non-violence. Non-violence is not a cloistered virtue, to be practiced by the individual for his peace and final salvation, but a rule of conduct for the society. It is to live consistent with human dignity and make progress towards the attainment of peace for which it has been yearning in the past. Violence and terrorism can be wiped away only through the practice of non-violence by individuals and the society at large.

Transformation of the self is the prerequisite for the reformation of the society, state and world. Gandhi insisted upon self-purification, mortification and sacrifice. One has to die and be at the service of others with no ulterior motive. Authenticity and integrity should be the distinguishing marks of a *Satyagraha*. For this Gandhi insisted upon eleven vows (*vratas*), which will be the foundation of Gandhian non-violent social order. Gandhi believed that these vows would effectively control the insatiable craving for power and wealth. There would be inner congruence in that person and it would be an instrument of peace and unity.[8]

Conclusion

Working for a culture of peace demands that we engage in a politics of peace and for peace. Politics of peace will be a people's politics. We consider people's movements for human rights, justice, freedom and solidarity as people's politics. People's movements whatever are the issues they espouse, are indeed peace movements. If peace movements have to reap their harvest of peace, they need to become people's movements?

The bottom line remains that in contemporary history many leaders in different countries have used Gandhian ideology to tackle problem of oppression and exploitation in their respective countries. Names like Nelson Mandela, Martin Luther King Jr. and many more comes to one's mind. But there are many more who are working at grassroots level making a qualitative difference to the situation.[9]

Gandhi's statue, Gandhian magazines, books, film on Gandhi, Chair on Gandhian Studies in many Universities across the globe is spreading the idea of Gandhian non-violence which in years to come would become a powerful force in the world. Future of mankind looks a bit less sombre and doleful when Gandhian star of peace would shed light and hope to people savaged by war of one type or another in troubled spots of the world. That does not exclude for example internal insurgency issue like Maoism/Naxalite in India. On and off intellectuals and conflict resolution practitioners suggest Gandhian mode of non-violence to combat the raging fires of violence precipitated by Maoist leaders and their followers.

Mahatma Gandhi's roadmap to peace runs contrary to worldly paradigm. One representative lodestar of this worldview is expressed eloquently in words of Nicols Machiavelli who wrote in his book *The Prince* that any man who tries to be good all the time is bound to come to ruin among the great number who are not good. Hence, a prince who wants to keep his authority must learn how not to be good and use that knowledge or refrain from using it, as necessity requires.[10]

Mahatma Gandhi showed to the world that there is another way to usher peace. Non-violence is the foundational premise where revenge or retaliation has no place in lexicon of peace activist. Peace

Making would be facilitated because liberty, not domination, is the key to Homo Sapiens survival. "Liberty would flourish and would lead to democracy."[11] Opposite to war is love, compassion, service and altruism and Mahatma Gandhi worked for this in his lifetime and this pathway has "helped us survive as a species for the past several hundred thousand years".[12]

NOTES

1. Joseph Benjamin, "US-USSR: A Quest for Nuclear Disarmament", *Indian Journal of Politics* (Aligarh), July-September 2005, pp. 145-154.
2. *The World Book Encyclopedia*, Vol. 15, 1996, p. 224.
3. *Ibid.*, p. 224.
4. Kanti Shah, "*Gandhi's Hind Swaraj—A Fresh Look*", Other India Press, Goa, 2009, p. 191.
5. Adrian Carminatti, "Gandhian Perspectives on World Peace", Unpublished M.A. dissertation, P.G. Department of Gandhian Thought, Nagpur University, (2003), Nagpur, p. 73.
6. *Ibid.*, p. 72.
7. *Ibid.*, p. 75.
8. *Ibid.*, p. 79.
9. T. Karunakaran, Director of Mahatma Gandhi Institute of Rural Industrialization, based in Wardha (Maharashtra) has been working at grassroots level. There are many more working at grassroots level.
10. Quoted in Robert Greene, "Power", Profile Book, and London, Preface XXIII.
11. Fareed Zakaria, "*The Future of Freedom*", Penguin Viking, New Delhi, 2003, p. 2.
12. Dean Ornish, "*Love and Survival*", Harper Perennial, New York, 1998, p. 130.

CHAPTER 11

Gandhi's Protest: Examination of Legacy of Gokhale and Tilak

B. ARUN KUMAR

Gandhi justified the citizen's right to not only warn and criticize the state when it embarked on a wrong course but also to protest it effectively so as to influence it to giveup its wrong designs and to work for the redress of the grievances that have arisen because of such intentions and actions thereupon. In carrying out this protest, Gandhi advocated an initial recourse to all the available means within the constitutional prescription. Thus, he recognized the recourse to petitioning, pleading and praying to those manning the administrative positions in order to influence them to take the desired step in the direction of ameliorating the grievances of the citizens. When the recourse to constitutional means failed to secure the necessary effect, Gandhi advocated the need to supplement these efforts by that of an agitation, the intensity and tactics of it being determined by the need of the hour or situation. However, in all such protesting, Gandhi was emphatic about an overarching conformity with truth and non-violence. He also insisted that all acts of defiance of law should be done in a civil manner. Before the act of defiance or disobedience was actually resorted to, Gandhi emphasized that the citizens should prove their law-abiding quality to the state. Moreover, this obedience, he recognized, was a prerequisite for the citizen to get convinced about the unjust or evil nature of the law through his personal experience of it while initially rendering obedience to it. All these nuances of protest were expounded by him through his philosophy of *Satyagraha*. In South Africa this protest was just a seedling, but in the course of Gandhi's political activism in India it gradually matured into a mighty tree with numerous limbs having their offshoots thrust deep down into the earth like the banyan.

A concomitant evolution was Gandhi's speculation on the principles that should inform the functioning of a good government. As his political philosophy matured, it started to more steadfastly conform to the idealized vision of his spiritual enterprise. Consequently, he recognized that if there existed a few principles, the conformation to which justified the existence of a government or state, then to the extent that the government or state transgressed these principles, it should be protested to bring it back to conform to these principles and seek the redress of the grievances that had so arisen on account of such transgressions. However, in protesting such an unjust and unrighteous state and government, Gandhi recognized that there were certain principles, conformation to which justified the protest so undertaken.

Before Gandhi commenced his political activism in India, there were already numerous individuals protesting the colonial regime of the British for its consistent neglect of Indians' aspirations and violation of certain principles which they believed should largely inform the functioning of the government. Broadly, these protests may be classified under the heads of moderate and militant protests. While each fold had many proponents, each unique in certain respects, yet in their essence they had certain common traits. The most prominent personalities whose views on protest largely included the general traits of their fold were Gopal Krishna Gokhale as the exponent of moderate protest and Bal Gangadhar Tilak as exponent of militantism in protest.

In Gokhale's recognition, the hallmark of any good government was its strenuous endeavour for the welfare of its people, identification with the needs and aspirations of its subject citizens; facilitating public participation in administration; and, in its functioning, the imbibing the notions of trust, conciliation and justice. Political governance, he recognized, transcended beyond legal connotation; it was a great moral responsibility and trust reposed on those who held the reins of the government. Therefore, it should be spiritualized by way of imbibing such principles of ethics like that of truthfulness, non-violence, honesty, altruism, etc., in its functioning. To a state conforming to these principles, Gokhale became a great champion of loyalty.

However, this notion of loyalty for Gokhale neither implied an uncritical adulation for those holding the rein of power, nor of a passive acquiescence or subservience to the unjust and oppressive rule. Instead, to an unrighteous, oppressive and unjust rule, Gokhale recognized the need for an active protest; and while doing so he was emphatic about the appropriate nature that this protest should assume. He denounced revolutionary and violent tactics for resisting the unrighteous and usurped authority. Instead, he advocated moderation and pragmatism. These were the underlying notions in his concept of "constitutional protest" through which he sought to not only check and reform the unjust government but also to preserve the freedom and integrity of the citizen's self and thereby uphold the spiritual values which their conscience perceived as inviolable.

Tilak, in contrast to Gokhale, was more militant in his views and activism. For Tilak, a general conformation to the principles of freedom, equality and justice concomitant with an endeavour to work for the decent and dignified existence of the subject individuals, largely determined the justification of any government's existence. A government flouting these principles, he recognized, should be actively resisted by the individual; it was his principal and moral duty. The aim of such a resistance should be to force the government to conform to the idealized principles and take the necessary steps towards the redress of grievances that had arisen as a consequence of government's negligence or transgression of the vital principles. One such principle was freedom. This freedom, *Swaraj* as Tilak called it, was the *elan vital* or *chaitanya* of a nation and indispensable for the existence and all-round development of the individuals. Therefore, he recognized *Swaraj* as the birth right of every individual and emphasized upon achieving it at all costs.

The nature of resistance for *Swaraj*, Tilak recognized, was largely determined by the prevailing conditions in a given political system. Thus, to a regime responsive to constitutional agitation, Tilak accorded recognition to such means of protest like that of requests, petitions, persuasions and passing resolutions. However, to a government unresponsive to such constitutional agitation, Tilak recognized the need to resort to any extra-constitutional means to effectively realize their goal. The only thing about which he was emphatic about was the purity of the goal itself. Thus, in his speculation on protest he is said to adhere to the doctrine of "the end justifying the means". Consequently, in his public activism Tilak is alleged of inciting violence against the colonial rule of the British.

The apparent inefficacy of existing protest to check the oppressive regime of the colonial rule, and to realize the cherished aspirations of the Indians, made Gandhi recognize the need for a more effective protest that would help in transcending the prevailing impasse. As he delved into the various nuances of his theory of protest—*Satyagraha*—he became more and more confident about its efficiency. The results of his various campaigns further testified his faith in its efficacy. Thus, he recognized it as the surest way to successfully realize any noble goal under any prevailing circumstance.

Gopal Krishna Gokhale (1866-1915)

More a political activist and social reformer than being a political philosopher in the accepted sense of the term, Gokhale's exposure to the liberal tradition of the West, his knowledge and close association with the nationalistic sentiments of his Indian predecessors and contemporaries and his personal experiences of both the beneficial and baneful effects of a colonial rule, influenced him to speculate upon both the principles that should form the basis of a good government and those that justified an action to resist or protest the government which did not measure up to these idealized principles. Any good government, in his recognition, had to strenuously endeavour for the welfare of the subject people; identify itself with the needs and aspirations of its subject citizens; facilitate public participation in administration; and, in its functioning, imbibe the notions of trust, conciliation and justice. Conceiving political governance as a great responsibility and trust reposed on those who held its reins, Gokhale recognized it more importantly as a moral responsibility than a legal one. Consequently, he emphasized upon its spiritualization. Although he was a great champion of advocating loyalty to the established order, this loyalty of Gokhale was neither an advocacy of uncritical adulation of those holding the authoritative position in the society nor of a perpetual subservience to the unjust and oppressive rule. Far from being a passive recipient, his loyalty was synonymous with patriotism.[1] "If Gokhale's response to the British rule was one of loyal acquiescence based on an overriding faith in the integrity and beneficence of that which was best in the British tradition, it was by no means the supine surrender of a sycophant or a mendicant to bureaucratic oppression. On the contrary his protest against the latter first of all led to his choice of a career in public service, and then sustained Gokhale through a lifetime of hopes deferred and apparent failures."[2] Gokhale's enunciation of loyalty thus did not presume the renunciation of the right to protest by the subject individuals; rather, it delved into the appropriate manner that it should assume. Being emphatic on moderation and pragmatism while taking recourse to protest against the state, Gokhale's advocacy of constitutional agitation was thus conceived not only as a means to check and reform the unjust or bad government while staying within the parameters of the existing regime, but, more importantly, also as a means for the subject individuals to preserve the freedom and integrity of their self and to uphold the spiritual values which their conscience perceived as something which cannot be compromised.

In its capacity as a means for seeking the authorities to take a desired step or seeking to refrain them from taking an undesired step, Gokhale's protest served as a communication channel for ventilating grievances and sought not the dislodging of those in power, but a continuation with them, and progressive participation of the protesters in the existing arrangement so as to ameliorate the specific grievances faced by them.

In his capacity as a subject citizen of a nation under colonial rule, he did not reject the values for which the British Empire stood; rather, he was opposed to the so called "un-British" type of rule which prevailed in his contemporary India. He, as a proud citizen of the British Empire, cherished the same values as his British counterpart did in Britain and sought for himself and his countrymen what a British already enjoyed in his native land or in the territory which fell within the domains of the British Empire. Thus Gokhale said, "I recognize no limits to my aspiration for our motherland, I want our people to be in their own country what other people are in theirs. I want our men and women without distinction of caste or creed to have opportunities to grow to the full heights of their stature, unhampered by cramping and unnatural restrictions".[3] Gokhale's protest, thus, only questioned the mechanics of British Empire's working in India, and not the value consensus that it represented. It being so, Gokhale recognized the immediate goal of his protest as lying within the parameters of "self government within the empire" and a government extirpated off its corrupt, exploitative and unjust facets.

All such emphases of Gokhale like that of causing the "least or the minimum disturbance of existing ideas",[4] "proceeding along lines which one understands however difficult the progress might be"[5], "one step enough for me"[6], etc., were a part of his recognition of refraining from dislodging those wielding power in the existing political arrangement. Consequently, he admonished every such claim for rebellion and revolution which were voiced by his more militant contemporaries and, instead, preferred recourse to protest and reform. It also influenced his understanding of the concept of loyalty. Interpreting loyalty from a broader point of view, Gokhale emphasized upon the need for the citizens to cultivate an active sense of loyalty to the existing order. He said, "Now loyalty is an active feeling. It implies not merely refraining from any hostile act against the order to which we are loyal, but also a readiness to rush to its support if its existence is in any way threatened. If we are loyal in this spirit, we may fight if the situation requires it with a clear conscience any individual measures or any series of measures of particular administration, with all legitimate weapons at our disposal".[7] This feeling of loyalty, he further emphasized, "is not one to be trotted out for official favour or demonstrated at official bidding. It must spring out of our very love for our country and it must be sustained by our clear recognition of what is necessary in our best interest".[8]

Gokhale's political realism also influenced him to advocate protest as an art of the possible, desirable and attainable.[9] Although as a test of a continuously progressive government.[10] Gokhale identified many of the increasing demands of the subject citizens being entertained by the authorities, his political realism influenced him to remark, "... whatever you may ask for, that is not the same thing as what you will get, or will be qualified to get or in practice maintain if you get. Let us, therefore, not go in pursuit of more idle dreams and neglect the opportunities which the present offers us".[11] Even these demands, he emphasized, could not be realized without a ceaseless endeavour for self-perfection so as to be worthy to realize it, and enjoy it when realized. Therefore, he also emphasized the need for the protesters to be self-reliant and be prepared for great sacrifices in order to realize the cherished goals. Thus he said, "Political privilege could not be had for the mere asking, and they had cost the other people prolonged struggles".[12] It was not sufficient, Gokhale recognized, for the aspirations of the protesters to be theoretically perfect ones; it was a question of not merely of dreams, but also of muscle and character, of capacity, of organization, of sacrifice.[13] It was with this recognition in mind that Gokhale established, the Servants of India Society and conducted its functioning; it was also the chief purpose of his public activism through the Congress platform.

This realism apart, Gokhale was also emphatic about the moral aspects of protest. He greatly emphasized upon the primacy of ethics in the conduction of all affairs of human life. Denouncing the recourse to unethical means as a matter of expediency to realize the envisaged goals, Gokhale advocated a steadfast or uncompromising adherence to the purity of means. Whether, it be the manner in which political administration was to be carried out or the act of checking controlling and influencing those holding authoritative positions in the political systems, the consideration of according primacy to ethics, Gokhale recognized, ought not be renounced at any cost. His advocacy of spiritualization of politics had this idea as its quintessential basis.

A natural corollary of Gokhale's political realism and spiritualism in politics was his advocacy of gradualism and constitutionalism as essential aspects of a protest. He often recalled the statement, "I do not ask to see that distant scene: one step enough for me".[4] Through this approach of gradualism and constitutionalism he sought to prevent chaotic and anarchic situations and causing "minimum disturbance to existing ideas".[15] Since violent struggles against the constituted authority, would lead to the undesirable trails of hatred, revenge and misery; as an alternative, Gokhale advocated a "constitutional agitation". A "constitutional agitation" was recognized by him as an agitation by such methods which one was entitled to adopt to bring about the desired changes through the action of constituted authorities.[16] It had both negative and positive aspects. Commenting on the negative aspect, Wolpert has written, "Gokhale defined such agitation to include all techniques short of physical force, rebellion, abiding or abetting a foreign invasion or criminal action".[17] Barring these three recourses, all other means were recognized by him as constitutional, the appropriateness of each means being determined by circumstantial factors.[18] Its positive facet lay in its advocacy of such recourses like that of prayer, petition, appeal, representation, negotiation, constructive criticism of the policies of the government and use of other peaceful methods within the ambit of all these recourses.[19] Not favouring a recourse to a direct confrontation with the government, Gokhale favoured a moral persuasion of those human agents who constituted it and a mutual goodwill, cooperation and conciliation for the amelioration of specific grievances faced by the protesters. Therefore he said, "... the idea that we should leave the authorities severely alone and seek to attain our goal independently of them is inadmissible and absurd".[20] Wolpert says, "He (Gokhale) rejected the 'violation of law' and 'rebellion' as legitimate means of agitation".[21] Consequently, as T.R. Deogirkar has opined, Gokhale's characteristic contribution to a rapidly changing India was the method of constitutional agitation.[22]

Recognizing the need to awaken the consciousness of the hitherto exploited, but apathetic individuals and, thereby, creating the force of public opinion to influence those in authoritative positions, Gokhale emphasized on the need for consolidation of the protesters. This consolidation implied a very intensive and extensive process of developing the resourcefulness of the protesters. Recognizing the importance of public opinion and united efforts, Gokhale sought, through his public activism, to awaken the public consciousness of the masses towards the various maladies affecting them and transform their apathy into creative and dynamic force to influence the authorities to take action for the amelioration of their grievances. He passionately advocated the individuals to sink their narrow differences and, in a cooperative endeavour, strive to secure the more general, pressing and noble objectives. In his speech on the political situation facing the Indians, which he delivered at Madras on 25th July, 1904, he thus said, "We have got to realize that on the one side of us are arranged forces of racial ascendancy, of monopoly of power, and on the other side is a vast mass of ignorance, apathy and moral helplessness. Between these two we have to work, to face, to try to overcome the forces marshelled against us on one side and quicken into life and to move into energetic action the vast mass on the other".[23]

Gokhale also recognized the importance of mobilization of resources from within to effectuate the demands of the protesters. Consequently, he emphasized upon each participant contributing to the protest in his own little, but best way. Thus he said, "If we all recognize our respective duties in this spirit we shall be able to turn out present efforts into a great, rousing movement for the political emancipation of this land. In the presence of such a movement all our petty personal differences will sink, all our squabbles will vanish, our faith will shine radiantly, sacrifices will be made to the extent they are necessary and the country will march onwards, will press onwards to the realization of that destiny of which we should dream by night and on which we should muse by day".[24]

Gokhale's political realism influenced him to emphasize upon the cognition of the realities of the existing political conditions before taking recourse to any particular means for the mobilization of masses. Accordance of importance to considerations of appropriateness and efficacy, he recognized, was very important before taking recourse to a particular means of protest. Therefore, for him all that was constitutional did not necessarily tantamount to be wise or expedient.[25] It was this consideration which influenced Gokhale to favour *Swadeshi*, when he finally did so, as a more effective and desirable means for consolidation and goal-realization than the recourse to boycott or other extreme means advocated by his contemporary militant nationalists. Thus Raman Murthi comments, "Differing profoundly from the extremist politician of India, B.G. Tilak, Gokhale viewed things and problems from a practical and rational angle".[26] Thus Gokhale did not want opposition to overstep certain well defined limits.

These advocacies of Gokhale, i.e. of active loyalty to the existing order, moderation in protest, faith in goodness of those wielding political power, cooperation with them, gradualism, constitutionalism, etc., did not, however, imply that Gokhale advocated passivity to, or acquiescence in, evil or injustice. Compromise with evil or injustice was not acceptable to him; on the contrary, regarding "blunt speech as a duty if the occasion so demanded",[27] he advocated the ultimate defiance of the oppressive regime when all constitutional means of agitation failed to prevent it from pursuing an unrighteous course. In his recognition this defiance was to be not only open but also concomitant with readiness to suffer the consequences which the laws of the land prescribed for such defiance. Emphasizing on the nature and importance of such a defiance, Gokhale thus said, "If we strongly and clearly and consciously feel the grave injustice of a law, and there is no other way to obtain redress, I think refusal to acquiesce in it taking the consequences of such refusal is the only course left to those who place conscience and self-respect above their material or immediate interest".[28]

Bal Gangadhar Tilak (1858-1920)

Tilak was an ardent champion of individual freedom, human equality and justice. A general conformation to these principles, together with a simultaneous endeavour to work for the decent and dignified existence of all the subject individuals, Tilak claimed, largely determined the justification of any government's existence or continuation. Any government failing to adhere to these principles or to realize the welfare of its subject citizens, Tilak contended, should be resisted. The aim of such an act of resistance, he recognized, should be to influence the government to conform to these idealized principles and take the necessary steps towards the redress of the grievances which arose on account of the transgression of these vital principles. The justness, or otherwise, of all such acts of resistance, Tilak claimed, was determined by the prevailing conditions in the given political system.

As a matter of first resort, Tilak preferred the redress of

grievances through constitutional means like that of humble requests, petitioning, persuasion, resolutions, etc., but when such means failed to bring back the government on the right track, he advocated a vigorous extra-constitutional agitation which, while exploiting the manifest potentials of all existing circumstantial factors, sought to exert pressure on the government to act in a particular manner as desired by the protesting subjects. Advocating a "responsible-cooperation" to the government, Tilak's protest, while attempting to consolidate on the gains conceded by the government, sought to influence the government to accede to all the demands that were made by the protesting individuals. This notion of "responsive-cooperation" simultaneously recognized such an interaction process between the government and the citizens that, on the one hand, it entailed upon the citizens the duty to cooperate and observe moderation in their actions while making demands to the government that had committed a few lapses in fulfilling the aspirations of the citizens, and on the other hand, conceded the right to the citizens to disobey, or to non-cooperate and take recourse to more stringent actions while seeking to realize their demands from the government that was reluctant, unresponsive and unsympathetic to their cherished aspirations. Whatever be the means advocated to Tilak to secure the redress of grievances of the protesting subjects, there exists in his advocacy a basic recognition of the inherent right of the subjects to make a critical evaluation of the performance of the government and to communicate this to it unequivocally. This, he recognized, should not be considered as a seditious act.

Weaknesses or inadequacies of the government, Tilak recognized, should be expressed without fear of the punishment prescribed for such acts. Conforming to the doctrine that 'eternal vigilance is the price paid for preserving one's liberty, Tilak emphasized upon the conscious existence of the citizens and recognized the need for the mobilization of this consciousness of the individuals for influencing the government to concede the demands of the protesters. Tilak recognized that the protesters had to make not only fearless and ceaseless efforts for the vindication of the essential principles lying at the core of their grievances but also be prepared to sacrifice even some of the best things held dearly in their life while doing so. Such a resistance to the government that deviated from its ordained moral or ethical functions, Tilak contended, was a bounden duty of the subject individuals.

Although embroiled in an active resistance to the unjust and oppressive regime of a colonial power, Tilak's advocacy of resistance did not limit itself to the mere considerations of freedom from a foreign rule. His nationalistic sentiments influenced him to prefer self-government, however, deficient it might be, to that of an efficient foreign government. However, he recognized no double standards so far as the reaction to an unjust government was concerned. There was only one prescription towards the unjust government, be it foreign or native, and that was the moral duty of fearlessly resisting its unjust and oppressive nature. Thus, Tilak's protest, assuming the form of a *dharma*, transcended the parameters of being merely a natural or inalienable right of a citizen, and was, more importantly, conceived as a bounden duty or moral obligation of the subject individuals. Therefore, he said, "Do not be afraid of speaking out things which are plain in themselves. There might be some trouble, but nothing can be had without any trouble".[29]

Tilak recognized the existence of mutual obligation between the ruler and the ruled. Thus, while he enunciated an active loyalty for the subjects towards the benevolent ruler, he entailed upon the ruler to do all the needful for the happiness and well-being of his subjects. A natural corollary of this enunciation was his recognition that if the ruler failed to fulfil his obligations towards the subjects and exploited or oppressed them, then the ruler committed treason towards the subjects. In all such cases, Tilak conceded to the people the right to impose their will on the ruler and even revolt against him.[30]

An oppressive and unjust government, Tilak contended destroyed the dignified existence of the individual. It not only curtailed his growth and development but also stifled all efforts by the individual to make just assertions in his life. Thus, it annihilated the qualities indispensable for the individual's meaningful personal and social existence. This loss of freedom, for Tilak, lay at the root of the nation's misery, poverty and humiliation.[31] Freedom from such oppressive and unjust regime, therefore, Tilak advocated, was the *elan vital* (*Chaitanya*) of a nation and as such essential for the existence of a society.[32] Consequently, Tilak's resistance to the British rule in India assumed the character of an active challenge to the existing nature of things under the colonial rule and sought to motivate it to act in the manner desired by the Indians, rather than being run on the basis of selfish colonial interest or personal whims or fancies of the British. He assailed not only their inherently unjust rule but also denounced the validity of their claim of being reposed with the providential duty to guide India out of the "dark ages".

Tilak's protest continuously endeavoured to serve as a communication medium to the authorities in the society seeking to convey to them the grievances of the oppressed and exploited Indians. He asked the government to respect and identify itself with the sentiments and aspirations of the Indian public and to simultaneously work for the fructification of their hopes. To a government seeking to function on these lines, Tilak asserted that his protest did not seek to overthrow the existing government. Thus, even in his most extreme demand of *Swaraj* or self-rule he visualized it as a programme for political achievement within the parameters of British sovereignty.[33] Thus, in his speech at Kanpur Home Rule Conference on January 1st, 1917 he said, "Now one aspect of Home Rule is to encourage you to acquire the freedom which you enjoyed in these various departments of life and to that standard by the co-operation of, and under the sovereignty of, the British rule. This result is not to be achieved by any unlawful and unconstitutional means, but I am sure by a desire and interest to raise your status to achieve this goal by means of the sympathy of the British people and by remaining a permanent part of the Empire".[34] Similarly, in his address at Yeotmal in 1917 he said, "The *Swaraj* of today is within the Empire and not independent of it".[35]

In order to seek a favourable reaction from a government, Tilak recognized the need for the maximum exploitation of as many means available in a given situation. These, as is evident from his political activism, varied from conciliatory and cooperative ones to those of the confrontationist types. Largely preferring an initial recourse to the constitutionally available means for the redress of grievances, namely, petitioning, passing resolutions, submitting memorandums etc., Tilak advocated the notion of "responsive cooperation" which, while deciding to accept whatever was conceded by the government, sought to continue to agitate for more and more till the whole of the demands raised initially was conceded. Elaborating its meaning he said, "We are expected to cooperate; but first there must be something to cooperate over. Let the authorities declare in what way they are prepared to cooperate with us and we will assure them that if they cooperate we will surely reciprocate. Cooperation is not a one-way traffic; it is mutual, what I call responsive".[36]

However, Tilak's own experience of the darker side of the colonial rule in India influenced him to concede the possibility of an existing regime becoming so unsympathetic, unresponsive and oppressive that such means of modest protest like that of prayer, petitioning, etc., failed to realize the cherished demands.

Tilak recognized that any advocacy which emphasized upon all political protest to be carried on within the bounds of a Constitution, especially when neither a Constitution nor a spirit of constitutionalism existed, was an absurd proposition. He was also emphatic about the essential distinction between the legal and a constitutional provision of a nation. While the latter, he conceded, provided some valid criterion for the evaluation of a political agitation as being within the permissible or acceptable level; the laws, especially when these were unjust and its enactment or amendment was subject to the will, fancy or caprice of those in power, could not serve as the valid criterion for the evaluation of justness or rightness of a political agitation. Such a view influenced him to contend that whatever was legal was not necessarily righteous and just. In such conditions of a given political system, Tilak suggested that the values of justice, morality, historical tradition and progress were capable of serving as the basis for the decision to take recourse to protest.[37] Consequently, Tilak advocated the transcendence of protest from the constitutional type to the extra constitutional type. In his recognition, when an existing government became unsympathetic and unresponsive, then militancy, not mendicancy, would become the need of the hour and moderation would transcend into the realm of extremism. Thus, he said, "For the last twelve years we have been shouting hoarse, desiring that the Government should hear us. But our shouting has no more affected the Government that the sound of a gnat. Our rulers disbelieve our statements or profess to do so. Let us now try to force our grievances into their ears by strong constitutional means".[38] Likewise, in his Calcutta speech in 1901, he said, "I say that we should force them (British) to fulfil their promises, but we should not make the application in such a way that it would be rejected. In demanding and begging there is a great difference".[39] Consequently, Tilak advocated the supplementation of constitutional means with those of passive resistance within the fold of which he envisaged the recourse to boycott, *Swadeshi* and national education.

So far as the advocacy of boycott was concerned, Tilak defined it in very simple words and said, "Do not help the Government, rule for yourselves. This is called boycott",[40] He recognized it as an alternative means for those who had neither the power nor the inclinations to take up arms against the evil or unjust government. Thus he said, "If you have not the power of active resistance, have you not the power of self-denial and self-abstinence so as not to assist the foreign (unjust) Government to rule over You? This is boycott and this is what is meant when we say boycott is a political weapon".[41] Tilak also recognized its positive and negative character. As a political weapon in its negative aspect he recognized it as implying a refusal to assist the government in such activities like that of collecting revenue, keeping peace, fighting beyond the frontiers of the nation, administration of justice and payment of taxes. On the positive side Tilak recognized its capacity, along with its complementary *Swadeshi*, to bring about solidarity among the protesting subjects as well as to build self-reliance and thereby destroy the hypnotic spell which made them accept the omnipotence of the unjust rulers. These were also envisaged as a means for economic salvation and as a powerful lever for liberation. Similarly, through national education Tilak sought to awaken the consciousness of the subjected people about their exploited condition, make them aware of the important national and international events happening around them, infuse into them courage, moral strength, spirit of social service and patriotism, and make them self-reliant. Through these tools of passive resistance, Tilak sought to realize *Swaraj* or self-rule which, in his view, was concomitant with the values of freedom, equality and justice.

When the policy of the government assumed the form of total apathy accompanied by brutal repression of even the moderate course of protest, then, Tilak recognized, constitutional agitation and rebellion became synonymous.[42] Such statements and his applause of some of the revolutionary acts of individuals, both in India and such other places like Russia and Ireland, have influenced a few scholars to opine that Tilak personally believed in, and favoured, the cult of violence so far as the resistance to the unjust and oppressive government was concerned.[43] This controversy is further deepened on account of the differing statements on the issue by Tilak's contemporaries. Tilak's activism too has revealed virtually conflicting views on violence. Thus, Tilak denounced the politics of senseless murder and never in his public activism took personal recourse to it even under the worst provoking times; yet, through his writings on a few occasions, he lauded the courage and patriotic sentiments of those who took to a revolutionary course; he even defended their acts. Through his literary writings, as acknowledged by some revolutionaries, he provided the impetus and incitement to resort to violence for pure or ethical goals like that of *Swaraj*. It is also a fact that he had close associations with most of his contemporary revolutionaries and had an important role in the plan to manufacture guns in Nepal with the consent of the King there. Such activities of Tilak have only complicated the controversy. However, one thing is certain; he was never an advocate of absolute *Ahimsa* nor recognized its extensive implication as conceived by Gandhi so far as the act of resistance to the unjust government was concerned. Another noticeable fact is his comparatively lesser militancy and belief in the futility of violence to settle political issues towards the last four or five years of life, that is, especially after his release from the Mandalay jail.

As senior contemporaries of Gandhi, and having tremendous popularity, both Gokhale and Tilak bequeathed to Gandhi their views on the nature and method of protesting the colonial regime. However, given the limitations of their protest, and his own convictions and views, Gandhi was influenced to borrow with a critical spirit from these and continuously improvise them to make the protest against the colonial regime more effective. In the process, many of the interpretations and improvisations that he made assumed radical implications. Gandhi did not fail to recognize the creative aspects of Gokhale's and Tilak's protest. Thus, *Satyagrahi* is characterized by a few indices of continuum of the spirit, temper and values which Gokhale and Tilak emphasized in their protest against the British Government.

Like Gokhale, Gandhi too believed in the "spiritualization of politics" and recognized the responsibility of political governance as a moral duty, which in turn implied that a government should not only function for the fulfilment of the cherished aspirations of its subject citizens but also conform to certain principles while discharging its appointed functions. While recognizing the need for the citizens to protest a government that flouted these principles, Gokhale was emphatic about the purity and "moderatism" or "constitutionalism" of the means that were adopted. Gandhi's theory of protest adopted Gokhale's advocacy as an indispensable part of the initial phase of protest against any unjust authority. However, to transcend any impasse that might persist despite the exhaustion of all available constitutional means of protest on account of the regime's reluctance to renounce its nefarious goals, Gandhi advocated the recourse to self-suffering, self-education and such forms of *Satyagrahi* like non-cooperation and civil-disobedience to realize the envisaged goals.

The voluntary self-suffering, non-violent and ethical aspect of such forms of *Satyagrahi* on which Gandhi was very emphatic, distinguished Gandhi's protest from that of Tilak's advocacy of an inevitable extra-constitutional protest in the colonial setting of the British rule. Gandhi, like Tilak, admired and preferred violence to cowardice, and dearly cherished the goal of *swaraj* for the Indians; but his recognition of the need to adopt nonviolence as a faith in preference to its adoption as a policy of cowardice influenced him not to laureate, like Tilak, the revolutionaries for their recourse to violence and also to denounce the justification of an unethical means to realize a noble end. The means being recognized by Gandhi as the end in the process of making, he claimed that pure means alone could ensure the purity of ends. He also recognized violence to be contradictory to truth and the concomitant values and, therefore, recourse to it as being incapable of ensuring the purity of the ends. It being so, Gandhi did not support or acquiesce in the recourse to violence while protesting an unjust or evil state.

Thus, Gandhi's theory of protest stands distinctly apart on

account of its predominantly moral, altruistic and non-violent emphases— some quintessential values about the inevitability and inviolability of which Gandhi was thoroughly convinced. It also emphasized on self-evaluation and consequently desired corrections. It also stressed upon self-purification and progressive self-realization so as to be able to create the desired changes in the heart of those manning authoritative positions in the government or state. Gandhi was an experimenter of truth and he applied rigour while borrowing the essence of moderate (like Gokhale) or militant (like Tilak) advocacy of protest so that these harmonize with the truth he understood from his phenomenological enterprise and historical juxtaposition. Gandhi's advocacy of the moral and ethical foundations on which abuse of authority may be protested and the manner in which this protest should be carried out is more comprehensive in its dealing when compared to Gokhale and Tilak. Today there are many individuals and non-violent movements in India and abroad who claim to be inspired by Gandhi or stake their claims to be Gandhian. His theory of protest provides a useful framework for evaluating the claims of these movements, viz., whether there are mere symbolic imitations of Gandhi and only a superficial commitment to the essential values emphasized by him. Having evaluated thus, we can decide the course of our support as part of reference public of these protest movements in contemporary society. For the protestors as such, the framework provides lessons on the grounds of justification of defiance of the state's dictates but also the appropriate manner in which the defiance should be carried out.

NOTES

1. Mathur, D.B., Gokhale: *A Political Biography: A Study of his Services and Political Ideas*, P.G. Manaktala & Sons Pvt. Ltd., Bombay, 1966, p. 388.
2. Stanely A. Wolpert, *Tilak and Gokhale: Revolution and Reform in the Making of Modern India*, Oxford University Press, Delhi, 1991, p. 299.
3. *Ibid.*, p. 197.
4. *Gokhale's Speech, The Work Before Us, in Speeches and Writings of Gopal Krishna Gokhale,* D.G. Karve & D.V. Ambekar (ed.), Vol. II (Political), Asia Publishing House, Bombay, 1966, p. 217.

5. *Gokhale's Speech, The Work Before Us, in Speeches and Writings of Gopal Krishna Gokhale,* D.G. Karve & D.V. Ambekar (ed.), Vol. II (Political), Asia Publishing House, Bombay, 1966, p. 217.
6. See Note 1, p. 395.
7. Gokhale's Speech, Students and Politics, in *Speeches and Writings of Gopal Krishna Gokhale*, D.G. Karve & D.V. Ambekar (ed.) Vol. III (Educational). Asia Publishing House, Bombay, 1967, pp. 196-97.
8. *Ibid*.
9. Note 1, p. 461.
10. For details see Gokhale's speech, Indianisation of Public Services, in *Gopal Krishna Gokhale (Political Thinkers of Modern India - 2)*, V. Grover (ed.), Deep & Deep Publications, New Delhi, 1991, p. 527.
11. Gokhale's speech, *The Reform Proposal*, Note 4, pp. 298-99.
12. Note 1, p. 219.
13. *Ibid*., p. 217.
14. As quoted by D.B. Mathur, Note 1, p. 394.
15. Note 1, p. 217.
16. See Note 1, pp. 217-18.
17. Note 2, p. 198.
18. Note 4, p. 218.
19. Note 1, p. 399.
20. Note 4, p. 218.
21. Note, 2, p. 201.
22. Deogirikar, T.R., *Builders of Modern India: Gopal Krishna Gokhale*, Publications Division, Ministry of Information and Broadcasting, Government of India, New Delhi, 1992, p. 5.
23. Gokhale's speech, *Our Political Situation*, Note 10, p. 571.
24. *Ibid*. p. 577.
25. Note 4, p. 218.
26. Murthy, V.V. Raman, *Non-violence in Politics: A Study of Gandhian Techniques and Thinking*, Frank Bros. & Co., Delhi, 1958.
27. Gokhale as quoted by D.B. Mathur, Note 1, p. 397.
28. Gokhale's speech, *Indians in The Transvaal*, Note 4, p. 414.
29. Kumar, Ravindra (ed.) *Selected Documents of Lokmanya Bal Gangadhar Tilak*, Anmol Publication, New Delhi (To be cited hereafter as *SDLT*), Vol. 3, 1992, p. 51.
30. For a detailed examination of this view see Shanta A. Sathe, "Tilak's Connotation of the Concept of Swaraj", in N.R. Inamdar (ed.) *Political Thought and Leadership of Lokmanya Tilak*, Concept Publishing Company, New Delhi, 1983, pp. 41-42.
31. Note 2, p. 297.
32. See Note 30, p. 36.

33. See V.P. Varma, *The Life and Philosophy of Lokmanya Tilak,* Lakshmi Narain Agarwal.Educational Publishers, Agra, 1979, p. 446.
34. *SDLT,* Vol. 3, p. 43.
35. *Ibid.*, p. 55.
36. Jog, N.G., *Builders of Modern India: Lokmanya Bal Gangadhar Tilak,* Publications Division, Ministry of Information and Broadcasting, Government of India, New Delhi, 1990, p. 171.
37. For details see Note 30, p. 40.
38. Note 36, p. 55.
39. *SDLT*, Vol. 1, p. 15.
40. *Ibid.*
41. Note 36, p. 101.
42. See *SDLT*, Vol. 1, p. 41.
43. For a detailed examination of the above view see V.P. Varma Note 5, pp. 446-50 and also T.V. Parvate, *Bal Gangadhar Tilak: A Narrative and Interpretative Review of his Life, Career and Contemporary Events,* Navjivan Publishing Company, Ahmedabad, 1958, pp. 491-502.

CHAPTER 12

Gandhian Concept of Women Empowerment

HIMANSHU BOURAI AND SHAKUNTALA

In Gandhian Philosophy stress is always laid on the individual as the starting point of social regeneration. To him the problem of the group is essentially the problem of the individual. The reason for this emphasis is that man is above all the soul, and the progress of society depends on the soul-force of the average individual. Unlike Marxists and Fascists who work towards the inner, Gandhi starts from the soul within and works his way out to the environment. But though in his plan of social reconstruction he attaches great importance to the individual with whom lies the first step, he also makes the institutional approach. Thus *Satyagraha* works from the individual to the social order and also from the social order back to the individual.[1]

Gandhi did not portray the classless and stateless society. He wanted to establish a non-violent society. The base of Gandhian structure of the society can be explained in the points stated below:

- Love means mutual affirmation and union on the basis of equality.
- Sacrifice means assertion of one's mental and moral self (e.g., civil disobedience).
- Justice means that individual has an unconditional claim to certain inherent and inalienable rights.

- Courage is readiness to suffer which means utmost assertion of one's individuality against the power-structure holding the individual in bondage.
- Difference relates to individuality realized on the basis of equality.
- Violence and wars are relics of barbarism. Pacifism is a human value, characteristic of a higher culture based on human brotherhood.
- Alliance with, and living with nature to gain self-knowledge and a spontaneous and happy life are as an antidote to man's alienation.
- Socialism: Interdependence of the individual and the society for the sake of the individual's self-development and self-expression.
- Love is the mutual affirmation and union of equals which has no nexus with power or domination. Love embraces the least and the most powerless individual. (*Unto This Last*)[2]

The main ingredients of his social philosophy:

- Gandhi worked for a social order which would remove the tragic isolation and powerlessness of the individual in a society based on mass production and mass consumption, which reduces him to a mere cog in a vast machine—a role that induces pseudo-thinking, pseudo-feeling and pseudo-willing, because man is caught in the hypnotic spell of taboos, conventions and status symbols of a materialistic regime of mass consumption and mass production.
- Gandhi wanted a throwback to non-proletarian forms of creative labour rooted in nature. This implied a restructuring of society into decentralized communities with, as far as possible, a decentralized organization of production and consumption.
- Since the individual's greatest strength rests in the maximum integration of personality and "authenticity" of living, self-knowledge is of the essence of social reconstruction. This, Gandhi thought, is the only way to counter the evil of pseudo-self, which plagues modern civilization.

- Gandhi believed in the "spontaneous" and "authentic" activity of the total personality, so that the split between "reason" and "nature" is eliminated. "Back to nature" and alliance with nature have biological and psychological implications, all of which was not recognized by Gandhi. He believed in the repression of certain essential parts of the self, on the implications of which he was quite rigid and dogmatic.
- The basis of Gandhi's social philosophy is the doctrine that positive freedom as self-determination (*Swaraj*) means affirmation of the uniqueness of the individual. Men are, no doubt, born equal, but they are also different.
- The cherished security of the individual must not be sought from a higher, extraneous power. It must come from spontaneous activity. It should be the result of freedom devoid of its present day illusions. It should have scope for life's tragic quality. It should be rooted in man's new sense of relatedness to his community of fellowmen.
- Spontaneous activity that does not recognize an extraneous, higher power does not mean anarchy. Destructiveness and craving for power and submission are the result of the isolation and insignificance of individuals failing to achieve their "identity". If this vicious chain of causation, which has a strange fatality about it, is broken, the qualities of dignity, courage, decency and kindness will assert themselves. At this point, one discovers a very close link between Gandhi's social philosophy and the social philosophy of anarchism.
- Gandhi did not believe that material "abundance" can usher in a non-authoritarian society and eliminate man's "alienation". Gandhi had a philosophy of work, wealth and happiness in line with the religious and ethical philosophies of the east as well as the west.[3]

Gandhian philosophy has its holistic approach. It is difficult to understand Gandhian views in watertight compartments because the whole philosophy is based on truth, non-violence and *Satyagraha*. Truth and non-violence are the only weapons for Gandhi to achieve any reconstruction, whether it is social, political or economic. To strengthen the society Gandhi, in his famous book *Hind Swaraj* has mentioned 18 constructive programmes in which one is about the 'women'.

Gandhi was outstanding among Indian leaders in respecting women as equals, and he was to choose women as some of his most trusted political comrades. Gandhi identified with the suffragettes because, although equal with men, they were treated as unequal; and also because they were not demanding privileges but were asking for their rights, wrongly withheld. Writing for his paper, *Indian Opinion*, Gandhi observed:

> Today the country is laughing at them and they have only few people on their side. But undaunted these women work on, steadfast in their cause. They are found to succeed and gain the franchise for the simple reason that deeds are better than words... if women display such courage will the Transvaal Indians fail their duty and be afraid of jail? Or would they rather consider jail a palace and readily go there? When that time comes, India's bonds will snap of themselves.[4]

When Gandhi returned to South Africa, he continued to follow the suffragette-campaign reporting their work in his paper, in particular the "women's parliament" as they were called. These took the form of rallies at Caxton Hall, London, followed by a mass march on parliament. The women were harassed on the march by mounted police, but plotted on, and into the central lobby, where they were arrested and again went to jail instead of paying fines. During his 18 weeks in London he spent much of his time meeting suffragette leaders like Emmeline Pankhurst and attending their rallies.

The women's movement was attaining a high pitch of militancy. The breaking of windows in public buildings was now a frequent tactic. Sentenced to jail, the suffragettes went on hunger strike. Gandhi reported this new development in the *Indian Opinion*. At first he made no mention of the window breaking, of which he thoroughly disapproved, but when they invaded Mr. Asquith's holding residence he felt compelled to condemn what he saw as violence. In explanation, he suggested "some of these women have grown impatient". But he added "there is no room for impatience in *Satyagraha*... Indian *Satyagrahis* must realize from this that the women are not *Satyagrahis* but are resorting to physical force. For a certainty, they will suffer a setback now". He continued to praise their courage and dedication but he condemned their change of strategy, as he saw it. If women gained access to politics through violence, then their entry into the political arena would not serve to alter the old game of power politics. They would be just like those men who had repressed them.

There was a split over the militancy issue, and General French's sister, Mrs. Despard, organized the non-violent women's freedom league. They adopted the tactic of the "vigil" what would properly be called "peaceful picketing" outside parliament, during all the hours it was in session. Gandhi praised Mrs. Despard's "spiritual resistance," as he termed it. This incident is an example of Gandhian means to achieve any thing. In his philosophy there is no place for violence or any other means which are ethically wrong. These principles also apply to women who are struggling for their rights.

Mahatma Gandhi believed in the fundamental equality of man and woman in the sense that they both possess immortal souls and the same intellectual and spiritual potential. In an article written in 1918 on the theme of registration of women Gandhi said: "[w]oman is the companion of man gifted with equal mental capacities... and she has the same right of freedom and liberty as he".[6]

The present social inferiority of women was seen by Gandhi as the historical consequences of discrimination that in no way indicates lesser capacities. Gandhi opined, "[t]he soul in both is the same. Each is a complement of other... but somehow as other man has dominated women from ages past, and woman has developed an inferiority complex. She has believed in the truth of man's interested teaching that she is inferior to him. But the seers among men have recognized her equal status".[7] In *Hind Swaraj* Gandhi said:

> I have included service of women in the constructive programme, for though *Satyagraha* has automatically

brought India's women out from their darkness as nothing else could have in such an incredibly short space of time, Congress has not felt the call to see that women become equal partners in the fight of *Swaraj*. They have not realized that women must be the true helpmate of man in mission of service. Woman has been supressed under custom and law for which man was responsible and in shaping of which she had no hand. In a plan of life based on non-violence, woman has as much right to shape her own destiny as man has to shape his. But as every right in a non-violent society proceeds from the previous performance of a duty, it follows that rules of social conduct must be framed by mutual co-operation and consultation. They can never be imposed from outside. Men have not realized this truth in its fullness in their behaviour towards women. They have considered themselves to be lords and masters of women instead of considering them as their friends and co-workers. It is the privilege of Congressmen to give women of India a lifting hand. Women are in the position somewhat of the slave of old who did not know that he could or ever had to be free. And when freedom comes, for the moment he felt helpless. Women have been taught to regard themselves as slaves of men. It is up to Congressmen to see that they enable them to realise their full status and play their part as equal of men. This revolution is easy, if the mind is made up. Let Congressmen begin with their own homes. Wives should not be dolls and objects of indulgence, but should be treated as honoured comrades in common service. To this end those who have not received a liberal education should receive such instruction as is possible from their husbands. The same observation applies, with the necessary changes, to mothers and daughters. It is hardly necessary to point out that I have given one-sided picture of the helpless state of India's women. I am quite conscious of the fact that in the villages generally they hold on their own with their menfolk and in some respects even rule them. But to the impartial outsider the legal and customary status of women is bad enough throughout and demands radical alteration.[8]

Women, Gandhi believes, make even better *Satyagrahis* than men, because, being mothers, they have greater courage of the right type and immeasurably greater spirit of self-sacrifice. Indeed violence is against their nature. If non-violence is the law of our being, the future is with women. On the other hand if women are men, forsake the hearth and shoulder the rifle for its protection, "it is a reversion to barbarity and the beginning of the end". But the way of *Satyagraha* is only for the woman who acquires the requisite self-control and lives a simple and natural life. In order to be non-violent she has to avoid the modern craze of painting herself and looking extraordinary. If she tries to be Juliet to half a dozen Romeos, she cannot develop the non-violent spirit in her. To become non-violent she must forget that she ever was or can be the slave of man's lust and extend her love to the whole humanity.[9] If a woman thus revolutionizes her way of thinking and living, she will find that purity is the best strength. Gandhi believes that "The veriest ruffian becomes for the time being tame in the presence of resplendent purity". He also holds that:

> . . . [I]t is physically impossible to violate women against her will. The outrage takes place only when she gives way to fear or does not realize her moral strength. Her purity makes her conscious of her strength. If perchance she finds herself in danger, she should resist the lust of the assailant even to the extent of immolating herself. Even if gagged or bound, the resolute would give her the strength to die. Similarly, the *Satyagrahi* relation or friend of such a woman should stand between the assailant and his intended victim. He should then either dissuade the assailant from his wicked purpose or face death.[10]

Even if a woman is attacked by a group of assailants, a part of the group trying to carry away the woman and the other isolating and beating her brother or relation, the plan of non-violent defence will remain the same. Non-violent self-defence consists in being prepared to die bravely and with honour. The *Satyagrahi* woman would protect herself without caring or waiting for aid from her brother or sister and face death. Surrender has no room in Gandhi's plan of life. A woman should take her own life rather than surrender.

But behind Gandhi's approval of suicide under such circumstances is the belief that one whose mind is prepared even after suicide will have requisite courage for such mental resistance and purity that her assailant will be disarmed. If the choice is between taking one's own life and that of the assailant Gandhiji would prefer suicide.[11]

This method of defence by soul-force is far superior to armed resistance. It will, in all probability, exhaust the assailant's passion and awaken his soul. It will very likely steel the heart of others to put on equally brave defence. Besides, death in non-violent defence will not make the position even worse as defeat in armed resistance will do. Defeat or death in armed resistance, instead of stilling the fury or violence, feeds it by counter-violence. Even if the woman and her defender die in the effort, it will be a glorious death, for they will have done their duty.[12]

Non-violence rules out suppression of women also. "In a plan of life based on non-violence, woman has as much right to shape her own destiny as man has to shape his." He wants the customary and legal status of women to be changed so that they are placed on a footing of equality with and become true helpmates of men in the mission of service. Independence would be incomplete without the co-operation of women.[13] While advocating equal satus for women, Gandhi went on to say:

> Nevertheless there is no doubt that at some point there is bifurcation. While both are fundamentally one, it is also equally true in the form there is a vital difference between the two. Hence, the vocation of the two must also be different. The duty of motherhood which the vast majority of women will always undertake requires qualities which men need not possess. She is passive, he is active. He is the breadwinner; she is the keeper and distributor of the bread. She is the care-taker in every sense of the term. The art of bringing up the infants of the race is her special prerogative. Without her care, the race must become extinct.[14]

Gandhi also said: "The man should look to the maintenance of the women to household management; the two thus supplementing and complementing each other's labour".[15] Although Gandhi did not advocate that women in general should work outside the home to earn a livelihood, he did support a larger role for women in public life. He supported female suffrage in 1921, but in 1930, he at first expressed doubts about permitting women to participate in front line activities in the second civil disobedience or *Satyagraha* campaign.[16] However, later, he changed his position, welcomed women and hailed their courageous role in the Salt March that commenced the same campaign.

This favourable experience was crucial to the development of his theory that women have a special contribution to make to *Satyagraha*. Between 1920 and 1940, Gandhi gradually came to advocate a greatly expanded role for women in public affairs. He said: "I would love to find that my future army contained a vast preponderance of women over men. If the fight came, should then face it with greater confidence than if men predominated. I would dread the latter's violence. Women would be my guarantee against such an outbreak".[17]

According to Gandhi, women have a special contribution to make to humanity as the embodiment of *Ahimsa* which would be lost by imitating man's ways. He said, "[s]he can run the race but she will not rise to the heights she is capable of by mimicking man".[18] Gandhi retorted that all that is written in the *Smrities* is not divine, there are false interpolations, and, in any case, scriptural injunctions which are obviously in conflict with true morality should not be followed.[19]

Gandhi insisted that the ultimate arbiter of right and wrong is the conscience of the individual truth seeker rather than any written authority. Gandhi believed that women are individuals who should have the liberty to make their own moral choices, and bear responsibility for them. Although the Hindu scriptures extol the role of the submissive wife who follows her lord meekly in all things, Gandhi was of the opinion that it is no part of woman's duty 'to placate a sinful husband'. In an article Gandhi pointed out: "The wife has a perfect right to take her own course and meekly brave the consequences when she knows herself to be in the right and her resistance is for a noble purpose". He went on to say: "Hinduism leaves the individual absolutely free to do what he or she likes for the sake of self-realization for which and which alone he or she is born".[20]

Even in the context of marriage, Gandhi was of the opinion that women should guard against serving as mere tools of sexual enjoyment for their men.[21] He urged women to refuse to play along by dressing to please men, which could only confirm their subordinate status in the world. In an address to women in Ceylon, requesting them to donate their ornaments to social services, Gandhi said: "What is it that makes woman deck herself more than man? I tell you, if you want to play your part in the world's affairs you must refuse to deck yourself for pleasing man. If I was born woman I would rise in rebellion against any pretension on the part of man that woman is born to be his plaything".[22]

Gandhi initiated his first *Satyagraha* movement on Indian soil in 1917, the same year that an all India women's delegation presented the demand for female suffrage to Lord Montague. The deputation to Lord Montague marked the beginning of a new era of national organization and active lobbying by the women's movement in India. During the next twenty years, Gandhi's stand on issues affecting women was very similar to that of leading women's organizations, such as the Women's Indian Association founded in 1918, and the All India Women's Conference founded in 1926. Gandhi shared the concern of women reformers for the abolition of *purdah*, child marriage, enforced widowhood, and discriminatory laws of inheritance. He also strongly supported their demands for improved educational facilities for women. The only major difference of opinion was on the question of birth control. Gandhi denounced *purdah* as a barbarous custom which does 'incalculable harm to the country'. He further pointed out that by interfering with the "free growth of womanhood of India we are interfering with the growth of free and independent-spirited men". He rejected the argument that *purdah* protects the virtue of women in the following words:

> "Chastity is not a hot-house growth. It cannot be superimposed. It cannot be protected by the surrounding wall of *purdah*. It must grow from within and to be worth anything it must be capable of witches tending every unsought temptation... men, to be men, must be able to

> trust their womenfolk, even as the latter are compelled to trust them."[23]

Child marriage, for Gandhi, was an immoral and inhuman act. Gandhi was not only opposed to the custom of child marriage, but he also believed that no young person, of whatever age, should be coerced into marriage against his or her will. He urged young people to take a firm stand in the matters of conscience, even if it meant going against the wishes of their parents that they should marry.[24] Moreover, Gandhi was of the opinion that all girls may not wish to marry, and their right to a calling outside of marriage should be respected by their parents and society. In a speech to college women, Gandhi remarked:

> "Every girl, every Indian girl is not born to marry. I can show many girls who are dedicating themselves to service, instead of serving one man."[25]

Gandhi referred to the prohibition of remarriage for child widows as a senseless and cruel custom which should be abolished forthwith. According to Gandhi, widowhood, imposed by custom, "...is an unbearable yoke, and defiles the home by secret vice and degrades religion".[26] In 1935, Gandhi said, "I have repeatedly said that every widow has as much right to remarry as every widower. Voluntary widowhood is a priceless boon in Hinduism; enforced widowhood is a curse".[27]

Gandhi was sensitive to the arguments of that favouring contraception that it would alleviate the suffering of the poor, the arguments against the use of artificial means of birth control weighed more heavily with him. After talks with Margaret Sanger in 1936, Gandhi expressed admiration for her sincerity, but he reiterated his belief that self-control is the only legitimate means of birth control.[28] According to Gandhi:

> Birth control by contraceptives no doubt, regulates, to a certain extent, the number of newcomers, and enables persons of moderate means to keep the world from the door. But the moral harm it does to the individual and society is

> incalculable. For one thing, the outlook upon life of those who satisfy the sexual appetite for the sake of it is wholly changed; marriage ceases to be a sacrament for them.[29]

Gandhi was of the opinion that women in general have more self-control than men and, in particular, they have more control over sexual desire.[30]

It is also noteworthy that Gandhi was an ardent supporter of compulsory education for girls as well as boys. In his Basic National Education Scheme elaborated in 1937, Gandhi proposed free and compulsory education for children of both sexes from ages 7 to 14.[31]

According to Gandhi, co-education was generally desirable, and he agreed with women educators that it should be universal in the preadolescent years. According to Gandhi, as far as possible, boys and girls should be educated together up to the age of sixteen, and should be given the option to decide whether they prefer to study together or in separate institutions in later years.[32]

Although Gandhi said little on the problem of independent incomes for women, he very definitely advocated fundamental changes in Hindu laws of inheritance to give men and women equal property rights. In a discussion of inheritance-laws, Gandhi opined that women "should labour under no legal disabilities not suffered by man... I should treat the daughters and sons on a footing of perfect equality".[33] Gandhi was a warm supporter of the demands of the organized women's movement in India, but he felt strongly that women should eventually define their own goals and take the lead in solving their problems. Gandhi's writings and speeches suggest that he visualized women's struggle to surmount the barriers limiting the full development of their human potential from two perspectives. On the one hand, he was of the opinion that female weakness is only superficial; if women would but draw upon their inner reserves of strength, no obstacle could block their progress. At the same time, Gandhi recognized that a programme of rights, such as physical mobility and access to learning, was necessary to stimulate them the desire for progress.[34]

In a discussion of unequal inheritance-laws, Gandhi pointed out the relationship between the desire to preserve property and discrimination against women in these words:

> But to began remove inequalities will be a mere palliative. The root of the evil lies much deeper than most people realize. It lies in man's greed of power and fame, and deeper still in mutual lust. Man has always desired power. Ownership of property gives this power. Man hankers also after posthumous fame based on power. This cannot be had, if property is progressively cut up in pieces, as it must be if all the posterity became equal co-sharers. Most women are married and they are co-sharers in spite of the law being against them, in their husbands' power and privileges. They delight in being ladies this and what not simply for the fact of being wives of particular lords. Though, therefore, they may vote for radical reform in academic discussions over inequality, when it comes to acting up to their vote they will be found to be unwilling to part with their privileges.[35]

Gandhi's views about equality and individuality are very clear. Gandhi has given his views on all aspects of life but he was not rigid about his opinion and said, "There is no such thing as Gandhism and I do not want to leave any sect after me. I do not claim to have originated any new principle or doctrine. I have simply tried, in my own way, to apply the eternal truths to our daily life and problems. There is, therefore, no question of my leaving any code like the code of Manu".[36]

In nutshell we can say that the ultimate decision-maker is an individual and, in that way, women also are individuals. They should take their decisions as an independent unit of the society with purity of heart and inner conscience which is the base of self-realization or the force of soul.

NOTES

1. Dhawan, G., *The Political Philosophy of Mahatma Gandhi*. New Delhi, p. 6.
2. Ganguli, B.N., *Gandhi' Social Philosophy*. New Delhi, pp. 8-9.
3. *Ibid*., pp. 12-13.
4. Patil, V.T. (ed.), *New Dimensions and Perspectives in Gandhism*, pp. 96-97.
5. *Ibid*., p. 98.

6. Gandhi, M.K., *Women and Social Justice*. Ahmedabad, 1942, p. 3.
7. *Harijan*, February 24, 1940.
8. Anthony, J. Parel, *Gandhi: Hind Swaraj and Other Writings*. Cambridge University Press, pp. 175-76.
9. Dhawan, G., *The Political Philosophy of Mahatma Gandhi*. New Delhi, p. 157.
10. *Ibid.*, pp. 157-58.
11. *Ibid.*
12. *Ibid.*, pp. 158-59.
13. *Ibid.*, p. 205.
14. *Harijan*, February 24, 1940.
15. *Harijan*, October 12, 1934.
16. *Young India*, July 21, 1921.
17. *Harijan*, December 2, 1939.
18. *Harijan*, February 24, 1940.
19. *Harijan*, November 28, 1936.
20. *Young India*, October 3, 1929.
21. Patil, V.T. (ed.), *New Dimensions and Perspectives in Gandhism*, p. 391.
22. *Young India*, December 8, 1927.
23. *Young India*, February 3, 1927.
24. *Young India*, April 11, 1929.
25. "Speech given to girl students", November 27, 1927.
26. *Young India*, August 5, 1926.
27. *Harijan*, June 22, 1935.
28. Harijan, March 14, 1936.
29. *Harijan*, March 21, 1936.
30. *Harijan*, May 2, 1936.
31. Patil, V.T. (ed.), *New Dimensions and Perspectives in Gandhism*, p. 399.
32. *Ibid.*, p. 402.
33. *Young India*, October 14, 1929.
34. Patil, V.T. (ed.), *New Dimensions and Perspectives in Gandhism*, p. 404.
35. *Young India*, October 17, 1929.
36. Tendulkar, D.G., *Mahatma*. Vol. 4. New Delhi: Publications Division, Ministry of Information and Broadcasting, Government of India, 1991.

CHAPTER 13

Gandhian Perspective of Satyagraha and Democracy

ASHUTOSH PANDEY

> My notion of Democracy is that under it the weakest should have the same opportunity as the strongest. That can never happen except through non-violence. No country in the world today shows any but the patronizing regard for the weak.
>
> —*Harijan*: May 18, 1940

This study is very significant and interesting, as Gandhi does not make any distinction between morality and politics and ethics and economics. He does not want only to raise the standard of democracy but the quality of democracy and the quality of living in such a system. In the light of these issues, Gandhian alternatives have been studied, discussed, examined and analyzed keeping in view the contemporary problems in Indian democracy.

Introduction

The idea of *Satyagraha* is the most important contribution of Mahatma Gandhi to political thought. The meaning of *Satyagraha* is holding on to truth, hence, truth force. Gandhiji also calls it the soul force. Gandhi was a democrat. Writing in the *Harijan*, he said that true democracy must be the rule of the people in its real sense.[1] The transfer of power from the Britishers was not the end but the means for improving the condition of all men and women. In his address to All India Congress Committee on August 8, 1942, he said, "the Congress does not believe in the domination of any group or any community. It believes in democracy which includes in its orbit Muslims, Hindus, and Christians—everyone of the communities inhabiting this vast country".[2] Democracy meant complete decentralization of political powers. It must begin from the bottom and not from above; this is why Gandhi laid emphasis on the Panchayati Raj. Such a democracy is possible only through non-violence. Democracy sustained by violence cannot protect the weak. "My notion of democracy", he said, "is that under it the weakest should have the same opportunity".[3] Democracy must provide social justice to all.

Gandhian Perspective of *Satyagraha*

Satyagraha is compatible with democratic political process because it is closely analogous to other methods generally considered the essence of democracy. For example, written and verbal communication with the public is an attempt to sway the majority to a particular view.[4] The concept of *Satyagraha* or insistence on truth has a very comprehensive meaning. To Gandhi truth is the ultimate reality. "It is his conception of truth that is central to his life and work."[5] He considered *Satyagraha* to be the best weapon for the evolutionary process of social change. *Satyagraha* is the natural outcome of his love for truth. It is necessary for the *Satyagrahi* to make all endeavours for the realization of truth through peaceful means. "If truth is the ultimate reality then it is imperative for a votary of it to safeguard the criteria and foundation of truth. A votary of God, who is the highest Truth and highest Reality, must be utterly selfless and gentle."[6] Gandhi said that *Satyagraha* was the inherent birthright of a person and it implied the exercise of the purest soul-force against injustice, oppression and exploitation, never according to Gandhi, *Satyagraha* for the sake of truth and justice, to be given up. But *Satyagraha*, although based on moral resistance to unjustified authority is also never to become a formula of social and political disintegration. A *Satyagrahi* must have first rendered intelligent, spontaneous and willing obedience to the laws of states.[7] He thought that a lover of truth must devote his life to experience truth and be prepared to face any kind of suffering. Resistance to evil must be done with personal suffering to awaken the conscience of the evil-doer. The *Satyagrahi* appeals to the soul of the evil doer. "The efficacy of *satyagrahi* depends upon the tenacity to resist evil which, while it abjures force, develops in the *satyagrahi* the faculty to face all risks cheerfully."[8] To Gandhi, certainly, the *Satyagrahi* obeys the laws of the state not because of the fear of penal sanctions but because he regards them as promoting the common good. Gandhi himself claimed people have been, by nature, law-abiding and stated that the capacity for civil resistance came from the discipline undergone in process of obeying the civil and moral laws of the state, "Democracy comes naturally to him who is habituated normally to yield willing obedience to all laws, human or divine. I claim to be a democrat both by instinct and training. Let those who are ambitious to serve democracy, qualify themselves by satisfying first this acid test of democracy."[9] But Gandhi was also believer in the categorical superiority of loyalty to the commands of conscience to man-made law. The dictates and commands of any government, if they conflicted with the sense of higher loyalty to conscience, had to be resisted. Thus, according to political teachings of Gandhi, *Satyagraha* is a perpetual law against anything repugnant to the soul. In his conception of democracy, he rejected the adoption of any form of government imported from either the western countries or the eastern countries as he found fault in them. He thought that if *Swaraj* was to be desired it should be built upon *Swadeshi*. Analyzing the models of government of the west and the east he said, "The motive lying behind the western type and the eastern type is the same—the greater welfare of the whole society and the abolition of the hideous inequalities resulting in the existing millions of have-nots and a handful of haves. I believe that this end can be achieved when non-violence is accepted by the best minds of the world as the basis on which a just social order is to be constructed".[10] Similarly, Gandhi also maintained that *Swaraj* was not an alien concept and it could be achieved by self-reliance. He felt that *Swaraj* could be attained by the people of India if they realized and accepted the importance of all things what were native to India. Thus he said, "We do not realize that *Swaraj* is almost wholly attainable through *swadeshi*. If we have no regard for our respective vernaculars, if we dislike our clothes, if our dress repels us, if we are ashamed to wear the sacred *shikha*, if our food is distasteful to us, our climate is not good enough, our people uncouth and unfit for company, our civilization faulty and the foreign attractive, in short, if everything native is bad and everything foreign is pleasing to us, I should not know what *Swaraj* can mean for us... It seems to me that before we can appreciate *Swaraj* we should have not only love but passion for *Swadeshi*".[11] Gandhi called his model of government "*Ram-Rajya*" after the political order which was in operation in ancient India and which used to ensure the betterment of all by providing them an ideal living condition. To Gandhi, it signified a social relationship that allowed *Poorna Swaraj* for each.[12] Gandhi considered that no government considered as good unless it safeguarded the interest of the poorest of the poor. According to him the government had to protect the interest of all and had to act as the servant of the people and not behave as their master. "Essentially, power had to go along with the purpose of service. The power elite had to live at the level of the masses to justify and legitimize the holding of power."[13] In Gandhian political society the individual, the minority and the rural areas, are given due importance and all are considered the integral parts of it. He thinks that if any part is overlooked then the whole suffers and there cannot be true *Swaraj* in such a society. Gandhi believed in the betterment of all and their involvement in political sphere. He prescribed for a social system in which all will be emancipated. To him, all the people must be uplifted to enjoy good life in the society. He propagated for a social order promoting the good of all. He called this concept '*Sarvodaya*'. The goal of Gandhi's *Sarvodaya* was the overall transformation of the entire race of mankind at all levels of human existence. It represents ideal social order based on self-control, self-suffering, love, renunciation and social justice.

T.K.N. Unnithan gave a short summary of the *Sarvodaya* philosophy which was founded by Mahatma Gandhi. He says, "In a world of increasing complexity he preached simplicity, in a world of increasing confusion he pointed to the simple qualities of character in which the solution might lie; in a world devoted to material goals he clearly showed their limitations, in a period of urbanization, he showed that decentralization meets other important needs that material gains can offer".[14] The Gandhian model of government was not an elite model where only selected few ruled the people unchecked by any moral precepts or any legal rules. Rather Gandhi emphasized that all are creations of God and all have equal importance and equal share in all things created by God. He did not overlook the downtrodden of society whom he called *Harijans*. Gandhi said, "None can be born untouchable, as all are sparks of one and the same fire. It is wrong to treat certain human beings as untouchable from birth".[15] He was of the opinion that "all the objects of the world are pleaded by God, there is none that is high and none that is low, all are absolutely equal, equal because all are the Creatures of that Creator".[16] Hence, to Gandhi democracy is not merely a form of government. It is also a gospel of the social system. It is a principle of self-reliance, equality, freedom, emancipation of all, and love for one's own things. It is a system where everybody performs his duty and gets his due. It is a social order where pure means are adopted to achieve good ending, i.e., welfare for all.

Gandhian Perspective of Democracy

Democracy in India, Gandhi believed, was something which served the welfare of all, would be marked by Minimum State intervention in social life. He criticized parliamentary democracy. However, this system was certainly an advance over monarchy and oligarchy. He remarked, "I do not believe in any government but parliamentary government is better than capricious rule".[17] So, he accepted parliamentary *Swaraj* as an immediate goal and a point in the struggle for *Swaraj*. In 1924, he said, "Parliament is indeed barren. I do not imagine that its nature can change India I live, however, in the hope that our Parliament will only remain barren and not give birth to wicked son. I cannot abandon practical considerations. The ideal is one only, namely *Ramrajya*... I am suggesting many ways to ensure that the voice of parliament is really the voice of the people, and not the hired voters. With the end in view I am searching for a device which will enable us to listen to the voice of the entire people. All systems are bound to be defective. We are looking for a system, which will yield maximum benefit of India".[18] Although in the *Hind Swaraj*, Gandhi was bitterly hostile to the patterns of functioning of the British Parliament, he prescribed for India a parliamentary government based on Universal Suffrage. His conception of *Swaraj* inculcated a government based on the consent of the people. This consent of the people was to be ascertained by the largest number of adult population. He wrote: "By *Swaraj*, I mean the government of India by the consent of the people as ascertained by the vote of the largest number of the adult population, male or female, native born of domiciled who have contributed by manual labour to the service of the state and who have taken the trouble of having their names registered as voters".[19] He felt that for the success of a democratic government it was essential that the representatives should be given only general instructions and should not be subjected to detailed dependence on the electorate. It would not be possible for the legislature to operate if the representatives were compelled to consult the constituencies on all issues. It can be said that he upheld the 'mandate' and not the 'delegate' theory for the representative. Gandhi wanted India to evolve "*True Democracy*" and laid down six conditions for its realization in India:

1. *Satyagraha* expressed through *Charkha*;
2. Growth of Village Industries;
3. Primary education through Handicrafts;
4. Removal of Untouchability;
5. Communal Harmony; and
6. Non-violent Organization of Labour.

Gandhi also advised the Indians not to copy the Western model. He remarked that one nation suited in one condition was not necessarily good enough of another differently suited. Accordingly, he suggested evolving a decentralized people's democracy on non-violent lines at the lower levels. Gandhi declared: "The end to be sought is human happiness combined with full mental and moral growth. I use the adjective moral as synonymous with spiritual. This end can be achieved under decentralization. Centralization as a system is inconsistent with a non-violent structure of society".[20] His opposition to centralization was based on a fundamental ground. He held: "Centralization cannot be sustained and defended without adequate force".[21] According to him centralization leads to the concentration of power in the hands of a few and that in its turn, robs the people of its supreme authority in the matter of determination of public issues. Not only that, in an over-centralized state man loses his human dignity and becomes a cog in the wheel of the vast and impersonal state machines. Man becomes depersonalized. That is why he stood for thorough decentralization of political power and economic production. He wanted to give a new direction to politics and for that he went to the roots. According to Gandhi, India cannot be imagined without its villages. To think of a developed India with its undeveloped villages is a ridiculous idea for him. Therefore, he championed the cause of an enriched village life. He propagated for making the village's self-sufficient and self-reliant. He maintained, "Every village of India will almost be a self-supporting, self-contained unit".[22] He stood for the improvement of villages and for the success of democracy; democracy should originate from the grassroots level. He believed that power to be effective and genuine from the standpoint of the masses, must lie with the people which could only be possible in small communities of villages. "Society based on non-violence can only consist of groups settled in villages in which Voluntary Cooperation is the condition of dignified and peaceful existence."[23] He projected the state as the servant of the people; it had the duty to carry out the will of the people. He was for the prevention of exploitation of any kind of the rural people. "Exploiting of villages is itself organized violence. If we want *Swaraj* to be built on non-violence, we shall have to give villages their proper place."[24] Hence, he cried for village *Swaraj*, Panchayati Raj or democracy from below. According to him, "True democracy cannot be worked by twenty men sitting at the centre. It has to be worked from below by the people of every village".[25]

He advocated that in democracy the independence must begin at the bottom. It means that at grassroots level people must be independent in making their policies and implementing them without any rigid and strict control from the above. Thus, every village, to him, could become a republic having the institution of Panchayat with sufficient authority and powers. It means every village had to be self-sustained and capable of managing its own affairs and even to the extent of defending itself against the whole world. Ultimately, it would be the individual who was to be the unit. He clarified that it did not exclude dependence on and willing help and cooperation from the neighbours or from the world too. It would be free and voluntary play of mutual forces.[26]

Thus, he wanted India to evolve a decentralized structure of power based on the effective reconstruction of self-reliant and self-sufficient villages. The village organization was to be based on the principle of constructive social and economic efforts, sacrifice and the abnegation of illegitimate self-interest. Similarly, he had also pointed out that the political structure of Independent India was to be not a pyramid with the apex sustained by the bottom. In the Panchayati Raj the toiling labourer and the rich capitalist had to be treated as equal. There was to be solidarist spirit of mutual independence and harmonious cooperation. The communal tensions which were spreading to the rural areas from the towns had to be eliminated. The self-sustained villages were to manage their own affairs. They were not to rely on the help of a central army for defence. They should morally develop themselves to the extent even of having the strength of perishing the attempt of self-defence.[27] He dreamed of village *Swaraj* where every village would have its own government in the form of Panchayat which would be independent in all spheres of administration. "The government of the village will be conducted by a Panchayat of five persons annually elected by the adult villagers, male and female, possessing minimum prescribed qualifications. These will have all the authority and jurisdiction required. Since, there will be no system of punishment in the accepted sense, this Panchayat will be the legislature, judiciary and executive combined to operate for its year of office."[28] In essence, the Panchayat of every village republic was a key unit for decentralization of legislative, executive and judicial powers. Every village with its characteristics of self-rule and self-sufficiency was supposed to represent the values of a true democracy, wherein authority and power were shared and exercised by different functionaries. The individual would have complete freedom to shape his destiny according to his wishes. His thoughts and actions would be pervaded by the spirit of non-violence in an atmosphere of genuine freedom. The spirit of self-sacrifice and patriotism would be the mainspring of all constructive actions in such a village republic. Gandhi argued that in such a setting it was possible to secure "perfect democracy" based upon individual's freedom. The individual is the architect of his own government. The law of non-violence rules him and his government. For the law governing every village is that he will suffer death in defence of his and his village's honour.[29] The only way, according to Gandhi, to emancipate the nation from its age-long torture and frustration, was to make the villages of India self-sufficient and self-reliant through the decentralized structure of village republics. Thus alone could the villagers also develop their intellectual powers and could acquire the social-economic consciousness necessary to contemplate a non-violent society of the future. Thus, according to Gandhi, decentralization was a technique for revolutionizing the psychology of the people for building a more perfect society.[30]

This deep attachment to the concept of decentralization indicates the radical and fundamental nature of Gandhi's theory of democracy because he wants to begin the reform at the bottom. According to him, the common masses have to feel the thrill of participation in the exercise of power. Thus alone can the universal will of the people become a reality. Gandhi not only gave his ideas through speeches and writings but he was a man who developed a model of 'exemplary' life by making his own life—including its most intimate aspects—a museum of national learning. He converted large and already widely discussed dilemmas of Indian social structure into charismatic symbols: he labelled the vast masses of untouchables as *Harijans* (sons of God) and launched a powerful movement to ameliorate their oppression, which became a plank for the national movement. He championed the cause of women and spoke of their liberation almost in the style of feminism. He made the symbolism of Hindu-Muslim unity a general plank of social solidarity. He made the indigenous homespun cloth (*Khadi*) emblematic of all who would aspire to be nationalists, a symbolism that still continues to prevail among political cadres. He developed a comprehensive programme of constructive work in the villages, and among tribes and *dalits*. He rarefied traditional concepts of sacrifice and austere living into minimum qualifications for nationalist workers. He ordered the educated middle classes to go into villages and serve the people. He transformed the whole appeal and draw of individual prayer into a routine institution of the nation during which his solutions for problems of politics were highlighted and diffused. Gandhi turned the symbolism of a pacifist, saintly India to a militant organizational style, indeed the well-knit organizational drive of the Congress, with a programme of action and a powerful identity and discipline.

This enabled him to include in the Congress all streams of ideological thought and all important social interests. It gave rise to a high tolerance of ambiguity in the concerns of the national movement, allowed dissent to become part of the overall consensual style of the Congress, and imbued the Congress with great flexibility and freedom to manoeuvre. By providing an overriding symbolism—that had the sanction of tradition and had passed the test of functionality—he built bridges all over. Gandhi had the great gift of transforming dimensions of time (the bridging of several centuries) into concrete dimensions of space (bridging the gap between the city and the village) and penetrating both with an idiom of modernization that had indigenous meaning, simplicity of communication and great organizational as well as personal potency. He constantly reinterpreted traditional concepts of authority, social obligation and self-realization, and furnished them with meaning that proved functional in the development of national consensus and political identity. Above all, he wielded tremendous personal authority—the Congress High Command and the vast band of Gandhian Workers—by resolving tensions and cleavages in the government through definitive solutions and formulae that could not be effectively challenged even by other popular heroes of the movement. Gandhi made prominent a certain consensual style in Indian tradition by grafting and reinterpreting this aspect in the context of modern politics and giving it an ideological colour by invoking labels such as 'non-violent struggle' and 'peaceful disobedience' waged by a 'servant of the people' even when he was combating a powerful enemy. As for his own rank and file in the Congress, he emphasized the great virtue of discipline in the maintenance of political potency; he accommodated men of diverse capacities and intellectual background, and always valued the cohesion and discipline of the movement above any ideological or doctrinal considerations, or even considerations of personal pride. He even symbolized and made functional the Indians', tolerance of humiliation and deprivation, and turned these into programmatic plans of 'Civil Disobedience' and mass imprisonment at the hands of the colonial power. All this enabled him to build distinctive structure of political organization. It was the latter that ultimately succeeded in gaining power from the alien rules and provided the nation with a framework of political authority.

The dominant model of democracy today emphasizes competitive elections and interest group pluralism. Voters choose who will represent and govern them for a period of time, and if satisfied will return the incumbents, if dissatisfied will turn to alternative candidates. Between elections, organized groups are expected to represent the interest of these members before various government agencies to influence public policy.[31]

Gandhiji's departure from this model at the institutional level is obvious. He wanted a small setting with a relatively simple economy, while the pluralists have been concerned with the problems of representation in large, highly diversified societies.

Conclusion

Gandhiji's contribution to democratic theory is not that he offers specific institutional alternatives to representative democracy and pluralism, although he does that. Rather, his importance comes from offering alternative ways of thinking about politics in general and democracy in particular.

Gandhi attempted to reintroduce political culture and political psychology as vital elements in the theory and practice of democracy. A restructured society, where no one saw responsibilities and everyone attempted to pursue his own interest, would be no great improvement for Gandhi. Those who had been at the bottom would have additional resources to enter the political conflicts of the day. The formula of politics would not change, but new winners and losers would appear. Accordingly, Gandhi emphasized structuring a community of common purpose and individual responsibility to the community.

As western democracies move towards the prospect of slower growth and increasing scarcities, the model of interest group politics may lead to phenomenal cleavages. To meet these new challenges, the need for restraint, responsibility, and community becomes more important than in easier, carefree times, and Gandhiji's theory of democracy may help to understand and meet these challenges.

Gandhi himself believed that *Satyagraha* was not only an effective and heroic mode of emancipation of the people of a weak country, but also.....a beacon light....for Europe with all its discipline, science and organization. If Europe but realizes that, heroic as it undoubtedly is for a handful of people to offer armed resistance in the face of superior numbers, it is far more heroic to stand up against overwhelming numbers without any arms at all, it would save itself and blaze a trail for the world.[32]

NOTES

1. The *Harijan*, January 18, 1948.
2. Tendulkar, D.G., *Mahatma*, Vol. VI, p. 159, New Delhi, Publications Division, Government of India, 1962.
3. Gandhi, M.K., *Non-violence in Peace and War*, Vol. I, p. 269, Ahmedabad, N.P.H., 1948
4. Cohen, Carl, "Essence and Ethics of Civil Disobedience" in *The Nation*, March 16, 1964, No. 198, pp. 261-62.
5. Santhanam, K., "Basic Principles of Gandhism" in Ramchandran, G. and Mahadevan, T.K. (eds.), *Gandhi: His Relevance for Our Times* (New Delhi: Gandhi Peace Foundation, 1967), p. 310.
6. Verma, V.P., *Modern Indian Political Thought* (Agra: Laxmi Narayan Aggarwal Publishers, 1996) (Eleventh edition), p. 343.
7. Gandhi, M.K., "A Himalayan Miscalculation" in *Autobiography* (Ahmedabad: Navajivan Publishing House, 1927), p. 392.
8. Munshi, K.M., "The Spiritual Basis of Satyagraha" in Ramchandran G. and Mahadevan, T.K. (eds.), *Gandhi: His Relevance for Our Times, op cit.*, p. 121.
9. *Harijan*, 27-05-1939, Vol. VII, No. 16, p. 136.
10. Hingorani, A.T. (ed.), the *Village Reconstruction* (Bombay: Bhartiya Vidya Bhawan, 1966), p. 129.

11. Hingorani, A.T. (ed.), The *Village Reconstruction* (Bombay: Bhartiya Vidya Bhawan, 1966), p. 115.
12. Jha, M.N., *Modern Indian Political Thought*, *op cit*., p. 197.
13. Sethi, J.D., *Gandhi Today*, (Second Edition), New Delhi: Vikas Publishing House Pvt. Ltd., 1979, p. 42.
14. Unnithan, T.K.N., *Gandhi in Free India*, Groingen: Wolters, 1965, p. 9.
15. Gandhi, M.K., *From Yervada Mandir*, Ahmedabad: Navajivan Publishing House, 1945, p. 31.
16. *Harijan*, 30-01-1937, Vol. IV, No. 51, p. 408.
17. *Harijan*, 21-07-1940, Vol. VIII, No. 23, p. 211.
18. *CWMG*, Vol. XIV (October 1917-July 1918), *op cit*., March 1965, p. 444.
19. *Ibid*. Vol. XXV, (August 1924-January 1925), p. 34.
20. *Young India*, 29-01-1925, Vol. VII, No. 5, p. 40.
21. *Harijan*, 18-01-1942, Vol. IX, No. 1, p. 5. 180. *Ibid*., 30-12-1939, Vol. VII, No. 47, p. 391.
22. Hingorani, A.T. (ed.), *The Gospel of Swadeshi*, Bombay: Bhartiya Vidya Bhawan, 1967, p. 5.
23. *Harijan*, 30-12-1939, Vol. VII, No. 43, p. 391.
24. Hingorani, A.T. (ed.), *The Gospel of Swadeshi*, *op cit*., p. 125.
25. *Harijan*, 18-01-1948, Vol. XII, No. 51, p. 519.
26. *Ibid*., 28-07-1946, Vol. X, No. 25, p. 236.
27. *Ibid*.
28. *Ibid*., 26-07-1942, Vol. IX, No. 28, p. 238.
29. *Ibid*.
30. Verma, V. P., *The Political Philosophy of Mahatma Gandhi and Sarvodaya*, *op cit*., p. 213.
31. The thesis that democracies rest on competitive elections is presented by Joseph Schumpeter, Capitalism, Socialism and Democracy, New York: Harper, 1950, pp. 250-73. The classic position of the pluralist view is advanced by Robert Dahl in several books including *Who Governs*? New Haven: Yale University Press, 1961, and after the revolution, New Haven: Yale University Press, 1970.
32. Gandhi, *A Pilgrimage for Peace*, Ahmedabad: Navajivan Publishing House, 1950, p. 56. Emphasis added.

CHAPTER 14

Gandhian Perspective on Corruption

ANIL DUTTA MISHRA

Introduction

Corruption is a buzzword in contemporary India with a new scam unfolding every now and then. Corruption affects all, whether poor or rich, have or have nots and honest or dishonest. The difference is only of magnitude and position. In India there is a stark contradiction between theory and practice and between appearance and reality. In the same system we have number of honest bureaucrats and at the same time number of corrupt bureaucrats. Honest bureaucrats are everywhere but unfortunately society did not give them due respect and regard. Corruption breeds corruption because even in the family no one likes honest sons or daughters. They are called unsocial, unfit for society and not fit for this world. If this is the situation then how can we remove corruption from government and society is a million dollar question and Himalayan task. From Gandhian point of view we have to remove corruption from individual level to national level. It will not be possible by Central Vigilance Commission (CVC), Comptroller and Auditor General (CAG) and other agencies to remove corruption from India until and unless we are able to change the mindset of people. The individual who lives at the cost of the family—is corrupt, of the community—is very corrupt, and of society—is very very corrupt. In *Young India*, September 19, 1921

Gandhi rightly wrote: 'Character, not brains, will count in the crucial movement.' In contemporary India we need, in fact, a man of character and self-esteem in every walk of life. Mahatma Gandhi believed in the need for creating a social climate against corruption, which meant creation of an atmosphere in which the corrupt could not thrive.

Meaning and Typology

The word corrupt has been derived from Latin word *corruptus*, meaning to abuse or destroy or to break. Corruption, which is such a complicated social evil, may be defined in simple term as misuse of public power for private gain. Corruption comes under many different guises: bribery, misappropriations of public goods, nepotism (favouring family members for jobs and contracts), and influencing the formulation of laws or regulations for private gain are common examples of wrong doing or misconduct. As per Interpole, "Corruption is any course of action or failure to act by individuals or organizations, public or private, in violation of law or trust for profit or gain". The *Social Science Encyclopaedia*, defines corruption in detail as:

> "In its most general sense, corruption means the perversion or abandonment of a standard.... it is common to speak of the corruption of language or of moral corruption. More narrowly, corruption refers to the abandonment of expected standards of behaviour by those in authority for the sake of unsanctioned personal advantage... Political corruption can be defined as the misuse of public office or authority for unsanctioned private gain. Three points about the definition should be noted. First, not all forms of misconduct or abuse of office constitute corruption. An official or a government minister who is merely incompetent or who betrays government secrets to a foreign power for ideological reasons is not generally considered corrupt. Second, legislators and public officials in most countries are entitled to salaries and other allowances. Corruption occurs only when they receive additional *unsanctioned* benefits, such as bribes....Third, *electoral corruption* needs to be defined differently from other forms. Whereas, most political

corruption involves the abuse of public office, electoral corruption is the abuse of the process by which public office is won."

The late Prime Minister Smt. Indira Gandhi said that corruption is a misuse of power. In other words corruption means the destruction, ruining or the spoiling of a society or a nation. A corrupt society stops valuing integrity, virtue or moral principles. It changes for the worse. Such a society begins to decay and sets itself on the road to self-destruction. Corruption is an age old phenomenon. Selfishness and greed are the two main causes of corruption. The mighty Roman Empire disintegrated when its rulers became corrupt and selfish. Nations having a tyrannical powerful ruling elite that refuses to punish the corrupt within it, face the menace of corruption. A corrupt society is characterized by immorality and lack of fear and respect for the law. Recently regimes after regimes have collapsed due to corruption. One must learn lessons from Egypt and other countries of Middle East. Corruption is an act of irresponsible attitude towards the people. In the world mostly corruption descends from higher level to lower, that is, from politicians to bureaucrats. This is going to exist in the world, till the people are so enlightened to become responsible and learn its ill effects to the whole society. By which the progress comes to a stand still or leads to economic and political disaster.

Political and bureaucratic corruption in post-Independent India is major concern for the survival of Democracy. High-level corruption and scams are now threatening to derail the country's credibility and its economic boom. A study conducted by *Transparency International* in India in 2005 found that more than 45 per cent of Indians had first-hand experience of paying bribes or influence peddling to get jobs done in public offices successfully. In 2010 India was ranked 87th out of 178 countries in Transparency International's Corruption Perceptions Index.

Corrupt activities are bid rigging, bribery in politics, business, or sport, cartel, collusion, an agreement between two or more persons, sometimes illegal and, therefore, secretive, to limit open competition by deceiving, misleading, or defrauding others of their legal rights, or to obtain an objective forbidden by law typically by defrauding or gaining an unfair advantage, cronyism, electrol fraud, embezzlement, influence peddling, nepotism, organized crime, patronage, price fixing, etc. We may add more and more. For better understanding we may classify corruption as under:

1. Political corruption, the abuse of public power, office, or resources by elected representative of government for personal gain.
2. Bureaucratic corruption is the abuse of power, office, or resources by government employees for personal gain.
3. Corporate corruption, corporate criminality and the abuse of power by corporation officials, either internally or externally.
4. Corruption (philosophical concept), often refers to spiritual or moral impurity, or deviation from an ideal.

Corruption in India is a consequence of the nexus between bureaucracy, politics and criminals. It is a consequence of everlasting greed of capitalist, corporate houses and less paid government officials and ignorance of poor and illiterate people. The causes of corruption are many and complex. Following are some of the causes of corruption. Firstly, emergence of political elite who believe in interest-oriented rather than nation-oriented programmes and policies. Secondly, artificial scarcity created by the people with malevolent intentions wrecks the fabric of the economy. Thirdly, corruption is caused as well as increased because of the change in the value system and ethical qualities of men who administer. The old ideals of morality, service and honesty are regarded as an anachronistic. Fourthly, tolerance of people towards corruption, complete lack of intense public outcry against corruption and the absence of strong public forum to oppose corruption allow corruption to reign over people. Fifthly, a vast size of population coupled with widespread illiteracy and the poor economic infrastructure lead to endemic corruption in public life. Sixthly, in a highly inflationary economy, low salaries of government officials compel them to resort to the road of corruption. Graduates from IIMs with no experience draw a far handsome salary than what government secretaries draw. Seventhly, complex laws and procedures alienate common people to ask for any help from government. Eighthly, election time is a time when corruption is at its peak level. Big industrialists fund politicians to meet high cost of election and ultimately to seek personal favour. Bribery to politicians buys influence, and bribery by politicians buys votes. In order to get elected, politicians bribe poor illiterate people, who are slogging for two times a meal.

Gandhian Perspective

Criminalization is a serious problem in contemporary Indian politics which is an offshoot of corruption. The *Vohra Report*, submitted by the former Indian Union Home Secretary, N.N. Vohra, in October 1993, studied the problem of the criminalisation of politics and of the nexus among criminals, politicians and bureaucrats in India. The report contained several observations made by official agencies on the criminal network which was virtually running a parallel government. It also discussed criminal gangs who enjoyed the patronage of politicians—of all political parties—and the protection of government functionaries. It revealed that political leaders had become the leaders of gangs. They were connected to the military. Over the years criminals had been elected to local bodies, State Assemblies, and even the Parliament.

Corruption has prevailed in all governments whether UPA or NDA. Corruption allows criminal activities such as money laundering, extortion and drug trafficking to thrive. Judicial corruption in India is attributable to factors such as "delays in the disposal of cases, shortage of judges and complex procedures". Justice delayed is justice denied.

As early as 1928, Mahatma Gandhi had written that corrupt practices would eventually be brought to the public knowledge and any attempt to cover them would meet with failure. Writing in *Young India* on 6 December, 1928, he prophetically stated, "Corruption will be out one day, however, much one may try to conceal it; and the public can, as it is its right and duty in every case of justifiable suspicion, call its servants to strict account, dismiss them, sue them in a law court, or appoint an arbitrator or inspector to scrutinize their conduct, as it likes".

Mahatma Gandhi on May 1939 said that "I would go to the length of giving the whole Congress a decent burial, rather than put up with the corruption that is rampant". This was the outburst of Mahatma Gandhi against rampant corruption in Congress ministries formed under 1935 Act in six States in the year 1937. The disciples of Gandhi ignored his concern over corruption even when he was alive. In post-Independence India, when they came to power used Gandhi cap but not his principle of pristine purity in public life. On 16th December, 1947, Gandhi spelt out that "it is the duty of all leading men, whatever their persuasion or party, to safeguard the dignity of India. That dignity can't be saved if misgovernment and corruption flourish. Misgovernment and corruption always go together. I have it from very trustworthy sources that corruption is increasing in our country. Is everyone then going to think only of himself, and not at all of India?...." Further on 31st December, 1947, Gandhi stated clearly that "self-government is not an end in itself, but only a means to good government. And true democracy is that which promotes the welfare of the people, the test of good government lies in the largest good of the people with minimum of controls. The test of autocracy, socialism, capitalism, etc., is also people's welfare or good government. In themselves, the various approaches are of no value. Any system of government can fail if people do not show scrupulous honesty and a feeling of brotherhood. There may be work, there may be men to do the work and also the tools with which to do it: yet in my view, any system which admits poverty and unemployment is not fit to survive even for a day..."

Mahatma Gandhi exhorted people to take proactive measures to expose bribery and sleaze and nip them in the bud. "Instead of suing one's calumniator in a law court for false allegations of corruption", he wrote, "the best and the only right course would be for the public to prevent actual corruption from taking place by maintaining a sleepless vigilance...", Mahatma Gandhi's prescription that people's watchfulness would be an antidote to corruption assumes critical significance for our time. The movement launched by Anna Hazare and others constitutes an important step to remain vigilant for the cause of a public life pulsating with values and ethics. The CAG, judiciary and other governmental department are doing good work as expected by founding fathers of Constitution.

It would be worth to note that a few days before his assassination on 30th January, 1948, Gandhi referred to the issue of corruption in a prayer meeting in Delhi. Gandhi said, "Corruption will go when the large number of persons given to the unworthy practice realize that the nation does not exist for them, but that they do for the nation. It requires a high code of morals, extreme vigilance on the part of those who are free from the corrupt practice and also have influence over corrupt servants. Indifference in such matters is criminal". What he said more than sixty four years back sounds so contemporary and meaningful for our generation. Corruption won't stop unless we choose to stop it. Make the right choices:

- Choose not to give or receive bribes.
- Choose to achieve things on the basis of personal integrity and self-esteem.
- Choose to speak out when you see corruption around you.
- Choose to live simple. One must remember that only great can live simple.
- Choose not to glorify corrupt sons and daughters.
- Choose to adopt ethical means at all levels.
- Lastly start *Satyagraha* to fight corruption and for good governance.

Corruption is a cancer, which every Indian must strive to cure. Many new leaders, when they come into power, declare their determination to eradicate corruption but soon they themselves become corrupt and start amassing huge wealth. There are many myths about corruption, which have to be exploded if we really want to combat it. Some of these myths are: Corruption is a way of life and nothing can be done about it. We have to change this perception by changing the mindset of individual and through individual the society and the nation. From Gandhian point of view following measures need to be taken which are as follows:

1. Foolproof laws should be made so that there is no room for discretion for politicians and bureaucrats.
2. The role of the politician should be minimized.
3. Application of the evolved policies should be left in the

hands of independent commission or authority in each area of public interest.

4. People should have a right to recall the elected representatives if they see them becoming indifferent to the electorate.
5. Electoral reforms should be carried out without further delay. Several reforms like: strict enforcement of statutory requirements, like holding in-party elections, making political parties get their accounts audited regularly and filing income-tax returns; denying persons with criminal records a chance to contest elections, should be brought in.
6. Bureaucracy, the backbone of good governance, should be made more citizens friendly, accountable, ethical and transparent.

The judiciary, the law enforcement agencies and the educational institutions have an important role to play to fight corruption by changing the people's perception. Talking with Saurashtra Delegation on January 9, 1948, Gandhi rightly said that people should be educated in freedom so that they could keep the ministers on their toes. One can learn the lessons from life of Mahatma Gandhi. Firstly, "My life is my message: leadership by example, based on principle, values, ideals and commitment. Secondly, primacy of ethics: work based on moral imperatives and ethical preference, integrity (against corruption/deception, and against attachment to power, privilege and possessions) transparency and openness of behaviour, development of conscience, responsibility, accountability and receptivity, and moral courage. Thirdly, life is an integral whole: a single standard of conduct for all. A single standard must be followed in public and private life, and in thought, word and action. Lastly, the spirit of service and social commitment. Focus on duties, tolerance, accommodation, trust, compassion, and forgiveness.

"*Power corrupts and absolute power corrupts absolutely*." So, the power should be well defined and there should be checks and balances at every stage of governance. Honest and dedicated persons in public life, control over electoral expenses could be the most important prescriptions to combat corruption. We have tolerated corruption for so long. The time has now come to root it out from its roots. In societies where traditional, religious, ethical teaching and standards of morality are weak, corruption often thrives. These values should be revived among their congregations and subjects and in this effort religious leaders and chiefs have an important role to play. The need of the hour, therefore, is to wipe off the tormenting system, which could be possible only after its thorough overhaul. For this our national leadership is expected to devise a political mechanism to create a social atmosphere by empowering of people in real sense. Piece meal approach will not serve any purpose. It is high time for the individual to change the chemistry of thought and action by adopting Gandhian values in our daily life. We have to start from somewhere to overcome the hurdle coming in the way to fight corruption.

Summing Up

Let me end with a saying that there is a need to reiterate Gandhian values and instead of merely garlanding the portraits of Gandhiji, Indians must translate his ideals into real life. The politician, bureaucrat and policy maker as well as general public must remember the seven social sins which Gandhi wrote in *Young India* of October 22, 1925.

- Politics without principles,
- Wealth without work,
- Pleasure without consciences,
- Knowledge without character,
- Commerce without morality,
- Science without humanity, and
- Worship without sacrifice.

REFERENCES

Heidenheimer, A.J., Johnston, M. and LeVine, V.J. (eds) (1989). *Political Corruption: A Handbook,* New Brunswick, NJ.

Kohli, Suresh (1975). "The Psychology of Corruption," in Kohli (ed.), *Corruption in India*, New Delhi: Chetana Publications.

Mishra, Anil Dutta, *Mahatma Gandhi on Ethics*, New Delhi, Concept, 2010.

The Collected Works of Mahatma Gandhi, Government of India, Publications Division, Vol. 90, p. 391.

World Bank (1997). *World Development Report: The State in a Changing World*, New York: Oxford University Press.

Chapter 15

M.N. Roy, Gandhi and J.P. : Politics of Power

AVANINDRA KUMAR JHA

This chapter throws light on the concept of 'Politics of Power' of three contemporary Indian Political thinkers—Mahatma Gandhi, M.N. Roy and Jay Prakash Narayan. Mahatma Gandhi and M.N. Roy represent the two different ways and methods of the politics of power. J.P. accumulates both methods in his view of *gramdharma*, which is the synthesis of the views of Gandhi and Roy.

Gandhi, Roy and J.P. solicited the idea of reconstruction in the society and politics by minimizing the gap between the power and the community. Gandhi always thought for the decentralized pattern of politics and democracy. He suggested for 'self-rule' and 'self-control'. He told to develop self-rule in each individual so that he could dispense with the rule from above. The *Gandhian theory of atma-niyantran* is the basic philosophy of his political structure. Gandhi wanted that the *Satyagrahis* should mould the politics of the country without assuming power themselves. Gandhi's idea about state itself is remarkable here. He wrote, "political power means the capacity to regulate material life through national representatives". He clearly explained it, "if national life becomes so perfect as to become self-regulated, no representation becomes necessary". In such a state everyone is his own ruler. He rules himself in such manner that he is never a hindrance to his neighbour. In the ideal state, therefore, there is no political power, because there is no state.[1]

M.N. Roy developed his own political creed of radical humanism. His new way of thought was his deviation from main line communism. Roy told, "Society is a creation of man in quest of freedom. Government for the people can never be fully a government of the people and by the people".[2] He considered the organized local democracy as the foundation of the pyramidical structure of the state.

Gandhi thought that the autonomous bodies should be the substance of the new state as this is the only means for ensuring variety and freedom on the one hand, and preventing bureaucratic oppression on the other. The autonomous institutions, based on the principle of decentralization, Gandhi hoped, would develop spontaneous energies of the people while training them in cooperative action. Panchayati Raj system would be a flexible response to social requirements and could be a link in social groupings or organizations around the concepts of autonomy and cooperation. Therefore, he pleaded that these *panchayats* should be given full powers.

Every village has to be self-sustained and capable of managing its affairs and he was convinced that in an ideal arrangement it would be "free and voluntary play of mutual forces". Gandhi thought that "such a society is inevitably cultured because in it everyone knows his wants and also realises that no one should want anything that others cannot have with equal labour".[3]

In an ideal system, Roy thought, "there will be no contradiction between collective responsibility and individual liberty, social obligations will be voluntarily undertaken and discharged in quest of individual freedom by upholding his or her potentialities, that is to say, by asserting individuality, each member of the society will increase his social utility and thus contribute to the sum total of collective well-being and progress".[4]

The creation of such a diffused political order will carry diffused economic structure, where the possibility of exploitation will be eliminated. According to Roy, in such a society there will be a minimum economic power to all. This economy will be based on "production for use and distribution with reference to human needs". Roy assumed that "a Political organization is necessary, but once the basic necessities have been fulfilled, the purpose of the state should be no more than to maintain conditions under which it will not be necessary for any man to kill another".[5]

Gandhi proposed the organization of society in an ideal way. "In this structure, composed of innumerable villages, there will be every widening, never ascending circles. Life will not be a pyramid with the apex sustained by the bottom.... But it will be the oceanic circle whose centre will be the individual always ready to perish for the village, the latter ready to perish for the circle of the villages, till at last the whole becomes one life composed of individuals, never aggressive in their arrogances but ever humble, sharing the majesty of the oceanic circle of which they are integral units...."[6]

Gandhi also narrates further that, "the outermost circumference will not wield power to crush the inner circle but will give strength to all within and derive its own strength from it".[7] Thus the Panchayati Raj System of Gandhi is the true democracy in his view, where the humblest and the lowest Indian is equally the ruler of India. Where intellectual and physical labour has no distinction.[8]

Roy praised the rights of individual. He thought about the freedom and decision making of individual. According to him, "the state will become harmonious in proportion as the individual grows as a free human being capable of making rational as well as moral judgments".[9]

Roy was conscious of the fact that in a large country with different castes, creeds and religions and millions of inhabitants, rule of the people by the people was not possible. It was for this reason that he suggested for indirect democracy in terms of peoples' committees. He said that while parliamentary democracy divides us into atomised individuals, the new democracy, as he called it, will make the freedom concrete by restoring popular sovereignty to them.

The individual citizens while discussing and planning local affairs in the framework of similar neighbouring committees, together constitute the country known as India and for whose administration they will be the instruments through which the electorate will exercise influence over the decisions of the state. So the state will in this way become coterminous with society.[10] In this way he was hopeful that the existing Panchayats could be built up as units of organized democracy. He considered that the sovereign power expresses itself through local people's committees in villages, towns and cities.[11]

M.N. Roy's concept of politics of power is a vertical structure, where power flows vertically. Gandhi's concept of power structure is horizontal, where power flows horizontally.

Gandhian model of local government or organization was social and based upon Hindu mythology. But Roy's concept was fully political and based upon communist order. But both of them advocated for cooperative commonwealth. Gandhian theory symbolizes social order where Roy's theory symbolizes political order. Both these ideas were synthesized by JP. He saw the draining away of the people into cities as one of the chief threats to the life of India. He advocated for the rehabilitation of the village community.

After separation from the Congress party, JP came forward with his socialist friends for rural upliftment. He considered that healthy development of democracy depends upon the minimum dependency upon state.[12] The hundred and fifty years long British administration had destroyed the people's power in India.[13] When the new Constitution of India was adopted in 1950, he opposed many articles of it. He was against the powerful central administration.[14]

In February 1948, JP organized a meeting in *Wardh*a for construction works, where he produced a national agenda for this purpose. In December 1949, JP and his socialist activists came out with Sarvodaya Yojana, in which a casteless, classless and cooperative society was proposed. In this proposal—agriculture, industry, taxation, banking and insurance system were also discussed. JP in his famous article *Samajwad aur Sarvodaya*, cleared that if socialism overlooks Gandhism in India, then it could not survive here. JP firmly advocated for a strong Panchayati Raj system.

JP has a set of human values, the values of democracy that can obviously be practiced more meaningfully in a small community than in a large one. JP also accepted the Gandhian theory of decentralization of political and economic power.[15] JP's tone of revolution was tamed by the Gandhian theory of non-violence. Moreover Gandhian theory of socialism was only against the theory of violence.[16] JP's concept of non-violent revolution manifested in his works in Musahari, where he was considered as the anti-revolutionary. But he had clearly shown that he was not against the revolution, but the means and methods of revolution. He anticipated that terroristic violence, in fact was more likely to provoke counter violence from the stronger section of society, leading eventually to some form of despotism.[17]

He found that "the very impatience of the Naxalites with the existing state of affairs had an appealing quality. Moreover, their attempt to participate in a revolution here and now has rendered at least some service, in that it has aroused the social consciousness of the people in general and prodded at the powers that be in particular to hasten the implementation of the land and other socio-economic reforms".[18]

His non-violent revolution was a means to achieve the new socio-economic order, where individual was more important than the power of state. So he advocated for meaningful small democratic communities. It is true that the small democratic communities will have to be integrated into the larger democracy of the nation. But the true foundation of democratic life can be established only in the small community.[19] JP had defined his concept of community centred on the individual. He says, "not so small so that there is no scope for variety of living and there is monotony as a result of smallness. No too large in which individual is lost, is alienated from his fellow beings, and then alienated from himself". He wanted to create a communitarian society and to substitute the politics of power, *Rajniti*, with the politics of humanity, *Lokniti*. His goal was *gram dharma*, 'the function of *dharma* was to hold together harmoniously the social order'. His concept of *Sarvodaya*, was a pyramidical structure of government, with the Gram Sabha as the first unit. This unit was with tiers of councils rising to the apex body, in other words, integration of all the institution at the lower level.[20]. The key economic concept of this structure was "the land revenue must be placed totality at the disposal of the village Panchayat".[21]

In *Swaraj* for the People, JP laid down the essential reforms needed to make a reality of local participating democracy. To achieve this goal, he stressed upon the need of education. He also wanted that all the political parties must start their career from the Gram

Sabha. He insisted upon the decentralization of power and economy, especially public funds. To eliminate the feudal powers of village community, he advocated for self-government and small community. JP proposed that land revenue should be placed 'totally at the disposal of the village Panchayat and the Panchayat Samiti'. Thus, the local government will be more effective and the sense of integration will be more profound. Hence, an attitude of mutuality and reciprocity would be strong. JP's view of local government was more realistic than Gandhi and Roy. Perhaps he synthesized all the good senses of both the thinkers. Roy's concept was not adequate for Indian system while the Gandhian concept was more moralist and mythological than realistic. JP produced a better solution for this great and vast land. JP's concept of rehabilitation of the village community is a better solution for the unemployment and economic crisis of India. His methods of the politics of power (*rajniti*) and politics of humanity (*lokaniti*) are totally reflected in his thought of *gram dharma*.

NOTES

1. *Young India*, 2 July, 1931.
2. M.N. Roy, *New Humanism: A Manifesto*; Renaissance Publishers, Calcutta, 1947.
3. *Harijan*, 28 July, 1946.
4. M.N. Roy, *New Beyond Communism* (ed.), Philip Spark, New Delhi, 1981, p. 100 also John Patrick Haithcox, *Communism and Nationalism in India*, Princeton University Press, Princeton, 1971, p. 8.
5. M.N. Roy, *Politics, Power, and Parties*, Renaissance Publishers, Calcutta, p. 37.
6. *Harijan*, 28th July, 1946.
7. *Ibid.*
8. Haugh, Tinker, Local Government and Politics, Political and Social Theory in India in Mare J. Swartz (ed.), *Local Level Politics: Social and Cultural Perspectives*, University of London Press, London 1969, p. 221.
9. M.N. Roy, *Politics, Power and Parties*, p. 38.
10. *Ibid.*, p. 61.
11. M.N. Roy, *Constitution of Free India*, London, 1945, p. 45.
12. Sudhanshu Ranjan, *Jayaprakash Narayan*, N.B.T., New Delhi, 1997, p. 81.

13. Jayprakash Narayan, *Meri Vichar Yatra,* Bihar Sarvodaya Mandal, Patna, 1978, p. 45.
14. *Indian Express*, 27 July, 1950.
15. Jayprakash Narayan, *Samajwad Sarvodaya and Loktantra*, Bihar Hindi Granth Academy, Patna, 1978, pp. 106-07.
16. *Harijan*. 1 June, p. 15.
17. Ajit Bhattacharya, *Jayaprakash Narayan: A Political Biography*, Vikas Publishing House, New Delhi, 1978, p. 167.
18. *Ibid*.
19. J.C. Kumarappa, *Swaraj for the Masses*, Varanasi, 1963, p. 34.
20. Haugh Tinker, *op. cit.*, p. 223.
21. J.P. Narayan, *Swaraj for the People*, Sarva Seva Sangha Prakashan, Varanasi, 1961, p. 10.

Chapter 16

Swadeshi in the Contemporary Times

NUTI NAMITA

India in the present millennium is in so many ways unrecognizable from its pre-independence era. The liberalization consequent upon globalization has unleashed an era of consumerism riding on the crest of ever increasing levels of material aspirations. In the name of growth and development, we are becoming victims of our own desires, fed by relentless endeavour of global enterprises merchandising all sorts of goods causing increasing income disparities and environmental degradation. While the liberalization of 1991 is considered to have been a watershed in Indian socio-economic trajectory of development, it is perhaps possible to compare it with India's opening of trade to the East India Company in the seventeenth century which eventually made India a colony of the British for almost two hundred years.

The overall opinion on fruits of globalization remains divided. While it, certainly, makes Indian economy outward looking, enmeshed with the international processes of capital accumulation and distribution; it is also seen as neo-colonialism whereby poorer countries are perceived to be exploited by richer nations and international agencies perpetuating further poverty and income disparities. The neo-liberal recipe for development consists of a series of measures like import-liberalization, reduction of subsidies and public expenditures, opening of economy to foreign capital and privatization of domestic economy even as economic recessions caused by developed world's profligacy causes global slowdown.

A revisit to Gandhi's thoughts, for these reasons, becomes salient. While India has, since its independence, grown in economic terms, the perennial issues of poverty, unemployment and backwardness persist. As current problems afflicting the developed and developing countries are inter-related, there is a need to reappraise alternative framework provided by Gandhi. We must ask the question: what caused these problems in the first place? What prompts dehumanization of science, technology, industry, etc., where material matters, not man? How the uncontrollable urge to have more even when our needs are limited leads to ecological disasters throughout the world? Does the Gandhian concept of *Swadeshi* retain its relevance in the era of globalization?

Swadeshi

In Gandhi's own word: "After much thinking I have arrived at a definition of *Swadeshi* that, perhaps, best illustrates the meaning. *Swadeshi* is that spirit in us which enables us to access goods and service of our immediate surroundings to the exclusion of the more remote".

To unravel the complete structure of *Swadeshi*, we need to remember Gandhi's thoughts on politics, economics and religion since he used this term with a wide connotation. He says: "There is no salvation for us without true *Swadeshi*, not the *Swadeshi* which can be conveniently put off. *Swadeshi*, for me, has a deeper meaning. I would like us to apply it in our religious, political and economic life. It is not, therefore, merely confined to wearing on occasions a *Swadeshi* cloth. That we have to do for all time, not out of a spirit of jealously or revenge but because it is a duty we owe to our dear country. We commit a breach of the *Swadeshi* spirit certainly if we wear foreign-made cloth, but we do so also if we adopt the foreign cut. Surely, the style of our dress has some correspondence with our environment. In elegance and tastefulness, it is immeasurably superior to the trousers and the jacket. An Indian wearing a shirt flowing over his *pyjamas* with a waist-cost on it without a neck-tie and its flaps hanging loose behind, is very graceful spectacle".[1]

Swadeshi and Khadi

Making of *Khadi* and its adoption is often equated with *Swadeshi* in popular perception. This is not the correct interpretation. According to Gandhi, whilst *Khadi* is an obligation for all time in India, surely it is equally an obligation to use India-made things wherever we can get them even though they may be inferior to foreign articles. One is reminded of countless *Swadeshi* items in the market that require our patronage even though these may not be attractively packaged and marketed. What Gandhi hinted was that it is not always better to use the best and the cheapest in developing countries that engage in indigenous production of consumer goods even if these may not have global standards. It is for us to use them and improve them wherever improvement is possible. The analogy could be that just as we do not give up our country for one with a better climate so also may we not discard *Swadeshi* items for better or cheaper foreign goods. Gandhi sums up this core argument on *Swadeshi* by stating that "the law of each country's progress demands on the part of its inhabitants' preference for their own products and manufactures."[2]

'*Swadeshi* is cornerstone of Gandhi's thoughts on economics; this is related with his doctrines such as non-violence, non-exploitation, non-possession, bread-labour and trusteeship. The most important principles which impressed Gandhi, and which even later became the guiding spirit behind all his ideas, was the principle of *Sarvodaya*—the good or rise of all.[3]

Contrary to popular opinion, however, Gandhi had no objection to the use of foreign capital, or even to the employment of foreign talent, if it was not available in India, though he wanted it to be under Indian control and used in the interest of India. But the use of foreign capital or talent is one thing and dumping of foreign industrial concerns is totally another. He would rather prefer the development of the industries in question to be delayed by few years in order to permit national capital and enterprise to group up and build up such industries in future under the actual supervision, control, direction and management of Indians themselves.[4]

Gandhi was unequivocal in his belief that India could not be free as long as it voluntarily encourages or tolerates the economic drain. If India could make a successful effort to stop that drain, she can gain *Swaraj* by that one act. He was referring to Indian enslavement by its greed for foreign cloth which led to a drain of wealth and decimation of local cloth industry and poverty of weaver classes.

Gandhi went beyond economic rationale for using *Khadi*. He vehemently opposed the sartorial rationale for using foreign made cloth; human vanity sometimes creates compulsion for using fashionable fine garments. He should train himself to see art and beauty in the spotlessly white *Khaddar* and to appreciate its soft unevenness. The householder must learn to use cloth as a miser uses his hoard. This reveals the philosophy and art of living. Similarly, even when the householders have revised their tastes about dress, somebody will have to spin yarn for the weavers. Everyone spinning during spare hours either for love or money can easily do this.[5] He further clarifies the same with the following explanation:

> "We are too much obsessed by the glamour of the West. We forget that what may be perfectly good for certain conditions in the West is not necessarily good for certain other and often diametrically opposite conditions in the East. Free trade, which may have been good enough for England, would certainly have ruined Germany. Germany prospered only because her thinkers, instead of slavishly following England, took note of the special conditions of their own land, and devised economies suited to them."[6]

In effect, Gandhi's *Swadeshi* while centring around the handspun *Khaddar* extends to everything that can be and is produced in India thereby embracing his whole concept of *Swaraj*.

> "We do not realize that *Swaraj* is almost wholly obtainable through *Swadeshi*. If we have no regard for our respective vernaculars, if we dislike our clothes, if our dress repels us, if our food is distasteful to us, our climate is not good enough, our people uncouth and unfit for our company, or civilization faulty and the foreign attractive, in short, if everything native is bad and everything foreign pleasing to

> us, I should not know what *Swaraj* can mean for us. If everything foreign is to be adopted, surely it will be necessary for us to continue long under foreign tutelage, because foreign civilization has not permeated the masses. It seems to me that, before we can appreciate *Swaraj*, we should have not only love but passion for *Swadeshi*. Everyone of our acts should bear the *Swadeshi* stamp. *Swaraj* can only be built upon the assumption that most of what national is, on the whole, sound. If the view here put forth be correct, we should have a big movement in our country for *Swadeshi*."[7]

According to Gandhi, much of the deep poverty of the masses is due to the ruinous departure from *Swadeshi* in the economic and industrial life. "If not an article of commerce had been brought from outside India; she would be today a land flowing with milk and honey. But that was not to be. It is England's declared policy that India is to be held in trust for her people. If this is true, Lancashire must stand aside. And if *Swadeshi* doctrine is a sound doctrine, Lancashire can stand aside without problems, though it may sustain a shock for the time being."[8]

Regarding *Swadeshi* and *Charkha* he has said, "I claim for the *Charkha* the honour of being able to solve the problem of economic distress in a most natural, simple, inexpensive and business-like manner. The *Charkha*, therefore, is not only useless, but it is a useful and indispensable article for every home. It is the symbol of the nation's prosperity and, therefore, freedom. It is a symbol not of commercial war, but of commercial peace. It bears not a message of ill-will towards the nations of the earth, but of good-will and self-help. It will not need the protection of navy threatening a world's peace and exploiting its resources, but it needs the religious determination of millions to spin their yarn in their own homes. I may deserve the curse of posterity for many mistakes of omission and commission, but I am confident of earning its blessings for suggesting a revival of the *Charkha*. I stake my all on it. For, every revolution of the wheel spins peace, goodwill and love. And with all that, inasmuch as the loss of it brought about India's slavery, its voluntary revival with all its implications must mean India's freedom".[9]

Again, Gandhi defines *Swadeshi* as, "I must not serve my distant neighbour at the expense of the nearest. It is never vindictive or punitive. It is in no sense narrow, for I buy from every part of the world what is needed for my growth. I refuse to buy from anybody anything however nice or beautiful, if it interferes with my growth or injures those whom Nature has made my first care. I buy useful healthy literature from every part of the world. I buy surgical instruments from England, pens and pencils from Austria, and watches from Switzerland. But I will not buy an inch of the finest cotton fabric from England or Japan or any other part of the world, because it has injured and increasingly injuring the millions of the inhabitants of India. I hold it to be sinful for me to refuse to buy the cloth spun and woven by the needy millions of India's paupers, and to buy foreign cloth although it may be superior in quality to the Indian hand-spun. My *Swadeshi*, therefore, chiefly centres round the hand-spun *Khaddar* and extend to everything that can be and is produced in India. My nationalism is as broad as my *Swadeshi*. I want India's rise so that the whole world may benefit. I do not want India to rise on the ruin of other nations".[10] Further, he adds that if India wants to be strong and able, India would send out to the world her treasures of art and health-giving spices, but would refuse to send out opium or intoxicating liquors although the traffic may bring much material benefit to India.[11]

Gandhi believed that the Indian economy at one time was dependent on its own resources for spinning and weaving cloth by its own handicrafts industry. Gandhi thought that this scenario no longer holds true under the British rule. He was saddened by the fact that the income from an average Indian, instead of contributing to its own economy, is sent outside to England. He further laments that emergence of machine mills in India deprives the handicraftsmen from earning profitably from their profession. Moreover, Gandhi is of the view that the fascination of all things made in England makes an Indian to spend less on food and more on clothes, consequently suffering a two-fold loss. "We are bound to perish if the twin industries of agriculture and spinning as well as weaving disappear from our homes or our villages."[12]

Similarly, Gandhi was skeptical of the growth of modern transport and communication system attendant upon the burgeoning trade throughout India. While development in transportation helps move goods and travellers, it also helps in the fast deployment of war machines and soldiers to every nook and corner of the world. The mass media of communications—from the printing press to computer chips and satellites—have become the instruments of propaganda, thought control, mindset and brainwashing; the *Time Magazine* imperialism or *CNN* neo-colonialism being the latest examples.[13]

The oft-repeated ideas of racism, ethnicity, sexism, sectarianism, dogmatism and jingoism have flourished and thrived through the media imperialism. These narrow-minded messages, which are used to boost huge and massive industrialization, have also caused communal antagonisms and blood baths on national and international levels. The obsession with too much liberalization has, among other factors, created conditions of recession in the developed countries.

Some argue that science, technology and industrialization are not inherently immoral; it is only their misuse that causes problems. True, the sword by itself does not kill people; people have to use it to kill people. But in the human context, the very purpose for the creation of the sword is to inflict pain or death on human beings. This destructive purpose of the sword will not change until the sword, in Biblical terms, is beaten into ploughshare. When it becomes a ploughshare, then it is not a sword by definition and purpose. Thus ends and means should be integrated, not dichotomized or distorted.[14] Hence liberalization and globalization as concepts should be studied and analyzed in the light of the facts given above.

Gandhi brings in his concept of self-control and control of our wants and links it to freedom. He argues: "The outward freedom that we shall attain will only be in exact proportion to the inward freedom to which we may have grown at a given moment. And if this is correct view of freedom, our chief energy must be concentrated upon achieving reform from within".[15]

While advocating his views on freedom, Gandhi was also being a realist and displaying a scientific temperament. For him a true votary of *Swadeshi* accordingly, "will never harbour ill-will nor he be actuated by antagonism towards anybody on earth... To reject foreign manufactures, merely because they are foreign and to go on wasting national time and money in the promotion of the manufactured goods of one's country even though it is not suited for it, would be a criminal folly and a negation of *Swadeshi* spirit".[16]

It is a telling commentary of India that instead of examining relevance of *Swadeshi* and the Gandhian approach of development, we pay only the lip service to Gandhi's doctrines and jettisoned the basic principle of self-reliance by adopting Western model of development through industrialization. We are now enmeshed with the systemic crisis of modern civilization and culture; the amoral modernity, that Gandhi had anticipated in the *Hind Swaraj*. Despite the collapse of socialism and crises of capitalism India again opted for liberalization and globalization. The ruling class in India is complicit in mostly free entry to multi-national corporations and companies over which no national governments have any control, losing out thus, their economic sovereignty.[17]

Now, as the cries of economic nationalism is growing around the world, the idea of *Swadeshi* becomes relevant as it reduces the dependence on other countries and strengthens the confidence and efficacy and enhances the spirit of self-reliance among the people. To do this, however, there is a greater need to understand Gandhi's approach to *Swadeshi* and its proper application. *Swadeshi* is *Swadharma* as well as a way of life. Besides, *Swadeshi* is a philosophy of life to live and let others to live. It leads to the process of sustainable development.

In fact, *Swadeshi*, *Swaraj* and *Satyagraha* were the chief methods employed to oppose British imperialist domination and to gain political independence and mastery within the country and above all to gain India's complete freedom in all respects. *Swadeshi* movement as an economic battle was necessary link to *Swaraj* for the political battle for freedom through the method of *Satyagraha*. Economic freedom, according to *Swadeshi*, is based on indigenously controlled development. The word *Swadeshi* has an appeal to all sections of Indians. *Swadeshi* to many means, "What we can do, let us do".[18] *Swadeshi* also means a set of policies that are good for the economic development of the country, not for some section of Indians, be it labour or capital. Rather, it gives a sense of pride and no one will be against foreign collaborations in those areas in which

India lacks the expertise. Unfortunately to many intellectuals it is backwardness, to most in media it is amusement, to almost all industrialists it indicates inefficiency and inferior quality, and to economists it is bad economics.

In the present context, from Mahatma Gandhi's *Swadeshi* to current debate on economic nationalism represents a long journey. Two of Mahatma's essays in *Young India* and *Harijan* make his position clearer. Then, as now, a primary concern was the economy. "The situation today is this. The Britisher is the top-dog and the Indian the under-dog in his own country... It can be said without fear of contradiction and without any exaggeration that he has risen upon the ruin of India's commerce and industries. The cottage industry of India had to perish in order that Lancashire might flourish. The Indian shipping had to perish so that British Shipping might flourish... what is equality of rights between a giant and a dwarf? Before one can think of equality between unequals, the dwarf must be raised to the height of the giant."[19] In fact, according to Gandhi, the true meaning of *Swadeshi* is the revival and preservation of village industries that is the lifeline of the rural economy and villages in turn constitute the heart of India. According to Gandhi, "What is needed is protection of the village crafts and the craftsmen from the crushing competition of the power driven machinery whether it is worked in India or in foreign lands. I claim that this is true, fruitful and cent-per-cent *Swadeshi*".[20]

According to Gandhi, one rule of *Swadeshi* is that in serving people we should give priority to those who live near us. There is also an opposite rule that we should serve first those who are distant from us and then those who are near us. Near in the first rule means physically near, and distant in the second rule means distant from us mentally. Both may mean the same thing. An enemy may be physically near and distant mentally; we should, despite his being distant, serve him first. The reason behind this rule of *Swadeshi* is that we cannot reach all human beings in this world. If you ignore your neighbour and seek to serve someone living far away, that would be pride on your part. We display good manners, culture and learning in serving first those who are mentally distant from us.[21]

On many occasions, Gandhi emphasized *Swadeshi* since he wanted to cultivate fearlessness in the people as in those days Indian people did not have the courage to stand up against the British Empire. Gandhi considered it the first and foremost quality to cultivate. Therefore, he gave it a religious connotation and initially emphasized upon the need to cultivate *Swadeshi* in religion also. In fact, Gandhi's *Swadeshi* aimed at giving an assurance of providing a minimum standard of living to every individual and to provide meaningful employment to all able-bodied citizens and to avoid waste and extravagance in utilizing natural resources. Gandhi reasoned that earth provides enough for everybody's need but not for anybody's greed. By this he wanted that India should not depend upon others but should stand on its feet itself and should have that *Swadeshi* is not a cult of hatred. It is doctrine of selfless service that has its roots in purest *ahimsa*, that is, love.[22]

To be fair to Gandhi, he has emphasized that he is not totally against the mechanization or adoption of new technology or the new terms of globalization but the emphasis of all these should be on the morality of the human nature, i.e., it should help the mankind to get more and more employment and work so that he can fulfil his basic needs—bread, cloth and shelter without any difficulty.

While relating *Swaraj* to *Swadeshi* and *Swadeshi* to *Swaraj* to the ground reality of India, Gandhi goes to the basics the individual being the basic unit of society; and village as the basic unit of human habitation. He always argued that inner change within the individual ought to be the starting point of outer change in society, and that only self-ruling individuals can usher in true *Swaraj*. And as individuals mostly live in villages, only self-reliant villagers practicing *Swadeshi* could become the building blocks of a nation.

Gandhi's concept of *Swadeshi* is found to be identical to that of *Swadharma* in the *Gita*. The *Swadharma* depends upon *Swabhava*, i.e., one's fundamental nature. People must follow in life such avocations, as would not do violence to the nature. The *Gita* says: "One's own *dharma* though imperfect is better than the *dharma* of another well performed. The *dharma* of another is fraught with fear." Gandhi says of this: "Interpreted in terms of one's physical environment, this gives us the law of *Swadeshi*, for *Swadeshi* is *Swadharma* applied to one's immediate environment".[23]

From the above, it follows that Gandhi's conception of *Swadeshi* was both ethical and economic. As a matter of fact, Gandhi made no difference between ethics and economics. He said: "I must confess that I do not draw a sharp line or any distinction between economics and ethics. Economics that hurt the moral well-being of an individual or a nation are immoral and, therefore, sinful. Thus the economics that permits one country to prey upon another are immoral".[24] "It is sinful to eat American wheat and let my neighbour, the grain dealer, starve for want of custom. Similarly, it is sinful for me to wear the latest finery of Regent Street, when I know that if I had but worn the things woven by the neighbouring spinners and weavers, that would have clothed me, and fed and clothed them."[25]

Indians had understood, long before Gandhi, that the poverty of India was principally due to the murder of their industry at the hands of the British and unless indigenous industries are revived, Indian masses would remain poor. When Gandhi read R.C. Dutta's *Poverty of India Under British Rule*, he was so powerfully affected that he began to shed tears. Along with the Annual Congress Sessions, therefore, it was customary to call an industrial conference. Resolutions were passed both in the Congress and at the Industrial Conference advising people to use *Swadeshi* instead of foreign goods.[26]

At another instance, Gandhi said: "Duties to self, to the family, to the country and to the world are not independent of one another. One cannot do good to the country by injuring himself or his family. Similarly one cannot serve the country by injuring the world at large. In the final analysis we must die that the family may live, the family must die that the country may live and the country must die that the world may live". He further said: "I work for India's freedom because my *Swadeshi* teaches me that being born in it and having inherited her culture, I am fittest to serve her and she has a prior claim to my service. But my patriotism is not exclusive, it is calculated not to hurt another nation but to benefit all in the true sense of the word".[27]

The neglect of *Swadeshi* and agriculture that has characterized our Government's economic policies since independence has progressively landed us in the present economic and financial crisis. It had led to our enormous adverse balance of trade with almost every country in Europe and America and with Japan in Asia. It has obliged us to take to deficit financing that has assumed critical levels and has led to inflation and the decline in the value of the Rupee. It has made the rich richer without in any way improving the real purchasing power of the poor. It has also brought about the devaluation of the Rupee.[28]

Once political independence from British rule has been achieved, surprisingly, one does not find any direct reference to the *Swadeshi* concepts as it had evolved during the days of the freedom struggle in the policy formulations and planning documents. However, it was there in a modified shape in the garb of the objectives related to achievement of self-sufficiency in crucial sectors, particularly the building up of core sector industries and scientific/technological capabilities. Moreover, during the initial phase of planning, there was a general reluctance to rely on foreign investments, except in crucial sectors of the economy, primarily those in the capital goods or infrastructure segments where production capabilities could not be built up without recourse to foreign resources, technology and imported inputs. Thus during this phase, although no direct reference to the *Swadeshi* principle was present, in its essential spirit, it was *Swadeshi*. However, it did differ from the historical phase of Gandhian *Swadeshi* in one very important respect. Its accent, under the influence of leaders like Nehru and others was on the development of indigenous technological, scientific capabilities and modernization of the industrial sector whereas Gandhian *Swadeshi* was by and large wedded not only to the idea of preserving the traditional industries, but preserving them in their old traditional mould and above all providing employments to many hands.

However, this does not imply that as part of planned development, traditional industries were to be completely sidetracked. In fact, as generally known, the Karve Committee was appointed to look into their problems and to devise schemes for their enlistment. The setting up of Khadi and Village Industries Board and devising the framework of its responsibilities owes its origin to 1950s. However, traditional industries did not form the lynchpin of development programmes, which addressed themselves much more to attempts at modernization and bringing about the necessary structural changes in the economy, which could be characterized as 'modern *Swadeshi*' starting with 1951 when the planning mechanism was initiated. The gradual transformation in an increasing range of relaxations during the 1980s took a distinctive break in 1991 when the policy of liberalization and greater role for the operation of free market forces were adopted. This brought about dismantling of a number of controls including those on foreign exchange, removal or substantial reduction in many of import duties, promotion of foreign investment and free access to foreign technology. Within this framework, the objective of self-sufficiency as a general principle could not find an automatic berth without contradicting the underlying law of comparative advantage and the principles of free market economy. The apparent conflict, between the principle of self-sufficiency and theoretical foundations of the law of comparative advantage, as viewed within the framework of neo-classical economics, arises since comparative advantage theory demands that the relative magnitude of domestic production and import of any commodity should be determined by the market mechanism in terms of the degree of comparative advantage that an economy possesses rather than being imposed exogenously through a policy decision. Self-sufficiency can thus be justified only in terms of certain grounds falling outside the realm of neo-classical economics. This should not be taken as an endorsement of superiority of the principle of comparative advantage over the principle of self-sufficiency.

In favour of the new economic policy it was suggested that there was no use of being out of step with the given socio-economic conditions in India and global developments. It was argued that official policy in India has in past imposed stringent austerity standards. The upper and middle classes in India suffered, in particular more deprivation than middle classes in any other third world country. Liberalization policy, beginning in mid-seventies and gaining strength in eighties had, therefore, to be developed into a structural adjustment programme, which stipulated that not only by putting pressure on those who had money and means to satisfy their consumption needs in terms of global standards but by satisfying their demands in the market, growth could be stimulated and accelerated. The promoters of new economic policy follow this line of reasoning. They also promised that as economic progress is achieved, it would also lead to alleviation in the conditions of majority of Indian people living at and below the subsistence level.

Here, it is important to appreciate the full implication of the new realities of globalization today. The nation-states have lost a substantial amount of economic, and through that, political sovereignty. They have to accept severe constraints on making their economic policies, expanding money supply, incurring fiscal deficits, determining interest rates or exchange rates, controlling domestic prices, restricting industrial activities besides their reduced ability to control international trade and capital flows. The effectiveness of any policy would depend on what is happening in the world economy and how other countries react. The costs of disregarding such constraints are very large and even the flexibility in taking political actions have become limited. The United States has been trying to crush Cuba for a long time, but with very limited effect, as Cuba managed to utilize the channels of international trade to withstand all the pressure. Iraq is another example. While sanctions largely worked in Rhodesia and South Africa, they do not seem to work today in Iraq. For less resourceful countries, the loss of autonomy may be very severe. The sanctions imposed upon India after the nuclear tests were not comprehensive and fully enforced. But if they were, and came anywhere near those imposed on Iraq, India would have crumbled. It is good that India does not have the dictatorial regime of Iraq though our democratic system is much more vulnerable to economic disruptions and economic disparities.

In the case of the globalization and liberalization, though the benefits are more difficult to measure, because they are largely potential, and they require appropriate policy designs to be translated into the actual practice. Globalization and liberalization expands the opportunities for a country to realize more output, more employment, more social development, or in short, higher levels of social welfare from the given resources in the country's command. But expansion of opportunities does not mean that they would be automatically materialized or realized. They would be needed for the state action, in policy design, planning and coordination of activities. There may be increased constraints on the state's autonomy but there will be no decline in the importance of the state's functions.

Coming back to *Swadeshi*, Gandhi involved the most common Indian in the economic growth of the country. Not only did he raise the self-esteem of the poorest of the poor by providing him employment and a means of livelihood, but he also aspired to make the whole country self-reliant in the long run. He had realized that unless the people themselves were involved there could not be true economic prosperity in India. He was fully aware that government imposed development schemes did not bring permanent solution to age-old problems. Therefore, he insisted on people's involvement and participation. This idea is still relevant today. To make India self-reliant, what is required is to make the people a party to all development projects. The people should get involved in deciding what they need and what methods are necessary to achieve their goals. This would bring us to the adoption of the rural self-government and the enrichment of the village life. While decentralization has constitutional mandate, the local self-government institutions remain subservient to the governments at top. The grassroots leadership remains enfeebled by design of the dynastic politics. To make India self-sufficient, self-reliant and India of Gandhi's dream, it is essential to make its villages self-sufficient and self-reliant.[29]

Side Effects of Liberalization and Globalization

The supporters of globalization do admit that their vision of connected economies and shared prosperity has not lived up to expectation. It has engendered a variant of dependency and unprecedented rise in influence of international corporations. The deepening economic crises and degradation of environment are now recognized as the effects of global economic disorder.

Relevance and Significance of Gandhi's Views

In a discussion with a Polish engineer, Maurice Frydman, in 1936, who did not appreciate the wisdom of Gandhi's technological choice, Gandhi explained how urban industrialism was bound to lead to the exploitation of the rural people and could not give them sufficient employment and what was needed was that "production for use", as he put it, localization of production, employment and consuming power on the basis of largely localized, mutually advantageous exchange of goods and services. To quote Gandhi: "Industrialization on a mass scale will necessarily lead to passive or active exploitation of the villagers as the problems of competition and marketing come in. Therefore, we have to concentrate on the village being self-contained, manufacturing mainly for use. Provided this character of the village industry is maintained, there would be no objection to the villagers using even modern machines and tools that they can make and can afford to use. Only they should not be used as a means of exploitation of others".[30]

Gandhi was not a reactionary machine-hater who sought a release of the human spirit in primitivism. He was in favour of capital-saving techniques, to begin with. He wanted the rural folk to make modern tools and machines to be used in rural industries. He did not want machinery to be a means to the exploitation of the masses of the population, but as a means to more and better employment accompanied by as little exploitation as possible.

When Gandhi was in Europe during 1931 in connection with the Round Table Conference, he had the occasion of discussing with an American journalist the advantages of localization of production and consumption, rather than their increasing centralization under a system of mass production. Gandhi argued that besides squarely facing the problem of mass unemployment in a poor country, such a system of decentralized production was a way out of the economic travails of even Western countries. He stated: "When production and consumption both become localized, the temptation to speed up production indefinitely and at any price, disappears. The endless difficulties and problems that our present day economic system presents would then come to an end".[31]

Referring to USA, Gandhi said: "She has reached the acme of mass production, and yet she has not been able to abolish unemployment or want. There are still thousands, perhaps millions of people who live in misery, in spite of the phenomenal riches of the few".[32] Gandhi's context was the great depression with its paradox of "poverty in the midst of plenty". The interviewer suggested that the fault lay in distribution. If distribution could be equalized, mass production could be "sterilized of all its evils". Whereas Gandhi's answer was forthright: "No, the evil is inherent in the system. Distribution can be equalized when production is localized, in other words, when the distribution is simultaneous with production. Distribution will never be equal so long as you want to tap other markets of the world to dispose of your goods".[33] Gandhi was thinking of non-exploitative production and exchange both within the country and across international frontiers. He said that "the Western nations have to use their skill for the good of those who do not have the skill" in order to generate production and employment where they are needed most. He used the same argument on behalf of the vast masses of the unemployed in India.

While Gandhi's doctrine of hand spinning is at times considered anti-development, he realized that rural unemployment could not be tackled without a whole range of village industries supplementing one another, and a proper cooperative organization. Again in 1934, he said: "I discovered that, without the revival of other industries, *Khadi* could not make further progress. For villagers to be able to occupy their spare time profitably, the village life must be touched at all points".[34] There was a tendency to encourage *Khadi* as a ritual or sacrament. But there was a contradiction in people's attitude. As Gandhi said: "While people used *Khadi* exclusively, they were using other things, irrespective of how and where they were made. *Khadi* was thus becoming a lifeless symbol. There were multitudes with spare time on their hands. Their involuntary and voluntary idleness made them a perpetual prey of exploiters".[35] What, was therefore, needed was corporate effort to generate concurrent development of rural industries.

Thus, while globalization is deepening systemic crises, Gandhi's approach to '*Swadeshi*' (self-reliance) with the promotion of local indigenous industry or small-scale (industries which are primarily built upon the principle of national self-reliance and self-sufficiency, *Swadeshi* and *Swavlamban*), minimum surpluses will lead to devolution and decentralization of economic productivity and distribution. And such productivity will certainly force science and technology to adapt to small-scale industries and consequently reduce the need for raw materials, energy and pollution besides stopping the forces colonization, militarization and wars.

Etymologically, the term *Swadeshi* may mean "of one's own country". However, country is not its connotation but a sub-characteristic called *uplakshan* in Hindi. Accordingly, *Swadeshi* includes all indigenous things both abstract and concrete, namely, native language, wisdom, culture, dress and other products also. The core of the concept, however, is 'self-reliance' and 'self-governance' that reduces the extent of dependence on others to the minimum.

Even if Gandhi did not invent the term *Swadeshi*, he enlarged it by infusing new meanings to it. His understanding and approach to *Swadeshi* seems to be very dynamic, scientific, and very convincing. In the field of economics, the principle of *Swadeshi* means that a person basically uses those things that are produced in his immediate neighbourhood and serves those industries by making them efficient and meaningful. In other words, we can say that *Swadeshi* was the lifeblood of a Gandhian village. Gandhi illustrates this:

> "*Swadeshi* is that spirit in us which restricts us to the use and service of our immediate surroundings to the exclusion of the more remote... In the domain of politics, I should make use of the indigenous institutions and serve them by curing them of their proved defects. In that of economics, I should use only things that are produced by my immediate neighbours and serve those industries by making them efficient and complete where they might be found wanting."

Gandhi further clarifies that the neighbour thus served, has in his turn, to serve his own neighbour. Accordingly, in practice it is never exclusive and it recognizes the scientific limitations of human capacity for service. However, the principle of *Swadeshi* demands that a person must give preference to local manufactures even if they are of inferior quality or more costly than articles of foreign make. There is no place for hatred for the foreign made things also. Therefore, he advises the use of foreign made articles if there is no substitute. He defined a *Swadeshi* article as any article which "subserves the interest of the millions even though the capital and talent are foreign but under effective Indian control". However, Gandhi did insist upon the exclusion of such foreign made commodities whose import was harmful to the indigenous industries. He pleaded strongly for stiff protective duties upon foreign goods in order to nurture national industries.

Further, it may be added that in advocating the complete boycott of foreign cloth, Gandhi had no ill-will at all. He said, "To reject foreign manufactures merely because they are foreign, and to go on wasting national time and money to promote manufactures in one's own country for which it is not suited, would be criminal folly and a negation of the *Swadeshi* spirit".[36] He further added:

> "A true votary of *Swadeshi* will never harbour ill-will towards the foreigner, he will not be activated by antagonism towards anybody on earth. *Swadeshism* is not a cult of hatred. It is a doctrine of selfless service, that has its roots in the purest *Ahimsa*, i.e., love."[37]

Thus, Gandhi's concept of *Swadeshi* is wider one and has wider connotation also. Regarding the exclusion of everything foreign, Gandhi does not leave any room for doubt when he says:

> "I have never considered the exclusion of everything foreign under every conceivable circumstances as a part of *Swadeshi*. The broad definition of *Swadeshi* is the use of all homemade things to the exclusion of foreign things, in so far as such use is necessary for the protection of home industry, more especially those industries without which India will become pauperized. In my opinion, therefore, *Swadeshi* which excludes the use of everything foreign, no matter how beneficent it may be, and irrespective of the fact that it impoverishes nobody, is a narrow interpretation of *Swadeshi*."[38]

Secondly, Gandhi is clear that his insistence on priority for the immediate neighbour will not mean injury to or unconcern for the interest of those who are not in the neighbourhood. However, each has to give priority to his or her neighbour, or base his or her action on concern for his or her neighbour, and there can be contradiction or conflict, and no unconcern or injury.[39] In this respect Gandhi fully believed that a man could serve his neighbours and humanity at the same time, the condition being that the service of the neighbour was in no way selfish or exclusive, i.e., did not in any way involve the exploitation of any other human being. Thus, considered, it would spread like the proverbial snowball gathering strength in geometrical progression encircling the whole earth. It followed that *Swadeshi* was that spirit which dictated man to serve his next-door neighbour to the exclusion of any other as already mentioned. Accordingly, *Swadeshi* is never exclusive. Regarding the third question of an element of hatred or chauvinism for the foreigner it may be added here that Gandhi's arguments in this case were as under:

> "I have never been an advocate of prohibition of all foreign things because they are foreign. My economic creed is a complete taboo in respect of all foreign commodities whose importation is likely to prove harmful to our indigenous interest. This means that we may not in any circumstance import a commodity that can be adequately supplied from our own country. For instance, I would regard it a sin to import Australian wheat on the score of its better quality, but I would not have the slightest hesitation in importing oatmeal from Scotland, if an absolute necessity for it is made out, because we do not grow oats in India. In other words, I would not countenance the boycott of a single foreign article out of ill-will or feeling of hatred."[40]

On the contrary, he pointed out that India produced a sufficient quantity of leather and "it is my duty, therefore, to wear shoes made out of Indian leather only, even if it is comparatively dearer and of an inferior quality, in preference to cheaper and superior quality foreign leather shoes. Similarly, I would condemn the introduction of foreign molasses or sugar, if enough of it is produced in India for our needs. It will be thus clear from the above that it is hardly possible for me to give an exhaustive catalogue of foreign articles whose importation in India ought to be prohibited. I have simply inculcated the general principle by which we can be guided in all such cases. And this principle will hold good in future, too, so long as the conditions of production in our country remain as they are today".[41]

Similarly, in the economic field, our activities are oriented towards the production and consumption of goods and services for the satisfaction of our wants. Let us see how Gandhi's philosophy applies to both these fields. In production, one will have to give priority to the utilization or employment of local resources in material and man-power. In consumption too one will have to give priority to what is manufactured locally. In both cases, the arguments that are put forward against giving priority to the neighbour or local man-power and resources, or to the local manpower because he is considered to be inadequately equipped in skills, his technology is inferior, and therefore, the quality of his products cannot be compared with the quality of the goods produced elsewhere, generally in other countries. The second argument is that indigenous products are costlier, more expensive. If we follow these arguments and switch to or prefer goods manufactured in other countries, we will put our neighbour out of employment and contribute to money drain that will benefit other countries at the cost of our nation.[42] As a result the spirit of *Swadeshi* would certainly demand that one should work for the improvement of our skills, improve our technology and improve the quality and excellence of our goods, and put up with poorer quality till such time as we improve the quality of our goods. In reality the spirit of *Swadeshi* thus acts as an incentive to improve our technology. And, there is nothing in the philosophy of *Swadeshi* that asks us to be content with archaic or ineffective technology or to abjure the upgradation of technology.

Summing Up

We have tried to show that Gandhian *Swadeshi* is both a principle of evolution or construction, a creative principle, as well as an instrument of struggle for the economic regeneration of the masses. *Swadeshi* is equally valid in all spheres of human activity and all spheres in which man is capable of evolution. The stream of culture demands that we should not uproot ourselves from our heritage, which has taken its shape and texture from the thoughts and efforts of those who are, and who were proximate to us. To be ignorant of this heritage or to repudiate it is inconsistent with the spirit of *Swadeshi* as it is the base on which one builds. Therefore, one should contribute to its improvement or enrichment. This needs a lot of introspection and one must be able to detect and remove deficiencies and whatever is untenable. Besides, one should not fear any exposure to other cultural heritage. Rather, one should absorb whatever one finds it better. However, one should not allow one's roots to wither away or be eroded. Gandhi has very beautifully presented his ideas in the following words:

> "I do not want my house to be walled in on all sides, and my windows to be stuffed. I want the cultures of all lands to be blown about my house as freely as possible. But I refuse to be blown off my feet by any. I refuse to live in other people's houses as an interloper, a beggar or a slave...Mine is not a religion of the prison house".[43]

Viewed thus, *Swadeshi* is the doctrine consistent with the law of humanity and love as envisaged by Gandhi. This involves love and service of motherland and mankind as a whole. This means that we can do the best to those who are immediately known to our neighbour and our countrymen and thus must be the first to receive our service. This, in fact, is nothing but humanism or love of mankind. So, *Swadeshi* is a dynamic concept in Gandhian thought and spirit.

Being a dynamic concept *Swadeshi* is much more relevant and significant in the present context in which multinational companies and corporations have already entered in every nook and corner all round the world. India is not an exception in this field. Some people think and claim that the days of *Swadeshi* have already gone and now it is the age of globalization and multinationals. They argue that *Swadeshi* is irrelevant and thus would be misfit under the present economic scenario.

Keeping in view this question, it is important to examine the results of the policies and decisions implemented since the dawn of Independence. It has been seen that even after more than fifty years of our Independence, it is very sad and distressing to experience that India, the so-called largest democracy in the world, still continues to be one of the poorest countries in the world.[44] It is the tragedy of the first magnitude that crores of Indians, representing a large percentage of the world population, are living below the poverty line. Similarly, the numbers of unemployed and under-employed are on the increase. At present there are several job seekers (including professionals like engineers, doctors, etc.) in the country. We are becoming bankrupt as a government with a huge amount of debt (external and internal); we occupy the unenviable position of ranking fourth in foreign indebtedness among the countries of the world. Coupled with criminalization of politics and corruption, India appears to have lost its moral compass.

The need of the hour is to reverse the country's economic policy with a view to redistributing income to attain economic freedom, to fulfil basic material needs of every citizen and to develop a self-reliant economy. Our political freedom is incomplete without economic independence. The deepening economic crisis should open our eyes. We should not ape alien models of economic progress. We should evolve an indigenous model based on our culture, our past traditions, present requirements and aspiration for the future. We must devise an economic system based on materialistic management and humanistic economics (integral humanism) and create an infrastructure in which and by which the inherent potentialities of man may find their highest fulfilment.[45] The man, the integral man, (and his happiness) must be the centre of this system. *Swadeshi* may provide an alternative.

Swadeshi, through decentralized rural industry and village arts and crafts, can provide employment and steady income and can also help in reducing the poverty of the millions. We should aim at gross village product (GVP) instead of GNP. Rightly did Gandhi declare in the forties, "Cut down your wants and at once all your economic problems will be solved". The theory of non-possession has a deep-rooted meaning in economy.

However, in spite of the logic in the above contentions, people are still doubtful about the concept of *Swadeshi*, which they ridicule as old fashioned, outdated and reactionary. The craze for foreign articles among the country's elite and middle class people has no limit. Moreover, their possession has become a status symbol.

Such an attitude is not a healthy one, as it will hamper the country's progress and development. We may lose our individuality and become slaves once again. Therefore, we must revive the spirit of *Swadeshi* and encourage the use of Indian goods, Indian resources and modernized indigenous technology wherever necessary. *Swadeshi* in consumption is essential for evolving a self-reliant economy. The positive content of *Swadeshi* should be used as the cornerstone for the reconstruction and promotion of our economy.

Further, where industrialization is a must, it must not be in blind imitation of the West. Nature is to be milked and not misused or abused. There should be integrated thinking in ecology, economics and ethics. Emphasis should be laid on labour intensive rather than capital-intensive industries under the present grim situation. The problem of unemployment and underemployment must be handled on war footing. Economic and industrial policies must be aimed at maximizing employment so as to enable the people to have more purchasing power having our focus on the needs of the poor masses.

Gandhi developed *Swadeshi* movement during our struggle for freedom as a weapon to cut the roots of colonial economic interests and exploitation as well as to utilize our own local resources and manpower to the maximum. Now the time has come to rebuild the same spirit of *Swadeshi* and self-reliance to defeat the nefarious design of neo-imperialist interests of multi-nationals and economically advanced nations. Sometimes, one has to face the music of too much liberalization as the side effects prove to be very dangerous and fatal ones. Our multi-crore security scams and other scandals are the best illustrations in this respect.[46] Undoubtedly, India needs rapid economic development, however, it is not possible without inculcating the spirit of *Swadeshi*, self-reliance and self-confidence. For this purpose there is an immediate need to understand the meaning of true *Swadeshi* which means lesser dependence on foreign goods and maximum use of our own resources keeping in view the basic needs of our immediate surroundings without neglecting the universal human element *Swadeshi* is the way to solve the problem of exploitation and inequality. Accordingly, there is a pressing need to examine and reexamine the growing impact and merits and demerits of liberalization and globalization.

REFERENCES

1. Collected Works of Mahatma Gandhi, (Ahmedabad: Navajivan Trust), November 1964, January 1915-October 1917, Vol. 13, p. 261.
2. *Young India*, May 30, 1929.
3. Sharma, M.L., "Gandhi's View of Swadeshi and its Relevance in the Present Context" in Arya, P.P. & Tandon, B.B. (eds.), *Multinationals versus Swadeshi Today—A Policy Framework for Economic Nationalism*, New Delhi: Deep & Deep Publications Pvt. Ltd., 1999, p. 494.
4. *Harijan*, 26.3.1938.
   See also: Tandon, B.B., "Swadeshi Today—Issues Before us" in Arya, P. P. & Tandon, B.B., *op. cit.*, p. 5.
5. *Young India*, January 19, 1921.
6. *Young India*, May 12, 1927.
7. Ahluwalia, B.K. (ed.), *op. cit.*, p. 83.
8. *Ibid*.
9. *Young India*, March 12, 1925. "I work for India's freedom because my *Swadeshi* teaches me that being born in it and having inherited her culture, I am fittest to serve her and she has a prior claim to my service. But my patriotism is not exclusive; it is calculated not only not to hurt any other nation, but to benefit all in the true sense of the word. India's freedom, as conceived by me, can never be a menace to the world."—*Young India*, April 3, 1924.
10. *Young India*, March 12, 1925.
11. *Young India*, January 8, 1925.
12. The Developed World controls 60 per cent of the World's Newspapers, 65 per cent of the World's Radios and 65 per cent of the Books published in the World. See Sean McBride *et al.*, *Many Voices, One World* (London: UNESCO and Kogan Press), 1980, p. 125. See also: Naidu, M. V., "Globalization: Threat or Promise?" in *Gandhi Marg*, Vol. 21, No. 1, April-June 1999, p. 22.
13. *Ibid*. pp. 22-24.
14. *The Selected Works of Mahatma Gandhi*, Ahmedabad: Navajivan Trust, Vol. VI: *The Voice of Truth* 1968, p. 441.
15. *The Selected Works of Mahatma Gandhi*, Ahmedabad: Navajivan Trust, Vol. VI: *The Voice of Truth* 1968, p. 339.
16. Menon, M.S.N., "Swadeshi Spells Success" in *The Tribune*, Chandigarh, March 10, 2002, Spectrum, p. 1.
17. Tandon, B.B., "Swadeshi Today—Issues Before Us" in Arya, P. P. & Tandon, B. B., *op. cit.*, p. 4.
18. *CWMG*, *op. cit.*, 1971, December 1930-April 1931, Vol. No. 45 (397: The Giant And The Dwarf), p. 342.

19. Hingorani, Anand T. (ed.), The Gospel of Swadeshi, *op. cit.*, Vol. No. 16, p. 93.
20. Hingorani, Anand T. (ed.), Service Before Self, *op. cit.*, Vol. No. 22, p. 53.
21. Gandhi, M.K., *From Yeravda Mandir*, Ahmedabad: Navajivan Publishing House, December 1999, p. 38.
22. Kripalani, J.B., "The Meaning of Swadeshi" in *Gandhi Marg*, July 1967, Vol. 11, No. 3, p. 284.
23. *Ibid.*
24. *Ibid.*
25. *Ibid.*, pp. 284-285.
26. *Ibid.*, p. 287.
27. *Ibid.*, p. 289.
28. Panda, A.N., "Swadeshi: The Gandhian Approach to Self-reliance" in Mishra, Anil Dutta (ed.), *Challenges of 21st Century—Gandhian Alternatives*, New Delhi: Mittal Publications, 2003, p. 189.
29. Ganguli, B.N., *Gandhi's Social Philosophy—Perspective and Relevance*, New Delhi: National Gandhi Museum, 2000, pp. 299-300.
30. *Ibid.*
31. *Ibid.*
32. *Ibid.*
33. *Ibid.*, p. 301.
34. *Ibid.*
35. Gandhi, M.K., *From Yeravda Mandir*, *op. cit.*, p. 38
36. *Ibid.*
37. *Young India*, 17-2-1929.
38. Varma, Ravindra, "Gandhi's Philosophy of Swadeshi" in Gangrade, K.D. & Radhakrishnan, N. (eds.), *Gandhi and the Changing Facets of India*, New Delhi: Gandhi Smriti and Darshan Samiti, 1998, p. 26
39. *Young India*, 15-11-1928.
40. *Ibid.*
41. Varma, Ravindra, "Gandhi's Philosophy of Swadeshi", *op. cit.* pp. 27-28.
42. *Young India*, June 1, 1921.
43. Manohar Lal Sharma, "Globalization and Swadeshi: A Gandhian Perspective" in *Social Sciences Research Journal*, (Chandigarh: Panjab University), Volume 7, No. 1 & 2, 1999, p. 132.
44. *Ibid.*, p. 133.
45. *Ibid.*, p. 134.
46. *Ibid.*

Bibliography

Andrews, C.F., *Mahatma Gandhi's Ideas*, London: George Allen & Unwin Ltd., 1949.

Anjaria, J.J., *An Essay on Gandhian Economics*, Vora & Co., Bombay, 1944.

Ashe, Geoffrey, *Gandhi: A Study in Revolution,* Bombay: Asia Publishing House, 1968.

Bandyopadhyaya, J., *Social and Political Thought of Gandhi*, Allied Publishers, Calcutta, 1969.

Bhattacharyya, Buddhadeva, *Evolution of Political Thought of Gandhi*, Calcutta: Calcutta Book House, 1969.

Biswas, S.C. (Ed.), *Gandhi: Theory and Practise Social Impact and Contemporary Relevance,* Indian Institute of Advance Study, Shimla, 1969.

Bondurant, Joan: *Conquest of Violence: The Gandhian Philosophy of Conflict*, Bombay, Oxford University Press, 1959.

Bose, N.K., *Studies in Gandhism*, Ahmedabad, Navajivan Publishing House, 1962.

Bose, N.K., *Gandhiji: The Man And His Mission*, Bharatiya Vidya Bhawan, Bombay, 1966.

Bose, N.K., *Selections from Gandhi*, Navajivan Publishing House, Ahmedabad, 1972.

Brown, Judith M., *Gandhi and Civil Disobedience*, London: Cambridge University Press, 1977.

Brown, Judith M., *Gandhi's Rise to Power, Indian Politics*, 1915-22, London: Cambridge University Press, 1972.

Chatterjee, Partha, *Nationalist Thought and the Colonial World*, Oxford University Press, New Delhi, 1986.

Chatterjee, Margaret, *Gandhi's Religious Thought*, London, 1992.

Chopra, Pran, *The Sage in Revolt: A Remembrance*, Gandhi Peace Foundation, New Delhi, 1972.

Choudhuri, *Manmohan, Exploring Gandhi,* The Gandhi Peace Foundation, New Delhi, 1987.

Datta, D.M., *The Philosophy of Mahatma Gandhi*, Madison: University of Wisconsin Press, 1953.

Dhawan, Gopi Nath, *The Political Philosophy of Mahatma Gandhi*, Ahmedabad: Navajivan Publishing House, 1962.

Diwakar, R.R., *Saga of Satyagraha*, New Delhi, Gandhi Peace Foundation, 1969.

Doke, J. J., *M.K. Gandhi—An Indian Patriot*, Madras: Natesan, 1909.

Durga Das, *India from Curzon to Nehru and After*, London, Collins, 1969.

Erikson, Erik H., *Gandhi's Truth: On the Origins of Militant Non-violence*, Faber & Faber Limited, London, 1970.

Fischer, Louis, *The Essential Gandhi*, George Allen & Unwin Limited, London, 1962.

Gandhi, M.K., *An Autobiography Or the Story of My Experiments with Truth*, Ahmedabad, Navajivan Publishing House, 1988.

Gandhi, M.K., *Hind Swaraj Or Indian Home Rule*, Ahmedabad, Navajivan Publishing House, 1975.

Gandhi, M.K., *Satyagraha in South Africa,* Ahmedabad: Navajivan, Publishing House, 1975.

Gandhi, Rajmohan, *Mohandas: A True Story of a Man, His People and an Empire*, New Delhi, Penguin, 2006.

Gandhi, Rajmohan, *The Good Boatman: A Portrait of Gandhi*, New Delhi, Penguin Books, 1995.

Gandhi, Tushar A., *Let's Kill Gandhi!: A Chronicle of his Last Days, The Conspiracy, Murder, Investigation and Trial*, New Delhi, Rupa, 2007.

Gangrade, K.D. and Misra, R.P., *Conflict Resolution Through Non-violence Role of the Universities*, Concept Publishing Company, New Delhi, 1990.

Ganguli, B.N., *Gandhi's Social Philosophy: Perspective and Relevance*, Delhi: Vikas Publishing House Pvt. Ltd., 1973.

George, S.K. and Ramchandran, G. *The Economics of Peace: The Cause and the Man*, Peace Publishers, New Delhi, 1992.

Ghosh, Sudhir, *Gandhi's Emissary*, London, 1967.

Gregg, Richard B., *The Power of Non-Violence*, Ahmedabad Navajivan Publishing House, 1960.

Green, Martin, *Gandhi: Voice of a New Age Revolution*, New York, *Continuum*, 1993.

Guha, Ramachandra, *India After Gandhi:The History of the World's Largest Democracy*, New Delhi, Picador, 2008.

Hardiman, David, *Gandhi in His Time and Ours*, New Delhi, Permanent Black, 2003.

Holmes, J.H.; Bridge, P.C., and James, F.E., *Mahatma Gandhi, World Significance*, Calcutta: C.C. Basik, The Research Home.

Hunter, Doris A. and Mallick Krishna, *Non-violence: A Reader in the Ethics of Action,* Gandhi Peace Foundation, New Delhi, 1990.

Huttenback, Robert A., *Gandhi in South Africa: British Imperialism and The Indian Question*, 1860-1914, Cornell University Press, London, 1971.

Iyer, Raghavan, *The Moral and Political Thought of Mahatma Gandhi*, Oxford University Press, Chicago, 1973.

Jack, A. Homer (Ed.), *The Gandhi Reader*, Samata Books, Madras, 1984.

Kalelkar, Kaka, *Stray Glimpses of Bapu*, Ahmedabad: Navajivan Publishing House, 1957.

Karunakaran, K.P., *Gandhi Interpretations*, Gitanjali Publishing House, New Delhi, 1985.

Keer, Dhananjay, *Mahatma Gandhi Political Saint and Unarmed Prophet*, Popular Prakashan, Bombay, 1973.

Khan, Afaque, *Gandhian Approach to Communalism: A Critical Study*, Ajanta Publications, Delhi, 1986.

Kripalani, J.B., *Gandhi: His Life and Thought*, New Delhi, Publications Division, Ministry of Information and Broadcasting, Government of India, 1968.

Mehta, P.J. *Gandhi and South African Question*, Madras, 1911.

Mishra, Anil Dutta, *Understanding Mahatma Gandhi:Speeches and Writings that Reveal his Mind Methods and Mission*, New Delhi, Concept, 2011.

Mishra, Anil Dutta, *et al*. *Revisiting Gandhi*, New Delhi, Abhijeet Publications, 2011.

Mishra, Anil Dutta, *Mahatma on Ethics*, New Delhi: Concept, 2010.

Mishra, Anil Dutta, *Revisiting Hind Swaraj*, New Delhi: Concept, 2010.

Mishra, A.D. (ed.), *Perspectives on Human Rights*, New Delhi, Radha Publications, 2002.

Mishra, Anil Dutta (Ed.), *Gandhian Approach to Contemporary Problems*, Mittal Publications, New Delhi, 1996.

Mishra, Anil Dutta and M.S. Dadage, *Panchayati Raj: Gandhian Perspective*, Mittal Publications, New Delhi, 2000.

Mishra, Anil Dutta, *Challenges of 21st Century and Gandhian Alternative*, Mittal Publications, New Delhi, 2003.

Mishra, Anil Dutta, *Fundamentals of Gandhism*, Mittal Publications, New Delhi, 1995.

Mishra, Anil Dutta, *Rediscovering Gandhi*, Mittal Publications, New Delhi, 2002.

Mishra, Anil Dutta, *Gandhian Approach to Contemporary Problems*, Mittal Publications, New Delhi, 1996.

Mishra, Anil Dutta, *Gandhism After Gandhi*, Mittal Publications, New Delhi, 1999.

Mishra, Sweta, *Democratic Decentralisation in India*, Mittal Publications, New Delhi, 1994.

Misra, K.P. and Gangal, S.C., *Gandhi and the Contemporary World: Studies in Peace and War*, Chanakya Publications, Delhi, 1981.

Mukerjee, Hiren, *Gandhi: A Study*, New Delhi: People's Publishing House, 1960.

Namboodiripad, E.M.S., *The Mahatma and the Ism*, New Delhi: People Publishing House, 1959.

Nanda, B.R., *Gandhi Pan-Islamism Imperialism and Nationalism*, Oxford University Press, Bombay, 1989.

Nanda, B.R., *Mahatma Gandhi: A Biography*, London: George Allen and Unwin Ltd., 1959.

Narayan, Shriman, *Selected Works of Mahatma Gandhi*, Navajivan Publishing House, Ahmedabad, 1956.

Nehru, Jawahar Lal, *Mahatma Gandhi*, Calcutta: Signet Press, 1949.

Ostergaord Geoffrey, *Non-violent Revolution in India*, Gandhi Peace Foundation, New Delhi, 1985.

Parekh, Bhikhu, Colonialism, T*radition and Reform: An Analysis of Gandhi's Political Discourse*, Sage Publications, New Delhi, 1989.

Parel, Anthony J., *Gandhi's Philosophy and the Quest for Harmony*, Cambridge: Cambridge University Press, 2006.

Parel, Anthony J., *Hind Swaraj and Other Writings*, Cambridge: Cambridge University Press, 1997.

Parel, Anthony J., *Gandhi, Freedom, and Self-Rule*, New Delhi, Vistaar Publications, 2000.

Polak, H.S.C., H.N. Brailsford and Lord Pethick, Lawrence, *Mahatma Gandhi*, London, Odham Press Limited, 1949.

Prabhu, R.K., and Rao, U.R., *The Mind of Mahatma*, Ahmedabad: Navajivan Publishing House, 1967.

Pyare Lal, *Mahatma Gandhi: The Early Phase*, Volume 1, Ahmedabad: Navajivan Publishing House, 1965.

Pyare Lal, *Mahatma Gandhi: The Last Phase*, in 2 volumes, Ahmedabad: Navajivan Publishing House, 1956, 1958.

Pyare Lal and Nayar Sushila, *In Gandhiji's Mirror*, Oxford University Press, Delhi, 1991.

Pyare Lal, *Mahatma Gandhi: The Last Phase*, Ahmedabad: Navajivan Publishing House, 1958.

Radhakrishnan, S. (ed.), *Mahatma Gandhi: Essays and Reflections on His Life and Thought*, Allahabad: Kitabistan, 1944.

Radhakrishnan, S. (Ed.), *Mahatma Gandhi 100 Years*, Gandhi Peace Foundation, New Delhi, 1968.

Rajendra Prashad, *At the Feet of Mahatma Gandhi*, Bombay: Asia Publishing House, 1961.

Rao, U.R., *The Way to Communal Harmony*, Ahmedabad, Navajivan Publishing House, 1963.

Rao, U.S. Mohan (Ed.), *The Message of Mahatma Gandhi*, Publications Division, Ministry of Information and Broadcasting, Govt. of India, New Delhi, 1968.

Raghuramaraju, A. (Ed), *Debating Gandhi: A Reader*, New Delhi, Oxford University Press, 2006.

Rolland, Romain, *Mahatma Gandhi: The Man Who Became One With The Universal Being*, (Translated by Catherine D. Groth), Agra: Shiva Lal Aggarwala & Co. Ltd.

Roy, Ramashray, *Contemporary Crisis and Gandhi*, Discovery Publishing House, Delhi, 1986.

Roy, Ramashray, *Gandhi: Soundings in Political Philosophy*, Chanakya Publications, Delhi, 1984.

Rudolph, Lloyd I and Rudolph, Susanne Hoeber, *Postmodern Gandhi and Other Essays: Gandhi in the World and at Home*, New Delhi, Oxford University Press, 2006.

Sethi, J.D., *Gandhi Today*, New Delhi: Vikas Publishing House Pvt. Ltd., 1978.

Sharp, Gene, *Gandhi Wields the Weapon of Moral Power : Three Case Histories*, Ahmedabad: Navajivan Publishing House, 1960.

Sharp, Gene, *The Politics of Non-Violent Action: Power and Struggle*, Part 1, Boston: Porter Sarget Publishers, 1973.

Sheean Vincent, *Mahatma Gandhi: A Great Life in Brief*, Publications Division, New Delhi, 1990.

Sitaramayya, Pattabhi, *Gandhi and Gandhism*. Allahabad: Kitabistan, 1942, in 2 Volumes.

Tendulkar, D.G., Mahatma, New Delhi, Publications Division, Ministry of Information and Broadcasting, Government of India, 1952.

The Collected Works of Mahatma Gandhi, New Delhi, Publications Division, Ministry of Information and Broadcasting, Government of India, 1965, (Vols. 1-100).

Verma, V.P., *The Political Philosophy of Mahatma Gandhi and Sarvodaya*, Agra: Lakshmi Narain Aggarwal, 1981.

Vinobha, Bhave, *Swaraj Sastra,* Sarva Seva Sangh Prakashan, Varanasi, 1963.

Watson, Francis and Tennyson Hallam, *Talking of Gandhi*, Sangam Books, Bombay, 1957.

Weber, Thomas, *Conflict Resolution and Gandhian Ethics*, The Gandhi Peace Foundation, New Delhi, 1991.

Weber, Thomas, *On the Salt March*, New Delhi, Harper Collings, 1997.

Weber, Thomas, *Gandhi as Disciple and Mentor,* New Delhi: Cambridge University Press, 2004.

Index